Praise for *America's 100 Years' War*

"For decades, Bradley Thayer has bloodied his knuckles fighting Communism in defense of the American spirit. This civilizational struggle spans generations, from the emergence of the Bolsheviks in the early twentieth century to the radical Marxists who operate today in American politics, fomenting division in our culture and violence in our streets. In this book, Thayer maps out the battle lines, provides a detailed profile of our ideological enemies, and hands us the proper weapons to defend ourselves. He reminds us that this long war can be won—that it must be won—but only if we have the courage and will to fight."

—Joe Allen, author of *Dark Aeon: Transhumanism and the War Against Humanity*

"Thayer has documented the most existential threat to our country at precisely the time when strategic decisions need to be made. China's 'People's War' and unrestricted warfare with no moral boundaries imposed by a Communist system devoid of God should scare you. His treatment of the last hundred years is all signal and no noise and he has done a service that will reawaken the American mind and compel us to make the pivot that requires courage and sacrifice. Outstanding work."

—David Brat, former U.S. Congressman, PhD economist, Vice President, Liberty University, and moral philosopher to "Steve Bannon's WarRoom"

"Brad Thayer nails it with a crystal-clear and downright terrifying diagnosis of the existential threat hammering the West. He traces one unbroken line of pure Leninist aggression straight from the Bolshevik Revolution I have specialized in studying to the halls of the modern Democratic Party and the corridors of Beijing. By ripping the mask off the CCP as nothing but a colonial impostor and exposing the neo-Bolshevik tactics that have captured our institutions, Thayer gives us the real roadmap to reclaim the American Trinity and win the Hundred Years' War. His rock-solid historical analysis—spotlighting the inevitable brutality of the Leninist project—turns this from mere commentary into the essential battle manual for preserving Western civilization and finally crushing totalitarianism once and for all."

—Jeff Clark, Vice President for Litigation at The Oversight Project and former Justice Department and Office of Management and Budget Leader

"The mayor of New York City is a Marxist revolutionary who belongs to a party that calls the United States a 'prison nation' founded by 'slavers' and 'racists.' Minneapolis is under siege by groups like the Party of Socialism and Liberation that wish to abolish capitalism and replace the republic with a 'new revolutionary government.' If you thought the fight against Communism was over, you were wrong. It has come home with a vengeance, and the fate of the republic hangs in the balance. Read this book. Now. Get smart on where we have been, where we are headed, and how the people who want to destroy America think and operate. And then, get involved. Today."

—Sam Faddis, retired CIA Senior Operations Officer

"Bradley Thayer has written a critically important book arguing that America's struggle against Communism constitutes the nation's longest war and its greatest enduring national security threat. This conflict was waged against the Soviet Union in the past and continues today against Communist China. However, the struggle is not confined to foreign adversaries; Americans also confront Communism within their own country. The war against Communism is a single, continuous fight. Thayer rightly contends that to defeat Communism at home and abroad—permanently—Americans must reclaim their identity as Americans and as inheritors of Western civilization."

—Michael T. Flynn, LTG, US Army (Retired)

"Brad Thayer gets it exactly right. Americans have been fighting a long war against Communism at home and abroad for a century. Our ignorance of Marxist-Leninist ideology has been very damaging for our national security and our freedoms. This book is a valuable tool for understanding past aggression by the Soviet Union and the existential threat posed by Communist China today. And it exposes how Communists have penetrated Western societies and what to do about it. A must read!"

—Bill Gertz, National Security Correspondent, *The Washington Times*

"Dr. Bradley Thayer has provided an exceptional analysis of the evils of Communism and what the American people must do to stop its destruction of their country and the world. This is bold argument. It is a clear assessment of Leninism, the Comintern, and the Chinese Communist Party, and a welcome embrace of American identity and Western civilization. The book is essential reading for all who want to understand the Chinese Communist Party and the ideological upheaval in American politics today."

—Dr. Lianchao Han, Former Vice President, Citizen Power Initiatives for China

"Thayer has placed the last hundred years in a remarkable new light. The great fight has been against Communists abroad and at home. Thayer tells us how to defeat them and allows us to appreciate the key role of Western civilization in this war."

—Ben Harnwell, International Editor, "Steve Bannon's WarRoom"

"Bradley Thayer has written a timely and profoundly important book. America, founded on ideals of liberty, individual rights, and limited government that have changed and continue to shape the world, now confronts one of its greatest existential threats: the persistent menace of Communism—frequently disguised as 'socialism' or 'progressivism'—whose core tenets remain antithetical to the American experiment. Thayer masterfully traces the conflict from the 1917 Bolshevik Revolution through the Cold War to today's paramount struggle with the Chinese Communist Party, revealing a continuous, adaptive Hundred Years' War that has never truly ended. With clarity and rigor, he exposes how Communist ideology has evolved, mutated, and embedded itself in institutions, culture, and policy, and how advances in AI have accelerated it. This book is a wake-up call and reminds Americans why the Founders' vision must be defended with vigor and how the United States can—and must—prevail once more."

—Patrick K. O'Donnell, historian and bestselling author of *The Unvanquished* and *Revolutionary Snipers*

"It has become increasingly clear that forces are assembled intent upon destruction of our Western—American—society, culture, and values. Bradley Thayer comes to the rescue to provide readers with suggestions to fight it and prevail."

—Drew Pinsky, MD, host of *Ask Dr. Drew*

"Only by understanding the nature of the threats waged against us can we hope to preserve the American Spirit, all that makes this nation great and free. Dr. Thayer lays out with superb eloquence, brilliant analysis, and exceptional research the dangers of Communism, the multifaceted fronts on which we are being subverted by its many guises, and the ways in which we must fight against it and win."

—Dr. Karen Siegemund, President of American Freedom Alliance

AMERICA'S 100 YEARS' WAR

How to Win Against Communism

Dr. Bradley A. Thayer

Foreword by Stephen K. Bannon

WAR ROOM BOOKS

War Room Books may be purchased in bulk at special discounts for sales promotion, corporate gifts, fund-raising, or educational purposes. Special editions can also be created to specifications. For details, contact the Special Sales Department, Skyhorse Publishing, Skyhorse Publishing, 307 Fifth Avenue, 4th Floor, New York, NY 10016 or info@skyhorsepublishing.com.

Visit our website at www.skyhorsepublishing.com.

10 9 8 7 6 5 4 3 2 1

Library of Congress Control Number: 2026943360

Cover design by David Ter-Avanesyan
Cover photo credit: Getty Images and Shutterstock

Print ISBN: 978-1-64821-280-2
Ebook ISBN: 978-1-64821-281-9

Printed in the United States of America

For Eike, once again.

Contents

List of Tables

Acknowledgments

Many people aided me in each step of the process of turning ideas into a book. I am grateful to Steve Bannon for his strong support, for providing the foreword and placing the book in context. I am as well to Ólafur Björnsson and Thomas Skypek for their thoughtful comments. Sandra Tolliver was of great help, as always. I am full of appreciation for the exceptional work of the American Freedom Alliance, its outstanding board, and especially its president, Karen Siegemund, for allowing me to serve as a fellow. Dan Fleuette is an exceptional artist, and I thank him for his comments and photography. At Skyhorse, I am grateful to president and publisher Tony Lyons for his interest in this book, executive editor Daniela Rapp for seeing the manuscript through to production with incredible skill and alacrity, associate publisher Abigail Gehring for employing her prodigious abilities in the service of this book, senior production editor Chris Schultz for her great work, and David Ter-Avanesyan for his sharp cover design.

Foreword

By Stephen K. Bannon

Major books change the way you think about politics and history. Bradley Thayer's book does this on almost every page. The intellectual firepower of the book is formidable. Its big arguments should change the way Americans consider their American history and America's enemy: Communism. The U.S. has been in a war with Communism for a century. It is America's longest war and is the ideology of America's two biggest threats: the Chinese Communist Party (CCP) and the modern Democratic Party.

This Hundred Years' War has been fought abroad. America has fought two cold wars with Communist great powers—fighting and winning the Cold War with the Soviet Union and now fighting one with the People's Republic of China (PRC).

This war is fought at home too. The Communists took over the Democratic Party's leadership, donors, political action committees, law firms, and allied non-governmental organizations under the guise of neo-Bolshevik "progressivism." As he writes, Communists have the worst ideas but are the most effective at advancing them.

Thayer argues that the war abroad and at home is one fight, one war against Communism. And everything depends upon whether Americans or Communists win.

To win we need to understand our enemy. That means comprehending what Vladimir Lenin and his fellow Bolsheviks unleashed on the world. Lenin was one of the greatest strategists, theorists, and politicians of the twentieth century. He created effective and professional Communist parties. He executed the world's first Communist revolution in Russia. He invented totalitarian government. He started a civil war in the West among those who support Western civilization and those who would destroy it. "Civilizational erasure" has deep roots in Leninism. He created the Third Communist International (the Comintern) to spread Bolshevism around the world. The Comintern forged, nurtured, and, in every sense that matters, led the CCP. Lenin made Joseph Stalin possible. And he ordered the creation of the Communist Party USA. He brought Communism to Russia and China and may well bring it to the United States if the Democrats succeed.

Lenin's thought captured the Democrats. To understand the Democrats' ideology of progressivism, their strategy, and their policies, Americans need to understand Lenin's idea of revolutionary defeatism, "the worse the better." That is, Lenin wanted to weaken Russia and hurt ordinary Russians to advance the revolution. The worse shape Russia and Russian were in, the better for the Bolsheviks. Democrats work to make conditions worse for Americans, immiserating them while importing their replacements through illegal immigration and H-1B visas, to advance their revolutionary agenda of bringing Communism to America. The Democrats are not alone. Thayer rightfully sees George Soros and his son running a modern Comintern to spread Communism under the guise of progressivism.

Another one of Thayer's blockbuster revelations is that the CCP is the product of Soviet imperialism. It is a colonial polity and has no more right to rule the Chinese people than he or I do. There is nothing Chinese about the CCP. It is a fraud, just as Mao Zedong was and Xi Jinping is today. It may be a big lie, but it is a formidable threat.

Thayer recognizes that Communism is anti-American, and completely at odds with American identity. He is right that Americans were better at fighting Communism in the past than today because American identity was stronger. The truth is, Americans dropped the ball and let Communists into our education system, media, businesses, and Democratic Party so that Communist ideology infiltrated all positions of power. For decades,

Communists were teaching American kids about American identity. That led to absolute corruption of American identity and beliefs. It resulted in lost generations of Americans. The Republican Party was no help. It was captured or intimidated by the Democrats to serve as nothing more than a speed bump while the neo-Bolsheviks in the Democratic Party raced with revolutionary discipline and at lightning speed to fundamentally transform America. They almost got away with it. But they might, if we lose in 2028.

The miracle of the Trump revolution is to give Americans the chance to defeat Communism abroad and at home and to restore American identity. The Make America Great Again (MAGA) movement may be thought of as a response to the conditions that the Communists caused, both within America and by the actions of the CCP. Where they want to weaken America, America First works every day to save it. Where they seek to hurt, humiliate, and ultimately destroy Americans, MAGA aids Americans. Democrats want a totalitarian future for America. Our movement restores Americans' love of country and the American people for a future as prosperous as any in our history.

To win the war, as Thayer argues, there is much to be done—but the key is to recapture American identity and restore the confidence of Americans in it and in Western civilization. Our victory begins with understanding the enemy and defeating him through the restoration of American identity to vanquish him completely. This is a victory Americans can and must win. The final victory over Communism is possible; now we must sustain the struggle to our victory. This is our fight. We will prevail.

Chapter 1

What Has Happened to America?

If I asked you which political thinker has had the biggest impact on American politics today, you might say the Founding Fathers, or Lincoln, or FDR, or LBJ, or Reagan. I wish they did. This book argues that the man who has the greatest impact on American politics is not even an American—he is Vladimir Lenin (born Vladimir Ulyanov, 1870–1924), the leader of the 1917 Bolshevik revolution in Russia. His ideas are responsible for the ideological upheaval in America and for the civil war being fought today over Western civilization. Lenin and his intellectual descendants are to blame for the deep problems we face in our country and our civilization. They are attempting a revolution and may get away with it.

Americans can feel it in their gut. Something very unusual is going on in American politics. During the Biden administration tens of millions of people entered the country with little or no effort by the government to determine who they were. Among those millions were tens of thousands of Chinese men, many of whom also certainly were members of the People's Republic of China's (PRC) military, intelligence services, or paramilitaries to collect intelligence and conduct covert action against the U.S. from within U.S. borders. It is certain that terrorists entered the country, as well as criminals, including those who murdered Laken Riley and Jocelyn Nungaray, among others. Never has an American president acted with such strategic and deliberate aggression toward the American people. It is almost as though those running the Biden administration did not like America or Americans and wanted to rapidly transform it.

After President Joe Biden's dementia caused him to implode in an unprecedented and curiously early June 2024 presidential debate with President Donald Trump, he was no longer useful to the Democratic elite. Vice President Kamala Harris was appointed to be that party's 2024 nominee for president. In the Democratic Party, no one voted for her to become the nominee, and yet she was. The Democratic Party and the mainstream news media united behind her in lockstep as though her appointment by the party's elite was perfectly ordinary, rather than something closer to the behavior of the Soviet or Chinese Communist Party's (CCP) Politburo.

And it is not just at the presidential level. From the election of Zohran Mamdani as mayor of New York City on the back of the Democratic Socialists of America's rise, to Alexandra Ocasio-Cortez and "the Squad" and their takeover of the Democratic Party, to the anti–Immigration and Customs Enforcement (ICE) protests in Minneapolis and St. Paul, to the violence of Antifa on the streets of America's great cities, the radical, anti-American Communist left is on the march in the U.S.

These incidents compel Americans to wonder both *what* is happening to their country, and *why* is this happening.

This book answers why these events are occurring. The answer is that Americans never defeated Communism, which has been at war with America since the Bolshevik Revolution of 1917. Now Americans must defeat Communism or be conquered by it. This is the central struggle of our age. Americans understand it intuitively. They grasp that at present, American politics is defined by a major ideological division in the United States, and the country is in a period of significant ideological upheaval. On one side, Americans work to preserve the principles, ideas, institutions, and values of the American Revolution of 1776. On the other, there are Communists advancing their policy of what they call "revolutionary defeatism"—the worse the better. They work to make things worse in America, not better. The more terrible things are in the U.S., the more divided, more violent, the more fractious, the more abysmal the economy, the more immigrants, the more H-1Bs to replace Americans, the more people transitioning to destroy themselves—the better.

The hideous structure that is the Obama presidential library in Chicago—a city famous for its great architecture—is no accident. It is entirely the point. It was one of President Barack Obama's last official chances to show his utter contempt and hatred for America and Americans by leaving a monstrosity as his legacy rather than something beautiful that honors America and its people. The more demoralized Americans, the uglier and dysfunctional their cities, the more anemic and shattered their identities as Americans, the weaker the United States, the more fragmented Western civilization, the closer they are to destruction and so more beneficial for the Communists.

This is a time in American history when Americans confront anti-Americans. American identity has become a battlefield. That matters because identity is the entelechy of the country. American identity is America—its people, its heart, and its essence—and threats to it are the most important national security matters the country confronts. In fact, national security depends upon American identity. The contest for American identity is the Founding Fathers versus the Bolsheviks, James Madison versus Vladimir Lenin. Which side is going to win this ideological conflict for the soul of America? For Americans and for Western civilization, there is no greater issue.

Americans must recognize the size of the threat. Communism was the shared ideology of the U.S.'s cold war foes: the Soviet Union (1946–1991) and currently the PRC. In sum, Communism is the most pernicious and most formidable enemy, foreign and domestic, America has ever faced. It is the ideology of the CCP and of the modern Democratic Party in the United States. Communists have the worst ideas but are the best at advancing them—and imposing them on the rest of us.

The fight against Communism is not a new fight for Americans. This book delves into the implications of the ideology of Communism as the source of the long war the U.S. has waged against it during the twentieth and twenty-first centuries.

Since the end of World War II, the major national security concern of the United States has been a long war against Communism. These periods of intense security competition are typically viewed as discrete conflicts. Indeed, there are major and salient differences between the Cold War with the Soviet Union and the cold war with the PRC today. However, it is also useful to perceive the similarities between them, particularly when the motivation of their ruling parties is a shared adherence to the same ideology.[1]

The cold wars fought in the twentieth and twenty-first centuries against the Soviets and the CCP, and the struggle against Communism at home, should be considered a Hundred Years' War against the ideology of Communism.[2] Viewing the war against Communism as one long war rather than as discrete conflicts, first, allows Americans to understand how dangerous the ideology of Communism is and provides insight into the causes and conduct of America's long war against it; second, illuminates the similar motivation and weakness of America's Communist enemies; third, demonstrates the great variation in the adequacy of the U.S. response; and fourth, informs a path to victory over Communism in the PRC and in the U.S.

The core argument of this book is that the United States has faced a hyper-aggressive ideology: Leninism, the dominant variety of Communism, which first seized power in Russia in November 1917. It then devised a vehicle, the Comintern (the Communist International, or Third International) to spread that ideology. It did so successfully, including to China. This ideology motivated the Communist peer competitors, the Soviet Union and PRC, as well as other Communist states, like Cuba, that have occupied the

1 On the ideological ambitions of the Chinese Communist Party and its leader Xi Jinping, see Lianchao Han and Bradley A. Thayer, *Understanding the China Threat* (London: Routledge, 2023), pp. 17–147.

2 The Hundred Years' War was a series of conflicts between England and France from 1337 to 1453 over territory and claims to the French throne. It ended with a French victory, and England losing all its territory in France except for Calais.

strategic attention of the U.S. national security community for the bulk of the last hundred years.

It also spread that ideology to the U.S., and the U.S. has been slow to respond to the advance of Communism. Year after year, Communism has advanced and now is experiencing a renaissance among America's youth, as Mamdani's victory shows. This compels the recognition that what Lenin and his Bolshevik comrades did was frankly remarkable. They provided the ideology for America's two most formidable foes—the Soviet Union and the PRC—while starting a civil war in the West between those who support and would save Western civilization and those who would destroy it and replace it with Communism.

The advance of Communism in Western societies shows that potential saviors of the West thus far lack the focus and intent the Communists possess, are ignorant of their objectives, gormless when it comes to political warfare, or even may be fellow travelers or captured by Communists. In any event, they are always three steps behind the Communists as they destroy Western societies through agitation, propaganda, organization, penetration, deception, terror, and other strategies and tactics they have perfected over a century.

I. Main Arguments and Outline

This book presents the history of the ideology of Communism, specifically Leninism, and the Communist International.[3] The ideology of Leninism, as perfected by Joseph Stalin (born Joseph Vissarionovich Dzhugashvili, 1878–1953) in the Soviet Union and employed by Mao Zedong (1893–1976)

3 This book refers to Leninism rather than Marxism-Leninism because it was Vladimir Lenin's interpretation of the writings of Karl Marx and Friedrich Engels wedded to his own ideas that defines the ideology of the Soviet Union and the PRC. Lenin provided Joseph Stalin a totalitarian state, which Stalin then perfected. Stalin is also important because he served as a role model for Mao Zedong for the establishment of totalitarianism and for the creation of a cult of personality. Unless otherwise noted, the study will refer to Leninism and Communism synonymously.

in the PRC, is the genesis of the respective Soviet and PRC confrontations with the United States, as well as the Communism in the U.S. Leninism caused and heavily shaped the contours of those conflicts. The ideology of Leninism explains why these Communist states fought against the U.S. and its allies—and why the PRC still does today. Indeed, the principal U.S. national security concern since 1945 has been a struggle against Communism—the ideology of two peer competitors, the Soviet Union and the PRC, as well as their formidable allies like Cuba, Czechoslovakia, the German Democratic Republic (East Germany), and Vietnam.

In any conflict, ideology is important. This is especially so today when America's traditional ideology is under assault. Fundamentally, ideology explains and justifies the legitimacy to rule the country's people. It informs personal identity and explains why people should support the state and why they should sacrifice for it. Ideology is the force that unifies and provides cohesion for the country and like-minded people around the world. As a corollary, it defines the domestic enemy, those who do not believe in the ideology, as well as the enemy abroad. In addition, it explicates the ultimate reason for conflict with other states—which states are allies, which are foes, and why enemies should be opposed. Ideology is also a tool in political warfare to expand a state's influence, as well as to challenge the legitimacy of other states with competing ideologies.

The role of ideology in great power hot and cold wars is fundamental. In particular, comprehending the ideology of Communism allows the American people to recognize the worldview and objectives of their peer foes—the Soviet Union and the PRC—and the threat within the U.S.[4] This is an important point and may be easily overlooked. Its importance is captured in Soviet dissident Natan Sharansky's remarks. Sharansky (born

4 As explained in detail below, this book focuses principally on Leninism; it will also address the thoughts of Antonio Gramsci and the Frankfurt School. At root, those approaches share the Leninist aim of totalitarian control and are outgrowths of Bolshevik thought.

Anatoly Shcharansky) was imprisoned in Permanent Labor Camp 35 at the time of President Ronald Reagan's "Evil Empire" speech on March 8, 1983, to the National Association of Evangelicals in Orlando, Florida. Sharansky recalled his reaction after Reagan's death in 2004:

> It was the brightest, most glorious day. Finally, a spade had been called a spade. Finally, Orwell's Newspeak was dead. President Reagan had from that moment made it impossible for anyone in the West to continue closing their eyes to the real nature of the Soviet Union. It was one of the most important, freedom-affirming declarations, and we all instantly knew it. For us, that was the moment that really marked the end for them, and the beginning for us. The lie had been exposed and could never, ever be untold now. This was the end of Lenin's "Great October Bolshevik Revolution" and the beginning of a new revolution, a freedom revolution—Reagan's Revolution.[5]

As Sharansky's reflections capture, the political ideology of the United States was inspiring for dissidents and others who resisted Soviet control in the country itself and in Central and Eastern Europe. From the outset of the Reagan administration, the U.S. sought to undermine the ideology of the Soviet Union, its Eastern European satellites, and the attractiveness of Communism in world politics.[6] Thus, the Reagan administration

---

5 Tom Rose, "The View from the Gulag: An Interview with Natan Sharansky," *The Weekly Standard*, Vol. 9, No. 21, June 21, 2004. At: <http://www.weeklystandard.com/Content/Public/Articles/000/000/004/224ncdel.asp>. Accessed September 21, 2025. Also see John Arquilla, *The Reagan Imprint: Ideas in American Foreign Policy from the Collapse of Communism to the War on Terror* (Chicago: Ivan R. Dee, 2006), p. 106.

6 In July 1981, the interagency "East-West Policy Study," sought to provide the U.S. with ideological initiative in the Cold War's political warfare. The study called for illuminating the profound deficiencies of the communist system in the Soviet Union. It argued that its ideological foundation of

understood how significant political warfare was in the fight against the Soviet Union. The Reagan administration sought to create the maximum possible internal pressure on the Soviet Union to augment U.S. and allied efforts to bring external pressure on Moscow and its Warsaw Pact allies.[7] In the end, these efforts were critical in defeating the Soviet Union.

Understanding Communism provides insight into the formidable motivation of the foe and the strategic choices and vulnerabilities of Communist countries and movements. Due to Communist ideology, conflict is ineluctable. To modify Leon Trotsky's quip about war—you may not be interested in Communism, but Communism is interested in you. Thus far, conflict with the CCP has been only in the realm of political warfare, but it certainly may become kinetic.

The war with Communism is fought within the U.S., too. In fact, the acceptance of Communism has never been greater among the American people. This book argues that was by design and should be thought of as

---

Marxism-Leninism was a perversely flawed ideology that led inevitably to dehumanization and alienation for the Soviet population, precisely the problems that Communist ideology was intended, at least by Marx and Engels, to address. Interagency Report, "East-West Policy Study," Washington, July 8, 1981, in *Foreign Relations of the United States 1981–1988 Vol. III, Soviet Union January 1981–January 1983* (Washington, D.C.: United States Government Publishing Office, 2016), pp. 171–179.

7 In 1982–1983, Reagan advanced classified directives that defined how the U.S. could undermine the Soviet Union from within by identifying and using existing economic, political, and ideological cleavages and vulnerabilities present within the communist system and within the Soviet bloc between a dominant Moscow and subservient Warsaw Pact satellites. The most significant of these was the National Security Decision Directive (NSDD)-75. NSDD-75 defined the strategic intent of the United States against the Soviet bloc, "the primary U.S. objective in Eastern Europe is to loosen Moscow's hold on the region while promoting the cause of individual human rights in all key countries of the region." NSDD-75, "U.S. Relations with the U.S.S.R." January 17, 1983, Box 91287, NSDD Files, Executive Secretariat Files, Ronald Reagan Presidential Library.

one of Communism's greatest victories—to get Americans to forget their past and their birthright in favor of Communist ideas and policies. As a result, the book argues that the U.S. is at a "1776 Moment" of ideological transformation.[8] The American Revolution of 1776 defined a change of political ideology from absolutism to political liberalism, the ideology of America's Founding Fathers and of Americans for most of their history. Today, the ideological transformation is from liberalism to neo-Bolshevism, which is often called progressivism by the neo-Bolsheviks themselves.[9] The ideological change occurring in the U.S. is profound and is as great as any in American history.

In the modern fight between the ideologies of Madison and Lenin, everything—the American way of life and American identity—depends upon who wins. In this book, I explain the differences between America's historical ideology of liberalism and the Bolsheviks and the neo-Bolshevism of progressivism to reveal the differences between them and the consequences of a neo-Bolshevik victory.

This book offers a solution, the restoration of the American trinity—which is the American Spirit, liberalism, and Western civilization—and the concept of political and civilizational confidence. For Americans, political confidence is support for the American trinity. Civilizational confidence is the belief that one's civilization is unique and provides a better grounding for political principles, religion, philosophy,

---

8 I first advanced this argument in Bradley A. Thayer "Our '1776 Moment:' Either a Liberal or Progressive America," *American Greatness*, January 21, 2022. At: <https://amgreatness.com/2022/01/21/our-1776-moment-either-a-liberal-or-progressive-america/>. Accessed October 31, 2025.

9 Neo-Bolshevik progressivism is distinct from the earlier use of "progressivism" in American political history during the Progressive Era (approximately 1890s–1920s). Major progressives like William Jennings Bryan, Charles Evans Hughes, Robert La Follette and Theodore Roosevelt, who led the Progressive Party (Bull Moose Party), were advocates of labor reforms, tariffs, exposing corruption, and stewardship of public welfare.

art, music, and aesthetics than other civilizations.[10] I also illuminate the role of American identity and civilizational confidence and the ideological fight against Leninism that the U.S. faces today. There is an inverse relationship between the strength of American identity and the power of Communism: The stronger American identity is, the weaker Communism's ability to subvert American identity. Likewise, the greater confidence held by Westerners in their civilization, the weaker is Communism's power to destroy it.

Chapter 2 examines the ideology of Communism, Leninism, and the Comintern, which acted through its agents, local Communist parties and front organizations, and which is responsible for bringing Communism to China and to the U.S. The Comintern was led by an Executive Committee to direct the development of Communism in other countries and to spread the revolution to them.

The hyper-aggression of the Communist movement, led by the Communist Party of the Soviet Union (CPSU) and now by the CCP, is essential for Americans to understand. Hyper-aggression is a deliberate term that captures the aggression along every azimuth. The PRC directed aggression toward the Chinese people through the tyrannical abuses of Communist rule but also was oriented toward other states by way of both political and kinetic forms of warfare. Leninism furthered revolution by destabilizing other countries through the Comintern. Today the Comintern does not exist formally, but it would be accurate to say that it has been privatized. Its work is now conducted by CCP-linked billionaire businessman Neville Roy Singham, who has funded the Communist revolutionary group The People's Forum, The Justice and Education Fund, among about sixty other entities that Singham and his

---

10 See Bradley A. Thayer, "*Quo Vadis* for Western Civilization: The Rebirth of the West's Confidence," *American Greatness*, November 18, 2025. At: <https://amgreatness.com/2025/11/18/quo-vadis-for-western-civilization-the-rebirth-of-the-wests-civilizational-confidence/>. Accessed November 18, 2025.

wife, Jodie Evans of Code Pink, support via a vast network. Singham sold his Thoughtworks tech company in 2017 and has used the proceeds to fund Communist movements and propaganda worldwide. No doubt the CCP helps to fund his networks, too. George Soros and his son Alexander have similar aims that they support through the Open Society Foundation and the networks they have created, nurtured, and sustained for many decades. The Emerson Collective, founded by Steve Jobs' widow, Laurene Powell Jobs, advances the same deleterious ends for traditional American identity.

As important as Singham, Evans, George and Alexander Soros, Jobs, and other groups like the Southern Poverty Law Center (SPLC) are, and their networks are formidable, the modern Comintern has received its greatest boost through artificial intelligence (AI). The large language models (LLMs) like OpenAI's ChatGPT and Google's Gemini are heavily biased toward the political left. Unless corrected, that bias will grow exponentially as do AI's abilities. They are gaining their content from an intellectual milieu that is grounded in Leninism and neo-Bolshevik progressive thought. Searches and content found will be slanted toward the left and so the Leninist feedback loop will be established.

Chapter 3 explores its impact on China, Maoism, and PRC leader Xi Jinping. It explains why Mao's thought is derivative; his thought was the direct result of Bolshevik thought. Mao was not a major Communist thinker, but he was a ruthless thug who employed all the tactics of Stalinism to gain and maintain power. Today, Xi employs that ideology in a typically Leninist approach. The chapter also considers the future of the CCP. There are three futures or paths that the CCP's Leninism may take in the next fifteen to twenty years. While the CCP's precise future path is uncertain, the world might witness a return to Stalinism, but this time an efficient Stalinism where Communist dictator Xi Jinping employs advanced technology, including AI, to create the surveillance superpower to police the CCP and Chinese population.

Chapter 4 explains the core of American identity. It is what I term the "American Trinity": the American Spirit, the ideology of political liberalism, and Western civilization. This is America's greatest strength. American identity rejects Communism, but has not been immune from penetration by Communists, which explains why American identity and each pillar of the American trinity is in an existential struggle: a fight between Lenin and Madison for the survival of the United States and the West.

Chapter 5 describes how Communists penetrated the U.S., employing the tactics of the Comintern—the Communist Party, the underground party, front organizations, fellow travelers—to capture the ideas industry of the country, that is, intellectuals, journalists, film, and popular culture, to advance the revolution. The chapter also addresses the neo-Bolshevik ideology of progressivism and how it successfully dominated American journalism, education, civil society, and generated the street muscle of Antifa.

Chapter 6 explains the implications of the book's arguments for Americans to win the Hundred Years' War against Communism. There are five significant implications, the first of which is that the costs of Leninism have been massive for the United States and Western civilization. This aggressive and hostile ideology has directly or indirectly killed about 200,000 Americans. In World War I, Lenin's withdrawal of Soviet Russia from the conflict permitted the Germans to sustain the war and shift forces against the Americans, British, and French, which made possible the five major Ludendorff Offensives in the spring and summer of 1918. Lenin's governance made possible that of Joseph Stalin. As a result of Stalin's alliance with Adolf Hitler, the Molotov-Ribbentrop Pact contributed to the origins of World War II in Europe. Additionally, it caused the Cold War with the Soviet Union, which included hot wars in Korea and Vietnam, as well as the current cold war with the PRC. Leninism contributed to or caused almost all of America's hot or cold wars in the twentieth century. Even more damaging, Leninism penetrated and challenged America's identity to the point where it might permanently change American identity.

In addition, Lenin started a civil war among Westerners who would sustain Western civilization and those who would seek to destroy it. The civil war is ongoing and reaches every aspect of Western societies and countries. The political and social history of the twentieth century is the history of this civil war. Both sides had successes. Leninists captured Russia, China, and most of Central and Eastern Europe. Westerners won the Cold War with the Soviets. In turn, the PRC rose to become the greatest rival to the U.S., and Communists successfully penetrated Western societies and altered their politics and destroyed their identities. The result is that today in the U.S., Canada, and Western Europe, elites are pursuing policies that are actively destroying their societies and civilization—the importation of tens of millions of immigrants from non-Western societies into their countries is the starkest indication of this. In contrast, in Central and Eastern Europe, elites are some of the strongest voices in support of sustaining Western civilization. The Bolsheviks took a sledgehammer to Western civilization, and their neo-Bolshevik progeny are far from finished with landing their destructive blows.

The second implication is that Communism is an illegitimate ideology and polity and needs to be seen and acted upon precisely as a failed but supremely dangerous political system. The U.S. objective in the fight against Communism is the same as in any of the previous titanic struggles: total victory. Total victory over Communism will require many steps, starting with understanding Leninism to know the enemy's ideology. Comprehending Leninism permits the most fundamental recognition of its vulnerability—that is, the CCP is an illegitimate regime. Chinese Communism is a Western derivative, colonial rule put in place by Soviet imperialism. The result is that the CCP is fundamentally incoherent and vulnerable to strategies that would capitalize upon its major divisions. Developing strategies to exploit this illegitimacy is a key role for Americans, people of goodwill around the world, and the U.S. and its allies.

The third implication is that there are strong historical parallels between the Cold War with the Soviets and the cold war with the CCP today. But there has been considerable variation in the ability of the U.S. to meet this threat. The U.S. did so superbly during the early Cold War, and during the Reagan administration, but has been far less effective in the struggle against the CCP. For many decades, the U.S. has been slow to perceive that the ideology of Leninism is a pernicious one that perceives the U.S. as a threat. Thus, wherever the ideology of Leninism is present, within the U.S. or abroad, there will be conflict with the United States. The deeper problem is that the understanding of Leninism is not taught to the American people, in undergraduate or graduate education, or in the civilian and military workforce of the U.S. government. That almost total lack of attention to the greatest ideological change in American history is so curious that one might conclude it was deliberate and evinced the strength of Communists in waging political warfare against the American people.

The fourth implication to win the war is that the U.S. must capitalize upon Communism's lack of political legitimacy and civilizational confidence. The West should advance messages for political warfare to drive a wedge between the CCP and the Han population, so that the Party can never capitalize upon the greatness of the Han civilization. Likewise, Communism within the U.S., today evinced in the neo-Bolshevism of the progressive left, is incoherent, illegitimate, and anti-American, and this must be made clear to the American people.

The U.S. must exploit this split through a political warfare campaign centered on three avenues of attack. First, the Chinese people have the right, obligation, and motivation to overthrow the CCP and replace it with a government of their choosing, which might be a genuine form of Han polity for post-Communist China. Second, because the CCP is not democratic, it lacks political legitimacy. Its absence provides the United States, its allies and partners, and international community with justification to support the removal of the CCP and to undermine the actions of the PRC in international politics and international organizations. The third element of the political warfare campaign messaging would be that the CCP has failed to become Han after more than seventy years in power.

That is, not only is the Party a colonial polity and a product of Soviet imperialism, but the pull of Western ideology remains too great for the Party to overcome. The CCP is inherently Western; it is not Chinese. It is the last colonial power.

The fifth implication is that the American people, and the peoples of Western countries more broadly, must regain their political and civilizational confidence. Americans must understand the core of their identity as the American trinity and Westerners must comprehend why Western civilization is the best civilization. Americans must fight for these ideals with an energy and alacrity that has not been seen in a half century. American political confidence and Western civilizational confidence must be introduced once again as a component of political warfare against Communists at home and abroad. The American government and allied states need to advance the message that the future for all peoples is better if the American trinity is preserved. Its power must be sustained in the present confrontation against domestic Communists, the neo-Bolshevik progressive left, and the CCP.

Chapter 7 offers the conclusions of the book and looks forward to a renaissance of American identity and of Western civilization. The stronger American identity is, the weaker is Communism. A robust American identity is the antidote to the poison of Communism. Victory over Communism is possible by faith and courage, by knowledge and understanding of the Communist threat and by American history and Western civilization. There is much that Americans can learn from their past that can inform the fight against Communism today.

The era of the "End of History" is over. Or at least it is in the sense that its author, Francis Fukuyama, employing the great philosopher G. W. F. Hegel's ideas, conceived of it—as the triumph of liberalism.[11] Hegelian

11 See Francis Fukuyama, "The End of History?" *The National Interest*, No. 16 (Summer 1989), pp. 3–18; and Francis Fukuyama, *The End of History and the Last Man* (New York: Free Press, 1992).

strife has indeed returned. What could not be seen in 1989 was not only the return of ideological conflict but that this conflict would occur within the United States. Also not foreseen was that Lenin's Bolshevism, either in the PRC or America's variant, or both, might define History's end.

After all, AI is being developed by Lenin's intellectual grandchildren and great-grandchildren. The neo-Bolshevik progressivism found among the tech billionaires of Silicon Valley is baked into the LLMs. There is variation, but broadly that is true of Sam Altman's OpenAI's ChatGPT, Dario Amodei's Anthropic's Claude, Google's Gemini and Bard, and, of course, the PRC's DeepSeek. As more people become dependent on AI, so, too, the influence of neo-Bolshevism will grow, and expand very quickly. Lenin very well might defeat Madison if the American people do not prevent it. The victories in 1989 and 1991 were great but they were only battles in the Hundred Years' War. The war is yet to be won. Now is the time to win it.

II. The Significance of the Book

Studying the dynamics of the Hundred Years' War is important because Communism is the most formidable threat the U.S. has ever confronted. Comprehending the ideological origins and nature of this long war allows the American people and U.S. national security decision-makers to understand the source of the confrontation with the PRC and its ideological cause at home. Just as in the Cold War, when Americans faced the Soviet Union and Communism within the U.S., Americans once again face this twin danger.

This is one fight. The struggle against the PRC abroad and Communism at home is a related and interlinked struggle against a hyper-aggressive ideology intent on destroying the American way of life and political system and replacing it with a totalitarian government. The CCP supports the neo-Bolshevik progressives within the U.S. as they labor to destroy the country. At the same time, the neo-Bolsheviks support the PRC. The American people must see the connections between the threat abroad and at home.

Analyzing this allows the American people to understand the economic and political limitations and illegitimacy of the Soviet Union, and why the U.S. was able to defeat it. The Soviet population and leadership no longer believed that they were in a titanic struggle to build Communism and to liberate the workers of the world. In essence, at some point during the mature Leonid Brezhnev years in the 1970s, the Soviets and their Warsaw Pact allies did not believe in their ideology, which was a profound weakness in the Cold War against the West. Very likely the "last Bolshevik," the chief of ideology and the Communist Party's Second Secretary, Mikhail Suslov, was the last who truly believed in Communism. Suslov died in January 1982. Men replaced him in his position but not in spirit—that was long dead, and anyone who has read or seen David Lean's adaptation of Boris Pasternak's *Doctor Zhivago* might wonder if, perhaps, it never existed.

As with the Soviet Union, the PRC's Communist ideology allows Americans to understand the PRC's illegitimacy, despotism, incoherence, and weaknesses. As a result, Americans may understand vulnerabilities in the relationship between the PRC and the U.S., and between the Chinese population and government. Those weaknesses and cleavages will contain strategic asymmetries that the U.S. and its allies may exploit to counter the ability of the PRC to advance its interests in the Indo-Pacific and globally. Military and diplomatic history possess many important insights for U.S. decision-makers today as they evaluate policy options in similar strategic situations. Ideological history does as well. The history of ideas, especially the ideology of its enemies, is directly relevant to the American people because ideology was the genesis of conflict with the Soviet Union and is today with the PRC.

The ideological upheaval of the "1776 Moment" must be studied to determine if there are substantial weaknesses or cleavages introduced by the change and which would provide strategic asymmetries for the PRC and the neo-Bolsheviks in the U.S., the UK, and Europe. Equally, the ideological change from political liberalism to neo-Bolshevik progressivism might reveal new strengths that would provide asymmetries for the United States in its confrontation with the PRC. The U.S. should defeat the PRC because the incoherence of Leninism is no match for the mind of Madison. Whether that will happen is the dispositive question of the twenty-first century.

The prodigious power and political stability of the United States do not mean that it is omnipotent or will have a united society in perpetuity. The robustness of a political system is anchored in the American trinity. Its comprehension permits Americans to have trust and concomitant support for the country's political institutions and political norms. I recognize that the United States faces challenges today as it has in the past.

This book centers on the American trinity. It acknowledges but does not consider economic prosperity, the broader health of the American economy, federal debt and other fiscal problems, or demographic changes such as population aging. Thus, it accepts that the United States faces significant challenges in the economic, social, and military realms and inevitably will suffer setbacks well beyond the adverse, near-term economic and social impact of Covid-19 or certain future shocks, be they pandemics or economic crises. As important as each of these factors is, the American trinity is the bedrock of a stable domestic political system and governs America's economic, social, and military considerations. As the American trinity remains strong or weakens, so, too, do the governing principles of economic and social life and America's national security.

I introduce the concept of political and civilizational confidence and its role in the Lenin vs. Madison fight. That understanding informs the American people of why American political and civilizational confidence are essential for grasping why the U.S. and its allies were able to defeat the Bolsheviks during the Cold War—and why the U.S. can defeat the Bolsheviks in Beijing and neo-Bolsheviks among the American left.

Lastly, the book makes two major assumptions. First, Communist ideology is the source of the CCP's objective to supplant the United States as the dominant power and remake international institutions so they further the rule of the CCP. As a result, the rivalry between the PRC and the United States will continue to intensify. The PRC's military capabilities are formidable even as the PRC's economy is in a downturn. The diplomatic, military, and technological fruits of its decades of growth threaten U.S. national security. The motivation for the current cold war, a period of intense security competition in international politics, and the continued growth of these capabilities are the consequences of the CCP's ideology. At present, the signs of increased security competition are ubiquitous beyond the military dimension and are found in ideology, diplomacy, economics and trade, intelligence collection, and power projection. At the same time, intense security competition between Beijing and Washington is not innate. It is driven by the CCP's ideology. Were China a democracy, or if China were to return to something akin to the traditional political system it possessed for many centuries, then security competition with the U.S. would be greatly reduced.

While the PRC is likely to remain a fierce rival of the United States, the PRC has entered a period of economic decline. The decline is evident, even if its full parameters are not. As a result, the country's economic doldrums may be gradual as relative power between the U.S. and the PRC again widens in favor of the U.S. Such a measured economic and demographic deterioration will not stop the PRC's ambitions, but it provides the U.S. with a more favorable security environment and an opportunity to capitalize upon a weaker PRC. Alternatively, the decline may be precipitous, leading to dramatic loss of power and an existential crisis for the CCP—even opening a pathway to its overthrow.

Second, the book assumes that Communism has not yet won, not by a long shot, but the West is in a fight for its life, and the resultant intense struggle will not be stopped by some *deus ex machina*. The American people must not depend upon a dramatic reversal in the CCP's ideology or in the grand strategies of the PRC. Neither will it be altered by a dramatic change of strategic course because of changes within the CCP, such as with

Xi Jinping's death, or epochal economic or political changes within the PRC or the United States and its allies. The American people, those of the West, and their supporters around the world, must shoulder the burdens of this fight, and steel themselves for it.

Chapter 2

Leninism and the Comintern

In George Orwell's *1984*, the masterful characterization of how totalitarianism crushes humanity, the protagonist, Winston Smith, writes in his diary, "I understand HOW: I do not understand WHY." So it is with all peoples living under totalitarianism. The "how" is witnessed every day and crushes the humanity out of those who live under its tyranny. Orwell's Smith understood the Party's strategy, its methods, its organization, its behavior; all are evident and critical to understand if we wish to avoid totalitarianism. But the *why* question, why was the Party doing this—Orwell's answer was, in essence, that is the nature of totalitarianism. A boot stamping on a human face, forever. This chapter explains Leninism, the "how" and the "why" the boot is stamping on the human face, forever.

The cause of the Hundred Years' War is Leninism. Hence, it is essential to understand its fundamentals and the Comintern, the vehicle to spread Leninism, including the CCP. That provides the foundation for understanding Maoism and Xi Jinping's thought, which are explained in chapter 3. To address these issues, this chapter has three objectives. It explains Communist ideology, and specifically Leninism, which was the first Communist movement to seize power successfully. It examines the role of the Comintern. And it presents the Comintern's essential role in creating, sustaining, and guiding the CCP.

This book's answer to Orwell is that Leninism is inevitably totalitarian, not due to the inevitable failure of its millenarian dream of life in the

Communist paradise, or because of the innate nature of totalitarianism. To be sure, there are strong proclivities, even certainty, for Leninism to become the world that Orwell described. Nonetheless, Orwell's question is compelling: Why are Communists totalitarian, the boot smashing the face of humanity forever?

The answer is that Communists seek power, the total control of people. That power is employed to destroy everything about the old order because they hate it. That hate is incandescent. Their loathing, contempt, and rejection of individual rights and freedoms, of faith and family, and of liberal democracy is so great that they must be destroyed. What comes afterward is totalitarianism in a form that deliberately maximizes cruelty, brutality, chaos, and incoherence, and, in fact, is intended by Leninists to cause the destruction of Western civilization.

That is the motivation for the civil war in the West that Lenin started and that the West's populations are fighting today from Europe to America and Australia.

I. Introduction to Communist Ideology

Since Karl Marx and Friedrich Engels developed Communist ideology, its central objective has been consistent.[1] It is to destroy the bourgeois societies of the West through a working-class, or proletarian, revolution to introduce the era of Communism. For Marx and Engels, this would be liberation for the working class and would bring an end to its alienation.

---

1 For this book, Marx and Engels' key works are Karl Marx and Friedrich Engels, *The Communist Manifesto* (New York: International Publishers, 2014 [1848]). These initial thoughts were developed by Marx and Engels, *The German Ideology* (New York: International Publishers, 2016 [written in 1846, first published 1932]); Marx in *Grundrisse: Foundations of the Critique of Political Economy* (New York: Harper & Row, 1972 [written in 1857–1858, first published in 1939]); and Marx, *Capital*, 3 Vols. (New York: International Publishers, 1980 [1867, 1885, 1894]).

Under Communism, there would be communal ownership of the means of production. This meant there would be no exploitation and no class conflict, the driver of revolutionary change. Communism would mark the end of history and the dawn of an irenic epoch due to the abolition of private property and the elimination of class conflict.

However, as history has shown, Communist rule is horrific for the people who suffer under it. Communism is innately aggressive by its own logic because it must destroy alternative political ideologies and polities for history to advance and its lofty and illusory goals to be achieved. The ideology is brutal in its suppression of human freedoms and liberties because it has no mandate from the people. There is no consent from the governed and so it is an illegitimate political system. Communist polities stay in power through coercion of the people, coercion that inevitably will result in brutality used against the citizenry and gross human rights abuses.

For Leninism, the Communist Party would be the vanguard of the proletariat. The Party would seize the state and bring all else, such as social life, culture, and attitudes, under its control. The ultimate intent was to destroy bourgeois life, capitalist states, and Western civilization. The intent of Bolshevism was to overturn everything, including all cultural, social, economic, political, and international relationships as they labored to create a "perfect society" through a Communist polity.

In the West, Communists recognized that the revolution would not come from workers rebelling on the factory floor as Marx and Engels envisioned or from a supremely disciplined Communist Party executing a *coup d'état*. Trade unions were complicit in suppressing the class consciousness of workers and so they could never fulfill a revolutionary role, and Western bourgeois governments and societies were too strong and Western Communist Parties too weak for a Bolshevik *coup d'état* by a Communist Party as in 1917. Workers were blinded by the material comforts of the West, what was called false consciousness, and so would never develop sufficient understanding of the true interests of their class.

Yet, as will be seen, Lenin and other Bolsheviks did provide them with the tools for a successful political warfare campaign to achieve victory in the West. To advance the revolution in the West, Communists would employ political warfare, first, through the ideas industry—K–12 education and universities, law schools, media, publishing houses, think tanks and foundations; and second, through culture—including Hollywood, art, literature, theater, TV, and social media. They would be penetrated and remade to advance Communism under the guise of neo-Bolshevik progressivism. Today, the form of the revolution in the West is found in the flowering of neo-Bolshevik progressivism in political parties of the left.

Leninism is critical to comprehend because it is responsible for the conditions in which the U.S. and Western Europe find themselves—from Mamdani to endless mass migration. Leninism is also essential for grasping the foundations of how the U.S. and the West came to be in this dangerous situation; that means understanding the importance of Bolshevik thought, the Comintern, and the CCP. The examination of Leninism allows Americans to understand that the CCP and its ideology are entirely dependent upon Leninism. The CCP was formed, led, and controlled by the Comintern, which also trained its key cadres. After a quarter century of nurturing the CCP, it was Stalin, the Comintern, and the Soviet Army, coupled with U.S. gross strategic mistakes, vacillation, and Communist traitors and fellow travelers within the U.S. government, that brought the CCP to power in 1949.[2]

Leninism and the cult of personality perfected under Stalin are so dominant that the Chinese Communist ideology of Maoism is derivative from them.[3] As illuminated below, Mao took his arguments on the peas-

2 The Comintern was officially terminated in 1943 to placate Stalin's allies in World War II, Great Britain and the United States. However, it was relaunched in 1947 as the Information Bureau of Communist and Workers' Parties, or Cominform.

3 The Soviet system as it developed under Stalin was a continuation of Leninism. Stalinism, the system that prevailed until 1953, or February 1956 when Nikita

antry from existing conceptions of the role of the peasantry in Communist revolutions. These date from Lenin's 1906 recognition of the role that class could play in the revolution. Later, he took his ideas regarding the Cultural Revolution from left-wing Bolshevik Alexander A. Bogdanov (born Alexander Aleksandrovich Malinovskii, 1873–1928) and then Stalin in 1928 at the start of the first Five-Year Plan.[4] It was Bogdanov and other "left-wing" Bolsheviks, like the Commissar for Education Anatoly Lunacharski, who made the argument, as Mao did forty years later, that the entire society—its attitudes, culture, history, customs, traditions, education, language, holidays, and venerated historical figures, including

---

Khrushchev denounced Stalin in the "secret speech," has not been affected in any essential way by the changes of the post-Stalinist era. Lenin was the creator of totalitarian doctrine and of the totalitarian state in embryo. Stalin's own peculiarities, that is, psychotic behavior, lust for power, vindictiveness, jealousy, and paranoid suspicion, were allowed to flower in the Soviet Union due to the system Lenin constructed. The despotic system that was the Soviet Union or the PRC today remains in force due to Lenin's founding. Lenin made the despotism possible irrespective of whether, in a particular year, official killings are counted in the millions, the tens of thousands, or thousands, whether torture is used as a matter of routine or only occasionally, and whether the victims are workers, peasants, intellectuals, party bureaucrats, or Uyghur and other Muslims. The principal difference between Leninism and Stalinism was that Lenin's political opportunism was to some extent restrained by doctrinal considerations. In Stalinism, and Maoism, doctrine was absolutely subordinated to the purpose of legitimizing and glorifying the Soviet leader and government, and everything they did.

4 Bogdanov was a Bolshevik in name for some of his life and in spirit for most of his life. In fact, he cofounded the Party in 1903 when they split from the Mensheviks, although Lenin expelled him from the Party in 1909. He supported the Revolution and remained influential in Bolshevik circles, especially in left-wing circles. He became a professor of philosophy at Moscow State University and was arrested and held by the Cheka for five weeks in 1923. He became interested in blood transfusions as a means of restoring health and vigor and, ironically, died due to contracting tuberculosis and malaria in 1928 as a result of a transfusion.

statues—had to be remade to be in accord with what was politically correct. That is, what the Party dictated.

Inherently, Communists cannot accept other ideologies and labor to eradicate them. Communists are required to confront and defeat them because only they possess a "scientific understanding of society" and know that purportedly they are on the right side of history. All other ideologies, whether secular like political liberalism or informed by religion, such as the era of absolutism or political Islam today, are iniquitous and dangerous because they lead to false consciousness among the working class and even Party members. In truth, Communists are aggressive because theirs is an illegitimate form of government. They must always have internal and external enemies to motivate their believers, to terrorize their citizens, and to sustain and justify their totalitarian grip on power.

For Communists, the war against the West has been waged since the 1917 Bolshevik Revolution. That has not altered even as the West's policies toward the Soviet Union have varied considerably. For example, the expectation by many in the West that wartime cooperation would continue after the defeat of Germany and Japan was soon shattered. This perpetual, restless aggression was well illustrated by Soviet leader Joseph Stalin's February 9, 1946, speech, in which he boldly delivered the first volley of the Cold War.

In his address, he made three major points: First, Marxism-Leninism was a fundamentally superior ideology and economic system to democratic capitalism; second, World War II was a test of all political systems and one that the Soviet system not only passed but that its viability was proved on the battlefield and in the sacrifices made by the Soviet people; and third, that war was inevitable as long as monopolistic capitalism existed. As capitalism had caused both world wars, it certainly would cause a Third World War.

Accordingly, the Soviet people had to prepare themselves for war and devote themselves to achieving the goals of new Five-Year Plans. There would be no peace within the Soviet Union, as the people would have to commit themselves to victory, and equally, as Lenin identified, there could be no peace with the capitalist states.

Stalin's speech was a shock to the Allies. World War II had ended with Japan's surrender only five months before. It compelled the State Department to query the Moscow embassy for analysis. U.S. diplomat George Kennan responded with his famous "Long Telegram" of February 22, 1946. It also generated Winston Churchill's famous "Sinews of Peace," better known as the "Iron Curtain," speech at Westminster College in Fulton, Missouri, on March 5, 1946.

While Stalin openly announced that the cooperation of World War II was over and that the Soviets were once again waging war against the West, the CCP did as well in rhetoric and actions. The CCP has been at war against the West since coming to power in 1949, and the U.S. fought kinetic wars with the CCP in Korea and Vietnam. Today, the U.S. faces the CCP in the realm of political warfare. The U.S. has been slow off the mark, while the CCP has been adroitly waging political warfare to undermine the U.S. That has to change immediately.

II. Leninism: The Ideological Cause of the Hundred Years' War

Leninism is partially anchored in the thought of Marx and Engels but is principally the result of the eponymous thought of Lenin. Lenin subscribed to most of the major elements of Marx and Engels' arguments. This includes class conflict and historical materialism, the evils of capitalism, and the inevitability of the Communist revolution that would bring the proletariat to power.

Although inspired by Marx and Engels, Lenin was far more than an adherent or interpreter of their philosophy. He developed his own ideas and forced them upon a political movement, in which he and his small group of supporters were usually in the minority. His political thought and his movement were supremely successful. Arguably, they were more so than the great liberal revolutions of 1776 and 1789. During the Cold War, Leninism was the great rival to liberalism or democratic socialism in the West. Leninism remains so in this century, due the CCP's embrace of the ideology. Although most Americans do not recognize it, Leninism has been waging political warfare against the U.S. since 1917.[5] The costs of that war have been substantial. It has also gone kinetic as the U.S. fought the fruits of Leninism in Korea and Vietnam—and it may well fight a kinetic war against the CCP sometime soon.

Lenin's ideas made ten major contributions to Communism, history, and contemporary international politics, and these are important for understanding the Hundred Years' War. They define him as a singular figure in the pantheon of Communism. Lenin was the most important theoretician and practitioner in the history of Communist political thought.[6] Marx was certainly the most important theoretician but was not a practitioner. Engels made important theoretical contributions and bankrolled Marx for much of his life but, like Marx, he was not a practitioner. Likewise, Stalin was a practitioner but only a modest theoretician. Only Lenin was the entelechy of both theory and practice. Table One summarizes the ideology of Leninism.

First, Lenin argued that the Communist Party must be the vanguard of the proletariat and it must make the revolution. In direct contradiction to Marx and Engels' catechism, Lenin argued that the working class alone could never develop sufficient class consciousness to foment the revolution.[7]

---

5 See V. I. Lenin's "Letter to American Workers," August 18, 1918, *Collected Works*, Vol. 28 (Moscow: Progress Publishers, 1965), pp. 62–75.

6 The focus of the study is on Lenin's contributions that are relevant to the Hundred Years' War against Communism, but his contributions include other important ones, such as his explanation for imperialism and his critiques of both left-wing and right-wing Communism.

7 Vladimir Lenin, *What Is to Be Done?* (Moscow: Progress Publishers, 1971 [1902]). Marx and Engels believed that the emancipation of the working class is the work of the working class itself. Lenin strongly disagreed. "By their own efforts," Lenin wrote, "the working class can only arrive at a trade union mentality"—meaning that they can only bargain with their employers, strike, and protest on a limited scale and will never reach revolutionary consciousness without the Communist Party. Lenin, *What Is to Be Done?*, p. 99.

Table One: The Ideology of Leninism

The Core Ideas of Leninism
1. The Communist Party is the vanguard of the working class (proletariat) and rules in their name due to the Party's "scientific understanding" of society which is the Party's self-justification for its tyranny. The Party causes the revolution through its supreme skill at agitation, propaganda, organization and willingness to employ terror and violence.
2. The Communist Party must advance "revolutionary defeatism" (the worse, the better) to undermine existing order.
3. Both the peasantry and proletariat are revolutionary classes.
4. The Communist Party must possess iron discipline and be ruled by "democratic centralism," no deviation from the Party line, all thought, speech, expression, and behavior must be politically correct.
5. Devised the template that subsequent Communist parties would follow.
6. Party had to possess an urgency and immediacy for offensive action *à outrance*.
7. Lenin saw the world through the fundamental *kto-kogo* (who-whom) question—who rules over whom, and who wields power over whom, which is how the Bolsheviks saw the world and identified whom they must attack to seize power.
8. Lenin was a totalitarian and so was ruthless in crushing resistance, which was a defining feature of subsequent Leninist regimes.
9. Lenin was the architect of the revolution and the institution builder to advance its spread both in theoretical and practical terms—he founded the Comintern (Communist International) and the united front.
10. Lenin starts a civil war in Western civilization between its supporters and those who seek to destroy it.

The Communist Party would have to lead the proletariat and peasantry to the Revolution and then rule in the name of the workers and peasants. As the vanguard of the proletariat, the Party was the organizer, leader, and ideologist to move the workers and peasants beyond the horizon of bourgeois society.[8] The Party would have to cause the revolution. Human agency was necessary; it would not unfold solely as a result of a historical process as Marx and Engels anticipated.

In Lenin's vision, the Party would cause the revolution through its potent tools: supreme skill at agitation, propaganda, organization, and terror and violence, which were always present and employed when needed. It would turn out that terror and violence were always needed once in power for the Communists to keep their control.

The Party was composed of a small, efficient, deeply committed intellectual elite who had a scientific understanding of history, politics, and society in light of Marxist principles. For Lenin, the Party was the source of political legitimacy and of inherently correct policy by virtue of its scientific knowledge of society. This was the founding principle of the Soviet state and is of the CCP today. This justifies the Party's monopoly of power and its position as the sole fount of knowledge concerning society and therefore the absolute authority for that society. At root, Lenin argued that the Party always knows better than the society itself concerning what are the latter's interests, needs, and even desires. The people may be too backward or obtuse to understand these, but the Party can divine them thanks to its scientific knowledge—this is "scientific socialism" and is the foundation of the Communist Party's claim to rule in Russia or in the PRC.

---

8 Lenin's *What Is to Be Done?* was heavily influenced by the failure of the Russian revolutionary movements of the 1870s, the example of iron leadership of the German socialists, and the writings of Sergey Nechayev, *Catechism of a Revolutionary* (New York: Pattern Books, 2020 [1869]). It could be argued that Lenin sought the German organization imposed upon Russian revolutionary enthusiasm.

This is a critical point: The Party justifies its rule by claiming that it possesses a scientific knowledge of society. Of course, this is absurd. Neither Marx nor Lenin had any knowledge of society, nor did they care about its members. Both sought to force societies into a Procrustean bed, no matter the costs to individuals or colossal damage to society. It is risible if it were not gravely serious for those who have suffered under Leninist tyranny.

Core Party members would be professional revolutionaries. Certainly, in Russia, the Bolsheviks were what Lenin wanted: a select community, an almost religious order of professional revolutionaries, crusaders of a materialistic faith, a selection of the most self-sacrificing, decided, and active of the intelligentsia.[9] All were committed to the revolution and replacing bourgeois and capitalistic rule with Communism by any means possible, including the violent seizure of power when historical conditions were correct.

Second, Lenin advanced the idea of "revolutionary defeatism," often popularized as "the worse, the better." The worse conditions were for the working class and broader population, the better were the conditions for revolution. It was impossible to fight for the revolution within a country at war, as Russia was against Japan in 1904–1905 and again against the Central Powers (1914–1918), unless one is prepared to accept defeat for the country. Defeat would provide the best opportunity for revolution.

Hence, it was the duty of the Communist to work for the defeat of their country, as revolution depended upon defeat. This perspective helped to isolate Lenin and his followers during the first three years of World War I. Later, Lenin's decision to work with the Germans and his acceptance of support from Berlin hurt the Bolsheviks in 1917, as many in Russia and in Europe called attention to Lenin's support from

---

9 They were the zenith of Bolshevik/CPSU leadership. Stalin would crush individuals with these qualities leading directly to the mediocre leadership of the CPSU for the rest of the existence of the Soviet Union.

Germany—calling him, with good reason, a German agent. However, the charge, while accurate, did not have the effect desired because Lenin's ruthlessness rendered it impotent. For Lenin, any action was acceptable to secure and hold power.

Ironically, given how the Bolsheviks actually seized power in November 1917, Lenin was opposed to spontaneous revolution, as occurred in the 1905 Russian Revolution. For Lenin, historical processes would never cause the revolution. The Party had to grasp history by the neck and force the revolution. Once in power, the Party would remain for all time and tolerate no opposition. The Party itself would function as a well-trained army in the hands of its leaders.

The political struggle for revolution was everything in Leninist thought. There were no other issues than the revolution and its maintenance once it had occurred. Philosophical questions, art, literature, film, law, medicine, religion, culture, all had no meaning in themselves but were merely weapons in the political struggle.

Third, Lenin embraced both the proletariat and the peasantry. While Marx and Engels dismissed the peasantry and "the idiocy of rural life," Lenin and Leon Trotsky (born Lev Bronstein, 1879–1940) saw their revolutionary potential.[10] Lenin and Trotsky perceived that the peasantry were co-equal class partners with the proletariat, as evinced in the 1905 Russian Revolution. A review of Maoism reveals the Leninist, or more broadly, Bolshevik, genesis of Mao's ideology. It was Lenin and Trotsky, not Mao or other Chinese Communists, who identified the importance of the peasantry in furthering the Communist Revolution.

Lenin was influenced by the 1905 Russian Revolution to write that a new type of bourgeois-democratic revolution based upon the peasantry was possible. Lenin's April 1906 pamphlet, *The Revision of the Agrarian*

---

10 Marx and Engels were famously contemptuous of the peasantry and the "idiocy" of rural life in the *Communist Manifesto* (1848) and subsequently.

Programme of the Workers' Party, was a truly revolutionary work.[11] It was a major modification of the Marx-Engels dogma. In fact, it was heresy. The peasantry could be attracted by promises of land nationalization and redistribution to become a revolutionary force.[12] Significantly, Lenin believed the peasantry could enter the Marxist conception of history as a progressive force. Ideally, the peasantry would be aligned with a strong proletariat, but where the proletariat is weak, then the peasantry could be in the vanguard of the revolution.

Thus, long before Mao or his CCP comrades, it was Lenin who identified how the peasantry could support the Party's revolutionary aims. Trotsky's arguments, also advanced in 1906, were similar and even broader. He advocated for non-proletarian social groups, largely the peasantry, to become part of the workers' government.[13]

Fourth, Lenin dictated that the Party must possess iron discipline, which requires what the Bolsheviks called "democratic centralism." That is, debates could happen within the Party at the appropriate level, but once the Party line was adopted, further debate was prohibited, and all members must adhere to the Party line without deviation or face the consequences which were quickly delivered by the secret police. All thought, speech, expression, and behavior must be politically correct, that is, in accord with the Party's dictates. In addition, Lenin advocated for an "inner Party" that would lead and decide the Party's direction and a larger "outer Party," which would not be involved in decision-making but would rubber-stamp

---

11 V. I. Lenin, "Revision of the Agrarian Programme of the Workers' Party," in V. I. Lenin, *Collected Works*, Vol. 10 (Moscow: Progress Publishers, 1962), pp. 165–194.

12 Karl A. Wittfogel, "The Marxist View of China (Part I)," *The China Quarterly*, No. 11 (July–September 1962), pp. 1–20, p. 15.

13 Leon Trotsky, *The Permanent Revolution and Results and Prospects* (New York: Merit, 1969). This was detailed in "The Proletariat in Power and the Peasantry," in *Results and Prospects*, published in 1906, pp. 69–75. Far more than Lenin in his contemporaneous work, Trotsky emphasized the subordination of the peasantry to the proletariat.

and enforce the decisions of the inner Party. The Party was never intended to be democratic but always directed by a small number of men, which, in practice, meant one man: first Lenin, and soon after his death in 1924, Stalin.

The Party was distinguished by its ideological unity, efficiency, hierarchical and centralized structure and their conviction that it represents the interest of the proletariat and the peasantry, whatever the proletariat and peasantry may think. It was a Party that deemed its own interests to be automatically those of the working class and peasantry and of universal progress, because it possessed the "scientific knowledge" that entitled it to ignore, except for tactical purposes, the actual interests, wishes, and aspirations of the people it appointed itself to represent. As described below, that is the great source of the illegitimacy of Communists wherever they are in power.

Fifth, Lenin's pathway to power and model of Communist Party rule created the template that subsequent Communist parties would follow. Lenin provided the theory and practice of Communist revolution, and the lens through which to view struggles for power. Most importantly, he demonstrated that it could be accomplished in a historically backward state for Marxists like Russia. If the revolution could succeed in Russia, it was possible everywhere. Lenin clearly stated why the Bolshevik Party rightly led the Communist movement and was the model for other Communist parties to follow, must heed the lessons of Bolshevik experience before and after the revolution. This, he said, is because Bolshevism:

> went through fifteen years of practical history (1903–17 [*sic*]) unequalled anywhere in the world in its wealth of experience. During those fifteen years, no other country knew anything even approximating to that revolutionary experience, that rapid and varied succession of different forms of the movement—legal and illegal, peaceful and stormy, underground and open, local circles and mass movements, and parliamentary and terrorist forms. In no

> other country has there been concentrated, in so brief a period such a wealth of forms, shades, and methods of struggle of *all* classes of modern society, a struggle which, owning the backwardness of the country and severity of the tsarist yoke, matured exceptionally rapidly, and assimilated most eagerly and successfully the appropriate "last word" of American and European political experience.[14]

Lenin offered the tools, the tool kit, and the instruction manual for revolution that was widely and immediately emulated as the path to successful revolution. Leninism had a near-monopoly on the path to Communism that inspired and generated successful revolutions around the world from China, to Hungary, to Cuba, as well as failed Leninist coups in Bavaria, the Ruhr, Saxony, Thuringia, Estonia, and Bulgaria, and the imposition of Leninism by the Red Army in Central and Eastern Europe. His legitimacy as preeminent prophet of Communist revolution was assured by the CCP, whose members still venerate him even after his statues were removed in Europe following the 1989 and 1991 revolutions in Europe and Russia.

Sixth, Lenin's vision of the Party was that it had to possess an urgency and immediacy for action *à outrance*. Lenin was defined by audacity, but a careful, premeditated audacity. Always favoring the offense, Lenin forged the hyper-aggressive Communist Party that the world came to know in the century following. Lenin's Party waged metaphorical and actual warfare on the Russian people, as well as those of the world. Lenin's Party made socialism within Russia with dramatic and long-lasting consequences for the Russian people.

His Party defeated his challengers within the larger Communist movement. This was principally Karl Liebknecht's (1871–1919) and Rosa Luxemburg's (1871–1919) effort, as they were his greatest rivals among

---

14 V. I. Lenin, "Left Wing Communism—An Infantile Disorder," in V. I. Lenin, *Collected Works*, Vol. 31 (Moscow: Progress Publishers, 1966), p. 26. Emphasis original.

Communists. They were "left-wing" Communists who argued revolution had to come from the working class, not led by a Communist Party. Their January 1919 Spartacus League (*Spartakusbund*) offered a brief window to an alternative to Leninism before it was brutally ended by the Weimar government and the *Freikorps*.

Luxemburg, a Polish-German revolutionary, was an opponent of the Bolsheviks because Lenin called for a Third International, the Comintern, based on professional revolutionaries. Luxemburg was suspicious of professional revolutionaries and intensely disliked their tactics of permeation and manipulation of the mass movement.[15] She believed in the spontaneous evolution of the proletariat toward revolutionary action. For her, the premature formation of a new international could only sever the small groups of revolutionaries from the masses. It would be a step backward for the revolution in the West. Of course, it was Lenin's vision that triumphed and became the template for the global Communist movement.

Rather than waiting for the workers, Lenin would force the revolution. He created the Comintern to spread the revolution to capitalist states and to overthrow imperialist rule in the Third World. Moreover, it was Lenin's Party that defeated the efforts of capitalist states to strangle the revolution in Russia and thus prevent it from spreading.

What Lenin accomplished in the last decade of his life was truly frenetic and awesome. Lenin prepared and then led his Party to power in the *coup d'état* of November 7, 1917, defeated the White armies, implemented War Communism, reversed it with the New Economic Policy (NEP), founded the Comintern, spread revolution throughout Europe, and attempted to

15 F. Borkenau, *World Communism: A History of the Communist International* (Ann Arbor: University of Michigan Press, 1962), pp. 86–87. In her writings that came to light a few years after her death, Rosa Luxemburg strongly criticized Lenin, first, for making the peasants satisfied proprietors of the land, which transformed them from a revolutionary to counterrevolutionary class. Second, she lambasted him for disbanding the Constituent Assembly and argued for rule by the Soviet regime combined with parliamentary democracy.

spread it to China, the United Kingdom, and the United States. It was Lenin who ordered the 1920 invasion of Poland as a necessary step to spread the revolution to Germany.

In fact, had the Red Army succeeded in reaching Germany, the history of the twentieth century would have been dramatically different. A Leninist revolution in Germany, had it been successful, would have reached its apotheosis, as Marxism predicted. Marxists recognized the German working class to be the vanguard of proletarian consciousness. Its radicalization, backed by the force of the Red Army, was a credible and imminent threat to the nascent Weimar Republic, which was proclaimed in 1918, and so was younger than the Bolshevik regime.

Furthermore, the Russo-Polish War was a great threat to the West and an exceptional opportunity for Lenin. The Red Army was led by its foremost soldier, twenty-seven-year-old General Mikhail Tukhachevsky, who pushed the Polish army from Kyiv to Warsaw in two months. British Foreign Secretary Lord Curzon drew a line in the sand warning the Bolsheviks not to cross. With typical boldness and impudence, Lenin ignored this warning.

With French support, led by General Maxime Weygand, who had been chief of staff to the Supreme Allied Commander, Marshal Ferdinand Foch, the Polish army delivered a catastrophic defeat to the Red Army. In August, the Poles attacked. Tukhachevsky's command disintegrated, incurring 150,000 casualties. Another 66,000 men became Polish prisoners.

It was a victory that was called one of the decisive battles of the twentieth century, for as much as Charles Martel's victory at Tours in A.D. 732 had defeated the Muslim surge into France, so the battle of Warsaw checked Communism's first overt westward thrust. In the fighting that followed, the Bolsheviks lost another 200,000 men before agreeing to an armistice in October, which became peace with the Treaty of Riga signed on March 18, 1921.

Seventh, Lenin was a student of power politics and that heavily informed his worldview. Lenin and the Bolsheviks saw the world through the fundamental *kto-kogo* (who-whom) question—who rules over whom, and who wields power over whom. Lenin was as clear-eyed a realist as could be found—he perceived everything as a power struggle, who was ruling over whom, and if Communists were not, his intent was to ensure they ruled over all others. This approach allowed the Bolsheviks to identity with precision their enemies. Yes, the bourgeoisie were the enemy, but Lenin's sharp eye allowed for targeting specific individuals or groups for their effectiveness. For Communists, who rules over whom is the perspective to study class conflict but also international politics. In every case, Communists should rule over other political parties in domestic politics or states in world politics.

Eighth, as a master of tyranny, Lenin was ruthless in crushing resistance, which was a defining feature of subsequent Leninist regimes. His ruthlessness was ubiquitous from the Bolshevik seizure of power in 1917 and included founding the Cheka (All-Russian Extraordinary Commission, which was the first Soviet secret police organization, the antecedent of the famous Committee for State Security [KGB]) from 1917 to 1922, when it then became the GPU (State Political Directorate).[16] Led by Felix Dzerzhinsky, the Cheka implemented the "Red Terror," executing many, many millions and filling the Gulag (Main Directorate of Correctional Labor Camps) with many tens of millions more.

It was most notably displayed during the Kronstadt Rebellion of March 1921. The rebellion was conducted by many of the very sailors who supported the Bolsheviks four years before. The Kronstadt sailors were a symbol of Red October and so their rebellion was especially dramatic and portentous. They were hungry and, because many maintained close ties

16 The GPU lasted for about a year and continued a cavalcade of name changes ending, at least for most of the Cold War, as the Committee on State Security, KGB. After the GPU, came the OGPU, the Joint State Political Directorate, then the NKVD, the People's Commissariat for Internal Affairs, next the MGB, Ministry of State Security, and finally the KGB. Soviet Military Intelligence, the GRU, or Main Intelligence Directorate, was a discrete intelligence service.

to their villages, they understood Bolshevik tactics, including the employment of brutal food requisition squads and the presence of rural famine. About 40,000 men, including sailors, soldiers, and armed workers, called for elections, which was unacceptable to the Bolsheviks. Moreover, they employed Lenin's 1917 revolutionary slogan, "All Power to the Soviets," which meant all power to the workers' councils (soviets), as part of their political demands.

Trotsky employed about 150,000 men to suppress the revolt. It took multiple attempts and significant casualties (at least 25,000 loyal Red Army soldiers), but the Bolsheviks crushed the rebellion before it could spread. The result was significant, and major changes were needed.

Lenin himself recognized that the rebellion was spontaneous and not a product of White leadership. It was a genuine uprising in the face of totalitarian oppression, famine, and harsh economic conditions. In response, Lenin implemented the NEP, which permitted the return of what was largely a free market. In a pair of shocking public speeches, Lenin acknowledged that War Communism had been a mistake and called for the transition "to commercial principles," to stop the economic freefall. The NEP was a form of state capitalism, but he maintained it was only a strategic retreat.

In place of food requisitioning, peasants were assessed a specified amount of their crops to be furnished to the state as a tax. Once met, they were free to dispose of what was left on the open market. Instead of equal pay, wages for workers were fixed to reflect ability, effort, and degree of responsibility. The large industries, the "commanding heights" of the economy, transportation, utilities, the financial system, and natural resources, remained under state control. Shops and many small industries were permitted to operate for private profit, which gave rise to a new class of small businessmen, the "NEPmen." Stalin would crush them starting in 1927 as the NEP was quickly replaced by the first Five-Year Plan.

Ninth, Lenin was the architect of the revolution and the institution builder to advance its spread both in practical terms, he founded the

Comintern, described in detail below, and in theoretical ones, the united front, which I will describe here. The united front is one of Lenin's and more broadly, the Bolsheviks' contributions. It is a tool to destroy Western governments and societies.

Lenin advanced the united front argument in a pamphlet, *Left Wing Communism—An Infantile Disorder*, which was written in 1920, and is an exceptional work for understanding the grand design as well as strategy and tactics in the Communist movement.[17] In essence, he provided the design, instruction manual, tools, and tool kit to execute a Communist revolution through a Bolshevik-type *coup d'état* or through the united front.

It remains relevant today for its instruction and for its influence on the Comintern and on subsequent Communist thinkers, including Mao and the CCP and its United Front Work Department, the Frankfurt School, and the modern neo-Bolshevik progressive thinkers. That influence is due to the united front, which has been profoundly important for the success of Communist movements around the global and in the U.S. today. It also captures the essence of Lenin as a revolutionary intellectual and political thinker.

Lenin was at different times was a rigid sectarian and an inspired opportunist. For many years before the Bolshevik Revolution, he was the leader of a small, isolated, and impotent sect. Yet he was also the author of the bible of Communist opportunism—*Left Wing Communism*. He demonstrated his greatest flexibility and creativity after the Revolution when he proved capable of employing contradictory dogmas, stressing the dictates of orthodoxy or its opposite as the need arose. At the same time, Lenin could not work without dogmas; he was both rigid sectarian and a

17 Lenin, "Left Wing Communism—An Infantile Disorder," pp. 17–117. By left wing Communism, Lenin meant the *Spartakusbund*, the thought of Liebknecht and Luxemburg, and their allies in the Netherlands, Sweden, and UK, who argued against the need for a disciplined Communist Party in favor of direct action by the masses. Lenin was not referring to the left-wing Bolsheviks like Lunacharski.

unapologetic opportunist. At any one time or in any one work, he appears to be absolutely rigid, static, and uncompromising. It is only when the entire span of his life and body of his work is considered that he reveals himself to be anything but doctrinaire and intransigent.

The historical context is important. In 1920, Lenin was asked whether the British Communist Party, then in the process of formation, should affiliate with British Labour Party. Most of the early British Communists had denounced the Labour Party for so long that they thought it was inconceivable that they should. To their surprise, Lenin strongly advised them to do so, on the condition that they could conduct free and independent Communist activity. What Lenin provided Communists was permission to work with and to penetrate "reactionary institutions" like the American Federation of Labor (AFL), or educational systems, or churches, or media, or parliament, or Congress—whatever works to advance the revolution.

The logic of the united front was originally based in Lenin's advice to the British Communists to enter into an electoral agreement with the British Labour Party. The intent was not designed to strengthen Labour. On the contrary, Lenin wrote that he wanted to "support" the Labour leader "in the same way as a rope supports one who is hanged."[18] Lenin's logic was that if Labour accepted Communist support, they would open the Labour Party to Communist agitation and propaganda, and thus aid Communism. If Labour rejected it, they could be exposed as enemies of working-class unity.

When Lenin first planted the seed of the united front, he conceived of the approach as useful for the only the weakest Communist Party, the British. There was still ample revolutionary optimism to spread the revolution through conquest. The Red Army was still advancing toward Germany. But when it was defeated outside of Warsaw in 1920, and when the Germany Communist uprising in the Ruhr in March 1921 also failed, the Bolsheviks and Comintern began to apply Lenin's direction broadly.

18 Lenin, "Left Wing Communism—An Infantile Disorder," p. 68.

As realists, the Bolsheviks saw that the direct path, the Bolshevik model, was not succeeding and likely would not be victorious in Europe. Thus, the attractiveness of the united front to provide worldwide "strategic maneuver" as Grigory Zinoviev (born Ovsei-Gershon Aronovich Radomyslsky, 1883–1936) called the united front. The united front was political warfare to spread the revolution by any means, including working with and penetrating groups and institutions, rather by a *coup d'état* or the Red Army. The united front was a change in tactics, not in strategic objective. It would take different forms in different countries but always to the same end of advancing Communism. The decline of the postwar revolutionary wave, the recovery of European capitalism, the internal crises suffered by the inexperienced Communist parties outside of Russia, and the victories of anti-Communists in Germany, Hungary, and Poland made the united front necessary.

The Communist conception of the united front must be understood from the Bolshevik perspective. As long as the Bolsheviks thought that they retained the offensive in the battle against world capitalism, it was never contemplated. It was devised as an expedient to move the Communists off the defensive after some major defeats and onto the offensive through new means, a political war of maneuver to find and exploit the enemy's weaknesses rather than a frontal assault against the strongest of point of the enemy's resistance, the government and state power.

Throughout the work, Lenin stressed the need for propaganda, agitation, and organization. Terror and violence were implicit and never far behind. These are the hallmarks of political warfare for Leninists and thus for the united front. Propaganda to advance the goals of the Bolsheviks and to define the enemy. Agitation, akin to Antifa today, meant being a physical force on the streets, on the factory floor, and in the barracks. Organization is the discipline of the Leninist Party to define the strategy and drive it forward no matter the opposition. Terror and violence are Communist muscle and always present. Strategically, Leninism always advances but that advance will not occur in a purblind manner, but in one that is reflective of local conditions. Organization does not necessarily mean through the Party, but through non-Party means. Soros' Open Society Foundation is a classic example of advancing the Communist agenda through a Communist Party in all but name. In fact, Soros' organization is a modern-day, privatized Comintern and ensures that his ideological comrades are well supported.

Lenin emphasized the importance of flexibility. He told the Communist parties of the West, particularly those of Germany and Great Britain, that they must accommodate the latest developments. They had learned to attack, and now they must learn to retreat—they must be flexible in their tactics.[19] When necessary, they must compromise, accepting the discipline of the altered circumstances.

Lenin stressed that legal and illegal means must be utilized to advance the Communist revolution. This included joining the parliament to advance the revolution from within the confines of government. When direct attack would not succeed, other approaches like the united front must be used. To recognize only one road, only the direct road, that will not permit tacking, maneuvering, or compromising, would be a mistake and do harm to the Communist movement.[20]

Communists must be open to new paths, indeed any path, to advance the revolution. The united front permitted everything to advance Communism. "From the standpoint of the development of international communism, our work today has such a durable and powerful content (for Soviet power and the dictatorship of the proletariat) that it can *and must* manifest itself in any form, both old and new."[21] He continued, "It can and must regenerate, conquer and subjugate all forms, not only the new, but also the old—not only for the purpose of making all and every form—new and old—a weapon for the complete and irrevocable victory of

19 Lenin, "Left Wing Communism—An Infantile Disorder," p. 102.
20 Lenin, "Left Wing Communism—An Infantile Disorder," p. 103.
21 Lenin, "Left Wing Communism—An Infantile Disorder," p. 103. Emphasis original.

communism."[22] Lenin argued that new means, new tactics, new technologies, must be employed in the revolutionary struggle, and which subsequent Communists in the West will employ—such as the culture industry, radio, television, newspapers, and film, and today's social media—to further and sustain the revolution.

Left Wing Communism was the most important pamphlet that Lenin wrote, rivaled only by *What Is to Be Done?* It is a basic training manual and one of the most profound pieces of writing on revolutionary theory in relation to questions of strategy and tactics. Its message of adjustment and accommodation was key for members of the Comintern like Mikhail Borodin, as he wrestled with the major debates and problems of advancing the revolution in China.

Tenth, Lenin and the Bolsheviks started a civil war in Western civilization between those who sought to protect the West and its greatness and the Leninists who sought to destroy Western civilization and remake everything. As will be discussed in detail in chapter 6, all of the hallmarks of Western civilization—Christianity, the free market capitalism, free thought, objective knowledge, science, philosophy, literature, art, the classics and classical education, law and jurisprudence, standards of architectural and artistic beauty, the rules, norms, and principles of international order—were to be destroyed. Attitudes, customs, culture, and even history itself had to be destroyed. Complete civilizational erasure is exactly what the Bolsheviks sought.

Nothing substantive could remain of the past so that there was nothing to remind people of the old order and that better life that it provided. A new man was to be created, and nothing could remain of the old one. Understanding that allows us to understand why American identity and Western civilization are such a threat to the neo-Bolsheviks today. They must be destroyed. Civilizational erasure was launched by Lenin and his descendants today continue the fight. The civil war over Western civilization

---

22 Lenin, "Left Wing Communism—An Infantile Disorder," p. 103.

remains with us. The neo-Bolshevik progressives are winning. It remains to be seen whether the final victory will be theirs.

It is remarkable historical fact that these measures occurred in a truncated period of time, the six years between November 1917 and 1923, the last full year that Lenin was alive and thus still the dominant voice within the Party. Lenin had given the movement the key to seizing power, a disciplined Party driving the revolution, and he had demonstrated that it could be accomplished in any country, and the Comintern would spread it to those countries.

The great powers immediately recognized the threat of Leninism, although there was considerable variation in the response to the threat. Winston Churchill called Lenin's dogma a "plague bacillus," and that was certainly the case for the United States and its allies, which have suffered from the Leninist bacillus since 1917.

Churchill described the danger of Bolshevism in his November 6, 1919, address to the United Kingdom's House of Commons: "Lenin was sent into Russia by the Germans in the same way that you might send a phial containing a culture of typhoid or cholera to be poured into the water supply of a great city, and it worked with amazing accuracy."[23] Churchill continued: "He gathered together the leading spirits of a formidable sect, the most formidable sect in the world, of which he is the high priest and chief. With these spirits around him, he set to work with demoniacal ability to tear to pieces every institution on which the Russian State and nation depended."[24]

---

23 Quoted in Martin Gilbert, *Winston S. Churchill*, Vol. 4, *1916–1922* (London: Heineman, 1975), p. 355.

24 Quoted in Gilbert, *Winston S. Churchill*, Vol. 4, pp. 355–356. Churchill's arguments were rejected by Prime Minister David Lloyd George, who kept Churchill in the Cabinet only because he considered he would be more dangerous on the other side of the House. On November 8, 1919, Lloyd George declared that "Bolshevism cannot be suppressed by the sword. . . . We cannot . . . afford to continue so costly an intervention in an interminable civil war . . .

Alert to the danger from its genesis in 1917, Churchill feared Lenin with good reason. Lenin was indeed a determined revolutionary who, with his Bolshevik comrades, sought to bring revolution to the world, including the United Kingdom. His ideology was also hyper-aggressive toward his Party, toward those he sought to rule—the workers and the peasants, and, of course, class enemies and bourgeois states.

Lenin's hyper-aggression was directed domestically and globally. Against the Russian people, he inflicted War Communism, famine, and a civil war.[25] His belligerence was aimed at the foundation of the international state system. Lenin argued: "We have always said that there are different kinds of wars. We condemn the *imperialist* war, but we did not

---

Russia is quicksand. Victories are usually won in Russia, but you sink in victories; and great armies and great empires in the past have been overwhelmed in the sands of barren victories." Quoted in Gilbert, *Winston S. Churchill*, Vol. 4, p. 356. Lloyd George's "sink in victories" in Russia brilliantly anticipates the conduct of the German invasion of the Soviet Union in 1941.

25 From the Soviet Union to the PRC, to North Korea today, famine is a feature of Communist rule. In the wake of the Bolshevik Revolution, there were major famines beginning in 1918 and increasing in 1919 and 1920. To combat it, President Woodrow Wilson authorized the head of the American Relief Administration (ARA), Herbert Hoover, whose organization was already feeding millions in Western Europe to expand to Soviet Russia. The 1921–1922 Samara (or Volga region) famine is estimated to have killed 5–8 million people. As the famine deepened by midsummer 1921, it was so severe that even the Politburo supported the appeal to the West for help. The ARA had ameliorated the famine by 1923. The causes of the early famine were World War I and the civil war. The source of the great famine of 1920–1921 was the peasants' "strike," against Bolshevik requisitioning. It is estimated that there was about a 40 percent decline in grain production from 1918 to 1921 as the Bolsheviks employed food as a weapon in the civil war and during War Communism. See Bertrand M. Patenaude, *The Big Show in Bololand: The American Relief Expedition to Soviet Russia in the Famine of 1921* (Stanford: Stanford University Press, 2002).

reject *war in general*."[26] He continued: "We are not living in a state but *in a system of states*, and it is inconceivable for the Soviet Republic to exist alongside the imperialist states for any length of time. One or the other must triumph in the end. And before that end comes, there will have to be a series of frightful collisions between the Soviet Republic and the bourgeois states."[27] There could be no peace with the enemy. He had to be destroyed.

III. The Comintern

In late 1977, U.S. Army Major General Edwin L. Sibert, chief of intelligence during World War II, first to General of the Armies Omar N. Bradley and then to General of Armies Dwight D. Eisenhower, reflected upon the problems of counterintelligence that he encountered from 1944 to 1946 during the great campaign in northwest Europe and then later during the occupation of Germany.

Sibert said, "As our intelligence operations developed, we began to see that there was an intelligence service in Europe—a substrata of society would be an accurate term for it—far more proficient and omnipresent than that of the Germans."[28] It was "the *apparat* of the old Communist International, which Lenin formed back in 1919 to spread the world revolution of the proletariat and peasantry. Those *apparats* were everywhere, even in our own ranks and those of Allied armies. It was plain to me that

---

26 V. I. Lenin, "Eighth Congress of the R.C.P. (B.): Report of the Central Committee," March 18, 1919, *Collected Works*, Vol. 29 (Moscow: Progress Publishers, 1965), pp. 146–164, 153. Emphases original.

27 Lenin, "Eighth Congress of the R.C.P. (B.): Report of the Central Committee," *Collected Works*, Vol. 29, p. 153. Emphases original.

28 Anthony Cave Brown and Charles B. MacDonald, *On a Field of Red: The Communist International and the Coming of World War II* (New York: Putnam's Sons, 1981), p. 9.

the members of the *apparats* were loyal not to their own leaders or capitals but to Stalin and the Kremlin."[29]

They were of concern to Sibert "because they were armed, disciplined, and experienced underground fighters. We had to consider the possibility that if there was a war between Russia and the United States at the conclusion of World War II, as many thought there would be, we would find these people fighting us in our rear as they had fought the Germans."[30] To address this, Sibert "brought the matter to the attention of both Bradley and Eisenhower, and Bradley asked me to prepare a paper on the subject of the Communist International in a hurry."[31] Sibert gave the problem "to my chief of counterintelligence, but when we began to look for people who knew anything about this phenomenon, we found that there was nobody in the higher command who knew very much about the International."[32]

Finally, "We had to go to British intelligence and to the records of the German intelligence services and to employ two Belgian trade unionists who were familiar with the problem. We had four million men, and we could not find one who could write a five-page report on the International."[33] The report was prepared, and paid for, "but when I put the bill in to the fiscal people, they wrote back to me to ask why I had found it necessary to make a report on an Allied organization!"[34]

Sibert comprehended that the U.S. military had not recognized the nature of the adversary, particularly the importance of political warfare and its great organizational abilities made possible by Leninist discipline and the Communist International. He was not alone in not grasping the size and scale of the threat.

---

29 Brown and MacDonald, *On a Field of Red*, p. 9.
30 Brown and MacDonald, *On a Field of Red*, pp. 9–10.
31 Brown and MacDonald, *On a Field of Red*, p. 10.
32 Brown and MacDonald, *On a Field of Red*, p. 10.
33 Brown and MacDonald, *On a Field of Red*, p. 10.
34 Brown and MacDonald, *On a Field of Red*, p. 10.

The Comintern was proclaimed only a few weeks after the end of World War I.[35] On January 24, 1919, Lenin announced the establishment of "the general staff of the world revolution of the proletariat," to be known as the Communist International.[36] It held its founding congress in Moscow in March 1919.

In summarizing the objectives of the Comintern, Lenin attacked the great capitalist powers. As an economic system, Lenin declared, capitalism was moribund, and even though the capitalist leaders had brought the world to ruin in the war, they were at that moment planning another calamitous war. It was the responsibility of the Comintern to overthrow capitalism and spread Communism to the world.

The Comintern aimed to destroy the political power of capitalism and replace all its institutions with soviets of the proletariat, in which political power would be placed at the service of the working class. The concept of the state itself eventually would be destroyed and replaced by a world soviet of proletarian nations, with headquarters in Moscow. To achieve this goal, Lenin stated that there must be a common bureau for the purpose of directing and maintaining coordination and systematic leadership of the Communist International, a center in which the interests of the Communist movement in each country would be subordinated to the common interest of the international revolution.

Lenin chose Zinoviev to head the Comintern. Under Zinoviev, the Comintern was to become a vast and powerful bureaucracy devoted first to propagation of Communist ideology as defined by the Communist Party

---

35 The First International (the International Workingmen's Association) was founded in London in 1864 (1864–1876). The Second International was created in Paris in 1889 (1889–1916). Both were plagued by tensions between Marxists, socialists, and anarchists.

36 V. I. Lenin, "Speech at the Opening Session of the Congress," March 2, 1919, in V. I. Lenin, *Collected Works*, Vol. 28 (Moscow: Progress Publishers, 1965), pp. 455–456. In exile, Trotsky founded a Fourth International to compete with the Third. Founded in 1938, it existed in various forms until the early 1960s.

of the Soviet Union. Second, it was the instrument to wage political warfare against capitalist states. Lenin himself defined the fundamentals: Since capitalism was for Communists an abomination, an illegal and immoral conspiracy against the people, and since capitalists held the political power of the great nations outside Russia, the Communist International would have to fight illegality with illegality by creating what came to be called "the Communist underground," united front groups, through other front organizations, and the activities of fellow travelers.[37]

Although the Soviet government would provide the Comintern with headquarters, funds, and even personnel, and although the Comintern would serve the objectives of the Soviet government, the government could not accept responsibility for the Comintern's actions, which, Moscow claimed, would be determined not by the Soviet government but by the Comintern's own Executive Committee of Communist International (ECCI).[38] As with any secret service, the government might have to disown any connection with the Comintern.

To be successful, Lenin decreed that the organization of the Comintern in Russia would have to be highly centralized and highly disciplined. Any disobedience for whatever reason was to be dealt with by what would come to be called "pitiless courts." Although originally the Comintern was to be responsible for its own discipline, as time passed, the Soviet secret police would come to be responsible for order but also would come to use the political world created by the Comintern for their own purposes in the fields of intelligence collection, political warfare, and covert action.

---

37 The Comintern addressed other issue areas as in labor. The Red International of Labor Unions (RILU), or "Profintern," a telescoping of the Russian name, started in Moscow in 1921. The Profintern was a child of the Comintern and was intended to carry out the general line of the Comintern in the trade union field.

38 For a detailed description of the ECCI and its membership, see Jane Degras, ed., *The Communist International 1919–1943 Documents, Vol. I, 1919–1922* (London: Oxford University Press, 1956), pp. 453–456.

As ordered by the Second Congress of the Comintern when it met in July–August 1920, unquestioning obedience to the Comintern by Communist parties was unrelenting and utterly binding. Every party belonging to the Comintern had to subscribe to irrefutable dicta: The Comintern was established solely to organize joint action by the proletariat to overthrow capitalism and establish dictatorship of the proletariat, which were then to form an international soviet republic that would "completely abolish all classes and realize Socialism, the first stage of Communist society."[39]

The essential task of the Communist International was to fight by every means including armed force for the overthrow of the international bourgeoisie and for the creation of an International Soviet Republic. There would be no federalism with a degree of independence for some parties. The goal could be obtained only if all parties in fact and effect became one unified Communist party throughout the world. Of all parties, the Russian party, the Communist Party of the Soviet Union, was preeminent. The Russian party was the model for all others because of its iron discipline and strict organization. All parties were subordinate to the ECCI, which was the "general staff" of the worldwide revolution, and which had the authority to expel individuals, groups, and even national parties.

As he faced the forthcoming Second Congress of the Comintern in 1920, Lenin was concerned about his revolutionary message.[40] The desired revolution in the West had either not developed or had failed. The revolutionary situation that had existed at the end of the Great War had passed, and the new situation required new tactics.

Lenin had to explain the new circumstances to the delegates. As discussed, he did so in *Left Wing Communism*, his Bible for understanding

---

39 Degras, ed., *The Communist International 1919–1943 Documents, Vol. I, 1919–1922*, pp. 109–110.

40 See Brigitte Studer, *Travellers of the World Revolution: A Global History of the Communist International*, trans. by Dafydd Rees Roberts (London: Verso, 2023), pp. 41–50.

the direction and tactics in the Communist movement. It remains relevant today for its instruction and for its influence on the Comintern and on subsequent Communist thinkers.

Closely identified with the strategy for the developed countries that Lenin advanced in *Left Wing Communism* was another for national liberation movements in the colonies of European powers. In Lenin's *Preliminary Draft Theses on the National and Colonial Questions*, he emphasized that the first priority for Communists, from whatever country, had now become the struggle of the global bourgeoisie against Soviet Russia.[41] Only the victory of the Soviet system could assure salvation for colonial peoples. Soviet Russia sought to enlist their help in undermining international capitalism, and that alliance and assistance must be given since Russia's continued survival was essential to their future.[42] In sum, colonial and nationalist movements must recognize Soviet supremacy and aid the Soviet Union to the best of their ability.

To reinforce the Comintern's dicta, Lenin at the Second Congress introduced what became known as the twenty-one points. They provided that the parties would be admitted to membership only if they were genuine Bolshevik parties with "highly centralized organization" governed by "iron discipline," and they had to be prepared to periodically purge and expel all unreliable elements to cleanse the party of petty bourgeois elements. On the matter of illegality, Lenin stated that Communists can have no confidence in bourgeois legality. Communists were required to create parallel illegal organizations, which, at the right time, would aid the Party to advance the revolution.

All members of the Communist Party were also members of the Comintern whether or not they wanted to be. Thus, they were obligated to

---

41 V. I. Lenin, "Preliminary Draft Theses on the National and Colonial Questions," in V. I. Lenin, *Collected Works*, Vol. 31 (Moscow: Progress Publishers, 1966), pp. 114–151.

42 Peter Hopkirk, *Setting the East Ablaze: Lenin's Dream of an Empire in Asia* (New York: Norton, 1984), pp. 108–118.

obey the Comintern's rules, orders, and dogma. An American Communist was bound to Moscow tightly and required to follow its orders just as a Russian or Chinese Communist. That was the firm direction that the Bolsheviks required of all parties.[43]

Of course, Comintern agents worked closely with Soviet intelligence, both the state security organization, first the Cheka but known as the KGB for most of the Cold War, as well as Soviet military intelligence, the GRU. The Comintern was a useful apparatus to recruit agents and sources. Foreign Communists who might balk at working for the Soviet Union's intelligence agencies might be persuaded that they were serving the cause of world revolution. In the 1920s, there was hand-in-glove cooperation between the Soviet intelligence services and the Comintern's International Relations Department, known as the OMS (International Liaison Department), which oversaw the financing of foreign parties and the activities of Comintern emissaries.

By the 1930s, agents of the Comintern had often served in the Soviet intelligence services and the reverse. They were able to make use of the Comintern and its operatives because, from its foundation, the Comintern had required Communist parties to maintain, where possible, a legal political organization, the Communist Party, and an illegal or underground apparatus. Among the twenty-one conditions required for admission to its ranks, the Comintern stipulated in 1920 that all Communist parties create an illegal apparatus to assist the Party. These underground apparatuses were intended defensively to protect the Communist movement from police repression and offensively to promote political subversion and aid intelligence collection.

Comintern agents often traveled on false passports, employing a *nom de guerre*, entered countries illegally, and served as coordinators, messengers from Moscow, and financiers secretly to distribute cash and valuables to local party leaders. The Comintern maintained clandestine courier services,

43 Studer, *Travellers of the World Revolution*, pp. 69–73.

secret mail drops, and systems of coded telegraphic and radio communications with Communist parties around the world. In addition, the Comintern trained cadres in Moscow and elsewhere to operate illegally, prepare safe houses and fake identification documents, and take other steps necessary to support the underground party and the Soviet intelligence services.

Communist revolutions were occurring or brewing in Saxony, Thuringia, Bavaria, and in the Ruhr. Within two weeks of the founding of the Comintern, the first Soviet state outside the Soviet Union was founded in Hungary under Béla Kun, before it was crushed in August 1919 by Czechoslovakian and Romanian forces at the instigation of French Prime Minister Georges Clemenceau.

Where Communist parties did not exist, the Bolsheviks would create them—the most important was the Chinese Communist Party. Where there were multiple parties vying for recognition, as in the United States, the Comintern would require a single party, the Communist Party of the United States of America, vet its members, and provide the Party line to which it had to adhere at all times and in all matters. Independence of thought or action was not permitted.

IV. The Comintern in China

Spreading the revolution to the East was, of course, a desirable objective to undermine British and French colonial governments and to balance the Japanese. The central problem for Leninism was that there was a small working class and a large peasantry that was seen by Lenin at least as pre-Revolutionary—lacking any conception of class. But that theoretical problem did not stop the Comintern from trying.

The idea was advanced by the Comintern for bringing the Communist revolution to China and India, not only to advance the revolution there but to occupy and weaken the imperialist powers and thus aid the Soviet Union. It inspired the Comintern's organization of the January 1922 First Conference of the Toilers of the Earth in Moscow. Naturally, China was a priority as a critically important state. Since China did not have a Marxist tradition, the Comintern would have to give it one.

Following the Comintern's Second Congress in 1920, the Dutchman Hendricus Sneevliet (code name Maring) was ordered to Shanghai at Zinoviev's direction to help Chinese Marxists establish a Leninist Communist Party. Sneevliet had earlier established the Indonesian Communist Party, and with his assistance, Chen Duxiu and Li Dazhao founded the CCP in July 1921 at a meeting in the Po Wen Girls' School in the French Concession of Shanghai.[44] The man who would claim to be the "Founder of the Nation," Mao Zedong, was anything but. He attended the meeting, but was appointed to none of the CCP's organizations, and was then a marginal figure in the Party.

This seemingly historically insignificant occasion turned out to have massive effects. The thirteen young Chinese men, all of whom were disillusioned with China's postimperial development, met in Shanghai to form the Chinese Communist Party and so started a movement that less than thirty years later would rule the country and a hundred years later would be a peer rival of the United States.

Sneevliet and Grigori Voitinsky (born Zarkhin), the head of the Far Eastern Bureau of the Bolshevik Party, a member of the Comintern, and the first formal envoy to China who arrived in 1920 and established headquarters in Shanghai, shaped the Leninist form of the CCP.[45] Voitinsky was also crucial in formulating cooperation with

---

44 In the early decades of the twentieth century, the French and International Concessions of Shanghai provided safe haven for Chinese intellectuals who had run into difficulties with the authorities. The city was also a gathering point for students leaving and returning from study abroad. Moreover, many publishing houses were located there and produced translations of Western books and periodicals, both liberal, Marxist, and Leninist. Hans J. van de Ven, *From Friend to Comrade: The Founding of the Chinese Communist Party, 1920–1927* (Berkeley: University of California Press, 1991), p. 59.

45 van de Ven, *From Friend to Comrade*, p. 61.

the Nationalist Party or Kuomintang (KMT, or Guomindang, GMD). Sneevliet was involved with the CCP until ordered to return to Moscow to be replaced by Borodin in August 1923. Sneevliet reported in July 1922 to the Comintern that activity outside of the Shanghai cell had ceased. Even attempts to recruit new members among the city's intellectual circles had stopped.[46]

So, while Chen and Voitinsky had labored to create a Leninist party that might have a seed for a nationwide one, the Shanghai cell had weakened to the point of disintegration. Borodin would grow the CCP not in Shanghai but in Canton. While Shanghai would remain important, Canton would be the focus of the CCP for most of the rest of the 1920s.

Moscow viewed Borodin as more successful, reliable, and in possession of an urgency of action that was unsurpassed. Borodin had already labored to found Communist parties in Spain and Mexico, and had been involved in Communist politics in Chicago, the center of socialist politics in the U.S. at the time. Borodin had a peripatetic existence for most of his life. In the United States, he lived briefly in Boston before heading to Chicago, living there from 1908 to 1917.[47] In Chicago, he had an assortment of jobs; most significantly, he ran an English language school.

Under Voitinsky's and Sneevliet's direction, there were at first intermittent contacts between the CCP and the Comintern. This was partly because of the Comintern's focus on Europe and the United States and partly because the CCP seemed too small to be effective—in 1922, the CCP had only two hundred members and only a few thousand as late as 1925. Indeed, Sneevliet reported to the Comintern that before the Third CCP Congress in June 1923, Mao expressed to him a complete disbelief in the possibility of a revolution in China without assistance from the Soviet Union: "Comrade Mao told me that Hunan has 30 millions [*sic*]

---

46 van de Ven, *From Friend to Comrade*, p. 62.

47 Dan N. Jacobs, *Borodin: Stalin's Man in China* (Cambridge, Mass.: Harvard University Press, 1981), p. 5.

and 30 till [*sic*] 40 thousand modern workers. He is at the end of his Latin [a Dutch expression which means to be at a total loss about what to do after making many attempts] with labor organization and was so pessimistic that he saw the only salvation of China . . . [being] intervention by Russia."[48]

But Sneevliet placed the CCP on the right path. He founded the CCP and addressed four necessary tasks to further its success. First, radicalized intellectuals had to perceive Communism as a coherent ideology that was superior to other, competing radical ideologies such as anarchism and more moderate forms of socialism. In China, there was fertile ground among intellectuals who were seeking radical solutions to resolve China's weakness. Second, the intellectual inquiry and publishing emphasis had to be replaced by Leninist action. Third, the dominance of interpersonal relations as the basis for party formation had to be replaced by a commitment based on ideology and subservience to the party. Fourth, there had to be a shift to Leninism as the ideology of the Party and the related requirement to form a Bolshevik Party.[49] Although not yet a major figure, Mao wrote in December 1920 to his colleagues in the New Study Movement in Paris that he agreed that a proletariat dictatorship along the lines of Soviet Russia was the only solution for China's weakness and rapid improvement.

Leninist thought was appealing, as was its organization and direction. The collapse of the imperial system with the end of the Qing Dynasty (1911/1912) left a political and organizational vacuum but also intellectual space for competition from new ideas, as young radicals like Mao wrestled with the means to salvage China's future from its humiliations. There existed already among Chinese intellectuals the inclination to link national rejuvenation with global or international salvation, and this

48 Quoted in van de Ven, *From Friend to Comrade*, pp. 122–123.

49 Tony Saich, *Finding Allies and Making Revolution: The Early Years of the Chinese Communist Party* (Leiden: Brill, 2022), p. 55.

added to the appeal of Leninism. Leninism could connect with national salvation while linking the struggle in China to a movement of great global significance.

In addition, the impact of the Karakhan Declaration or Karakhan Manifesto (July 25, 1919), by Lev Karakhan, the deputy commissar for foreign affairs, was monumental. This relinquished Russian rights in China, including Chinese territories seized by tsarist Russia, extraterritoriality, economic concessions, Russia's share of the Boxer indemnity, and the return of the Chinese Eastern Railroad (CER), which later would become a major bone of contention between China and the Soviet Union. It created a favorable view of Russia and of Leninism in China. This was because the Karakhan Declaration defined revolutionary Russia as different from the imperialist great powers that colonized China and still maintained their spheres of influence.

Given the Comintern's centrality, its role was fundamental, if problematic, in CCP histories.[50] Once the CCP was ensconced in 1949, official historians advanced a narrative that blurred the origins of the CCP and the role of the Comintern, which saw China as an essential cog in the wheel of global revolution. While it is debatable whether a CCP would have emerged eventually, it is certain that without Soviet ideological, military, and economic support, it would not have come together so soon and thrived so well. Certainly, it would not have assumed its Leninist form so quickly.

Deciding that the CCP could achieve little on its own, at Zinoviev's direction, Li approached Sun Yat-sen (Sun Zhongshan), the leader of the KMT, which had evolved from a revolutionary league to the dominant political party in China based on Sun's "Three Principles:" nationalism, democracy, and the people's livelihood. The KMT's major political goals

---

50 While the Comintern was essential, Soviet support for the CCP in time also came from Narkomindel (the Soviet Foreign Ministry) and the Profintern (the International Labor Organization).

were to free China from the remnants of imperial rule, defeat the warlords, create a constitutional republic, and improve the conditions of the peasantry.

The Comintern's action in support of the KMT was ordered by Lenin, who had started a correspondence with Sun, as did the People's Commissar for Foreign Affairs Georgy Chicherin.[51] At the Comintern's Second Congress, Lenin advanced the argument that in colonial or quasi-colonial states, Communist parties would have to work with bourgeois ones because they would be too weak otherwise.[52] Lenin's *Preliminary Draft Theses on the National and Colonial Questions* stressed the necessity for the Comintern to enter a temporary alliance with bourgeois democracy in the colonial countries; that is, the CCP would have to enter into an alliance with the KMT, with the KMT as the dominant partner.[53] That was the united front that the CCP would maintain for much of the 1920s until Chiang Kai-shek moved against it.

Sun welcomed Li as he sought to learn from Leninist party-building and aid that the Soviet Union could provide. In fact, in March 1923, Soviet aid began flowing to the KMT as a result of the agreement reached in January between the KMT and Comintern. Also in 1923, Sun sent his Chief of Staff Chiang Kai-shek to Moscow to study the organization of the Communist Party of the Soviet Union and the Red Army. Seen at the time as a pro-Bolshevik leader, when Chiang returned to China later in the year, the Comintern sent an old hand with him:

---

51 Jacques Guillermaz, *A History of the Chinese Communist Party 1921–1949*, trans. by Anne Destenay (New York: Random House, 1972), pp. 76–77.

52 Hopkirk, *Setting the East Ablaze*, pp. 100–107.

53 The Asian delegates opposed Lenin's interpretation and their principal spokesman, Mahendra Nath Roy, argued that two distinct movements were to be found in the dependent countries, and they grew further apart. The first was the bourgeois-democratic nationalist movement, aimed at establishing a bourgeois order. The other was the mass struggle of the poor peasants and workers for their liberation.

Borodin. Chiang had played little other than a military role in KMT until the summer of 1925.

The Comintern advisers' influence was particularly strong and successful in two fields, both of which were essential to the development of the KMT: propaganda and military affairs.[54] Propaganda, which until then had been left to the initiation of local officials, was centralized, organized, disciplined, and controlled by an office of which Mao was once temporarily in charge.[55] In the military arena, Soviet advice and material aid helped Sun to develop the KMT's army.

Chiang owed his rising fortunes to Sun but also Borodin and the Soviet Union. Famously, at a victory banquet in December 1925, Chiang acknowledged his debt to the Soviets and specifically to Borodin. At this occasion, he declared that the KMT should accept Russian direction of the Chinese revolution and compared the Sino-Soviet relationship to that among the Allied powers in World War I. As commander in chief, Chiang said Borodin's position was like Marshal Foch's and that Sun had said, many times, that Borodin's views were his views.[56]

In January 1923, the ECCI passed the "January Resolution," which proclaimed the KMT to be the only serious revolutionary party in China and that it was necessary for the "young CCP" to coordinate its actions with the KMT.[57] The class conditions were not right in China. The labor movement was weak and not sufficiently differentiated as a social force. The peasants were not radicalized.

---

54 Guillermaz, *A History of the Chinese Communist Party 1921–1949*, p. 80.

55 Later in February 1926, Mao was also the editor of a KMT magazine, *Political Weekly*. Guillermaz, *A History of the Chinese Communist Party 1921–1949*, p. 80n3.

56 Jacobs, *Borodin*, p. 186.

57 "ECCI Resolution on the Relations between the Chinese Communist Party and the Kuomintang," January 12, 1923, in Jane Degras, ed., *The Communist International 1919–1943 Documents, Vol. II, 1923–1928* (London: Oxford University Press, 1960), p. 5.

Thus, the central task was the national revolution and the CCP members had to remain in the KMT. The CCP was not to become entirely mixed with the KMT and was not to unfurl its own banner. However, it was to work with the KMT to influence it to work with Soviet Russia to fight European, American, and Japanese imperialism in China. The CCP would continue to organize workers, but its political interests would lie with advancing the nationalist revolution. The united front between the KMT and CCP would allow the KMT to unify China successfully under a national-democratic regime and accelerate capitalist development. In turn, this would allow the proletariat to mobilize to cause the Communist revolution.

To promote a Communist revolution in China, Zinoviev established a Comintern general staff in Canton. Borodin was the leader and General Vasili Blyukher was his military adviser to Chiang. In addition to Blyukher, Borodin had the help of an imposing group of Communist luminaries, including Mahendra Nath (M. N.) Roy. M. N. Roy had failed to bring revolution to India but, as a favorite of Lenin, had been elected to both the Comintern's Executive Committee and its Presidium. These men were as foreign to China as were the British or any other imperialist power a century before.

One of Borodin's first moves was to establish control of the KMT's military forces, which he accomplished almost as soon as he arrived in China in October 1923 by placing Red Army advisers on the staffs of all Chiang's armies. Thereafter, he penetrated and yielded control of the KMT along classic Leninist lines.

Borodin established a Committee of Nine to run KMT affairs. He induced the KMT congress to accept CCP members and was said to have personally written the KMT's constitution and statutes, which the KMT congress approved. He advanced through the KMT congress an ideology based on collaboration with the Soviet Union, collaboration with the CCP, and providing support for the workers and peasants, in which the latter was overwhelming—only one in two hundred Chinese men could be considered working class.

The role of the peasantry had been emphasized by the CCP and by intellectuals before its founding. Chen argued strongly for the CCP to maintain its independence while collaborating with KMT. Chen supported the emphasis that Lenin's *Preliminary Draft Theses on the National and Colonial Questions* placed on the role of the peasantry. Only a rural revolution could arouse the most people to free themselves and so, for success, the revolutionary movement had to be based on the action of the peasant masses.

Borodin established a Party press and propaganda department, in which Mao occupied a major position. Through General Blyukher, Borodin helped Chiang establish the Whampoa Military Academy, in which a Communist, Zhou Enlai, received the post of assistant political director. Borodin also ensured that the academy's curriculum incorporated Leninist revolutionary studies and graduated politically reliable officers who were to come to dominate the staffs of the KMT's armies.

As those armies advanced and won victory after victory over the warlords, they followed what was a revolutionary doctrine for Chinese armies: not molesting or preying upon the people. As a result, the people welcomed the KMT. With them came CCP functionaries who quickly occupied key positions in local government.

Meanwhile, at Borodin's direction, the KMT began to strike at the foreign colonies, particularly the British, through labor agitation. Beginning in 1925, Borodin began a series of strikes that led to disorder. However, this was the high-water mark for Borodin.

In March 1926, Chiang began to check the influence of Comintern agents and the CCP. The Communists sent a gunboat to arrest Chiang in what is known as the March 20th, 1926, Incident. But Chiang moved first, arresting twenty-five Communist tutors at Whampoa, including Zhou, and placing Russian advisers under house arrest. Under Chiang's direction, the KMT's Central Executive Committee on May 15, 1926, took stern measures to prevent further Communist penetration of the

KMT.[58] The Comintern was divided. At the fifteenth CPSU conference in October 1926, Bukharin, backed by Stalin, stated that the central task in China was to fight foreign imperialism and therefore the national-revolutionary united front had to be maintained. In contrast, Trotsky argued that now was the time for the CCP to be an independent proletarian party—that is, a revolutionary party discrete from the KMT and fighting against it.[59]

In the course of the Northern Expedition, Chiang saw the opportunity to establish his control of the KMT and of China, after a police raid on the Soviet embassy on April 6, 2027, revealed the depth of the Communist penetration of China. The raid discovered critically important information, including the shipment of arms to southern China to foment a Communist revolution, and plans to seize the British concession along the Yangtze River, and to eliminate Chiang himself.[60] On April 12, 1927, Chiang moved against the CCP in what was termed the Shanghai Incident or Shanghai Massacre. That started a cascade of actions against the CCP in which it was decimated, with much of the Party destroyed, and was fiercely condemned by the Comintern.[61] It also marked a stark division between the

58 Later the Trotskyist opposition sharply reproached Stalin for being too passive in the wake of the March 20th Incident. Chiang's success drew the majority of the KMT to his side, inclining the KMT still further to the right, and paved the way for Chiang's bold strike against the CCP a year later. See Leon Trotsky, *Problems of the Chinese Revolution* (New York: Pioneer Publishers, 1932), pp. 221 and 347.

59 "Extracts from the Resolution of the Seventh ECCI Plenum on the Chinese Situation," December 16, 1926, in Degras, ed., *The Communist International 1919–1943 Documents, Vol. II, 1923–1928*, pp. 359–364.

60 This raid generated the British government to order a similar raid on May 12, 1927, on the All-Russian Co-Operative Society (abbreviated Arcos) which demonstrated Soviet efforts against Britain and led to the "Arcos Affair" and the termination of diplomatic relations between the Soviet Union and Great Britain.

61 "Extracts from an ECCI Statement on Chiang Kai-shek's Anti-Communist Coup," 15 April 1927, in Degras, ed., *The Communist International 1919–1943 Documents, Vol. II, 1923–1928*, pp. 359–364.

left-wing and right-wing KMT, with Chiang leading the right-wing faction in Nanjing in opposition to the left-wing KMT headquartered in Wuhan. In July, the left-wing KMT expelled the Communists from their ranks, leaving Chiang in complete control of the KMT, although the Comintern ordered the CCP to leave the Wuhan government but not to leave the KMT, despite Chiang's purge, to develop further the agrarian revolution and to arm the workers and peasants.[62]

This ended the First United Front between the CCP and the KMT, severely weakening the CCP. Later in the year, the Autumn Harvest uprising and Guangzhou uprising, or Canton uprising, both failed. Mao led the September 1927 Autumn Harvest uprising in Hunan and Jiangxi provinces. He established the short-lived Hunan soviet, with the intent to establish a base for a peasant uprising and redistribute land to the peasants from the landlords.

After initial success by the Communists, the KMT crushed the soviet. Mao was forced to retreat to the Jinggang Mountains. The failed uprising led Mao to recognize that the CCP needed an effective army, as did Zhu De, the founder of the Red Army, formally known as the Chinese Workers and Peasants Red Army, on August 1, 1927.[63] The Red Army broke off from left-wing elements of the KMT's National Revolutionary Army (NRA).

Thus, the Comintern *de facto* led the CCP and provided guidance for important Chinese Communists, including Mao, who was emerging as an important, but not yet dominant, leader by 1927.[64] Revolution in China

---

62 "Extracts from an ECCI Resolution on the Present Stage of the Chinese Revolution," July 14, 1927, in Degras, ed., *The Communist International 1919–1943 Documents, Vol. II, 1923–1928*, pp. 390–396, 395.

63 In February 1947, the Eighth Route Army and the New Fourth Army, major Communist forces, would merge and become known as the People's Liberation Army (PLA).

64 Mao would have his ups and downs, not securing full control until he forced the Party to bend to his will through the Yan'an Rectification Movement 1942–1945. After that, he was in firm control of the CCP and would only face major challenges to his leadership during the failure of the Great Leap

had become a top priority for the Soviet Union, and its vehicle would be the KMT rather than the weaker CCP, which sustained a united front with the KMT until July 1927. Despite the Comintern's denunciation of Chiang's coup, in every sense that mattered materially, Stalin would favor the KMT.[65] In sum, for the 1920s and 1930s, Stalin saw the KMT as a more effective mechanism of revolution, anti-imperialism, and an effective force that could balance Japan's growing aggressiveness.

The Fifth CCP Congress was held in 1927 in Wuhan. It was so small that it was held in Borodin's apartment, where the CCP Politburo had gathered. Roy and Borodin were sharply divided. Roy fiercely argued from his long-held principles, dating to the Second Congress of the Comintern in 1920 when he debated Lenin. As discussed, Lenin argued for class cooperation in colonial countries. The peasants and working class had to work with the national bourgeoisie. What Lenin had advanced in 1920, Borodin supported in his debate with Roy, and this was in accord with the Comintern's orders.[66] It is a measure of Roy's stature, stemming from his debate with Lenin at the Second Congress of Comintern, that Borodin had to debate him, given that Borodin was the Comintern's representative in China.

Roy's thesis was that in underdeveloped countries, the national liberation forces should not trust the national bourgeoisie to free their country from colonial rule.[67] The peasants must be the backbone of the revolution, and they must be won over through confiscation of the land from the landlords and given to the peasantry.

Forward and the great famine, 1957–1962, and from Lin Biao in 1971. Karl A. Wittfogel, "The Marxist View of China (Part II)," *The China Quarterly*, No. 12 (October–December 1962), pp. 154–169, pp. 166–168.

65 "Extracts from the Resolution of the Eighth ECCI Plenum on the Chinese Question," May 30, 1927, in Degras, ed., *The Communist International 1919–1943 Documents, Vol. II, 1923–1928*, pp. 382–390.

66 "Extracts from an ECCI Resolution on the Present Stage of the Chinese Revolution," July 14, 1927, in Degras, ed., *The Communist International 1919–1943 Documents, Vol. II, 1923–1928*, pp. 390–396.

67 Hopkirk, *Setting the East Ablaze*, pp. 194–215.

Roy supported his position with the undeniable fact that the peasantry in Hunan and Hubei had already rebelled against the landowners and driven them out. Perhaps as many as 15 million peasants had joined the newly established revolutionary peasants' unions. What was done there could be repeated elsewhere, if only the CCP would stop temporizing and unequivocally back the peasants' revolution.[68]

In response, Borodin argued that such a decision would end the alliance with KMT, which remained for Stalin and him the only hope of advancing the revolution in China. To maintain the alliance, it was essential not to encourage the peasants and workers but to curb their excesses. Borodin called for confiscation of all landlord-held plots except those belonging to the KMT or the NRA, their relatives and friends, and the land of small landlords. This meant, in effect, that practically all land was exempt from confiscation. As for military action, Borodin argued for the resumption of the Northern Expedition, which also had the virtue of moving closer to the Soviet Union should escape become necessary. Borodin won the debate and his policies were followed.[69]

But just as his policies were at their zenith, Chiang's actions—and Stalin's—eliminated Borodin's progress. Chiang's growth might allow him to target and then evict the Comintern agents. The Wuhan refugees arrived in Moscow at a time of crisis. The final scenes of the post-Lenin struggle for power were being enacted. The outcome was already clear, but the opposition would make one final effort to overturn the verdict. One of the chief causes of opposition was Stalin's "treacherous" and "antirevolutionary" mishandling of the China situation. The opposition pushed it with vigor. No matter how legitimate the reasons for pursuing his China strategy, Stalin was vulnerable because he had forbidden the arming of workers and peasants while cooperating with the bourgeoisie.

68 Jacobs, *Borodin*, p. 253.
69 Jacobs, *Borodin*, pp. 253–254.

If that policy had succeeded, all would have been well. But it did not. The Chinese revolution and its representative in Moscow were not only an embarrassment for Stalin but, with the showdown with Trotsky at hand, a possible danger as well.[70] Stalin was tired of China, which seemed to be a morass, just as he was fatigued by the whole international revolutionary effort. Under Stalin, the wave of the immediate future was a de-emphasis on the international in favor of a focus on the domestic revolution. Stalin threw his prodigious energy into the consolidation of his power, advancing "socialism in one country," that is constructing Communism in the Soviet Union through the first of the Five-Year Plans and planning the liquidation of the kulaks, or so-called rich peasants, but used against anyone who opposed collectivization.

Ultimately, Mao could not have achieved success in 1949 without the Comintern and Soviet assistance, including direct military aid and the employment of Soviet territory and later Manchuria as a protected area and direct line of communication for the Communists. Stalin's pressure on the quasi-independent state of Xinjiang was also supremely helpful for the Communists. Before Stalingrad, Xinjiang's leader was supportive of Chiang Kai-shek, and after, supportive of Stalin to the great benefit of the CCP. Of course, gross U.S. strategic mistakes toward the KMT and a supremely adroit political warfare campaign waged by the CCP and their allies also directly contributed. Those measures weakened the KMT and the perception of the KMT in the eyes of the Truman administration. These factors caused the final success of the CCP.

---

70 Trotsky also vacillated on China, a point which is often forgotten in the characterization of the incandescent debates between Stalin and Trotsky. It should be said that both underestimated the difficulties posed by Chiang's bold actions and the support enjoyed by the KMT at this time.

Chapter 3

The External Communist Threat: Communism in China

Leninism's success in China was one of its two greatest. Russia was the other, and the U.S. potentially would be the third. Leninism remains immediately relevant to understand the PRC's past and present actions. This chapter places the CCP in historical and present contexts. It places Mao in the correct context as well. Mao's "thought," what the world knows as Maoism, was just a Bolshevik knockoff. Mao's thought is derivative—his purported contributions were the direct result of Bolshevik thought and action.

That matters because the world needs to perceive Mao as he was. Mao was not a major Communist thinker, but a ruthless thug who employed all the tactics of Stalinism to gain and maintain power. In sum, he owed everything to Stalin, whom he feared, and the Comintern. In addition, the chapter analyzes "Xi Jinping Thought" and how Xi employs his ideology in a typically Leninist approach. Lastly, I present three futures or scenarios that the CCP's Leninism may take in the next fifteen to twenty years, if the Chinese people and their allies do not overthrow the CCP by then.

The world might witness a return to Stalinism—this time an "efficient Stalinism"—where the bulk of the Chinese people and the CCP itself can be kept under the thumb of the CCP's leader through advanced surveillance technologies. Stalin required millions of people to act as his spies.

Artificial intelligence (AI) may well reduce that number by many orders of magnitude. That would reduce the cost of Stalinism but employ more efficient and ubiquitous surveillance of the CCP and Chinese population—and thus, greater terror.

I. Maoism Is a Product of Bolshevik Thought

Leninism and the history of the Comintern are critical to understand because Mao's thought was wholly defined by the Bolsheviks' theoretical ideas and strategy and tactics for revolution. Thus, clearly Mao's thought is imitative and derivative. He did not make major original contributions to Communist thought.[1] At its core, Maoism is the application of Stalinism to China. What is termed Maoism is drawn from the Bolshevik debates in the first decade after the Bolshevik Revolution.

Even Mao's purportedly original idea of the Cultural Revolution—which he called one of two of his great achievements, the other being the 1949 revolution—was derived from Bogdanov's and other left-wing Bolsheviks' thought and their advocacy for the permanent change of Russian culture through such a purging.[2] Bogdanov advanced his idea in direct opposition to Lenin and, of course, Lenin defeated him.

In fact, Lenin was acutely aware of the role of culture in advancing the revolution. He saw cultural change as one of the means by which the Bolsheviks could consolidate power and promote Communist development.

---

1 For example, see Mao Tse-tung [Mao Zedong], "Report on an Investigation of the Peasant Movement in Hunan," March 1927, *Selected Works of Mao Tse-Tung* (Peking: People's Publishing House, 1965), Vol. 1, pp. 23–59; Mao, "On Practice" July 1937, in *Four Essays on Philosophy* (Peking: Foreign Languages Press, 1966), pp. 2–22; Mao, "On Contradiction," *Selected Works of Mao Tse-Tung* (Peking: People's Publishing House, 1965), Vol. 1, pp. 311–347; and Mao, "Introducing *The Communist*," *Selected Works of Mao Tse-Tung*, Vol. 2 (Peking: People's Publishing House, 1965), pp. 285–296.

2 See Zenovia A. Sochor, *Revolution and Culture: The Bogdanov-Lenin Controversy* (Ithaca, N.Y.: Cornell University Press, 1988).

But for Lenin, it was a matter of degree and balance among competing pressures.

In contrast, Bogdanov argued that a true Communist revolution had to set for itself a much more radical, immediate, and difficult goal—the transformation of attitudes, customs, and culture—what Mao would term in the Chinese context the "Four Olds": ideas, customs, culture, habits. For Bogdanov, only then could the Party forge a truly proletarian society. Bogdanov and other left-wing Bolsheviks like Lunacharski advanced ideas in direct opposition to Lenin and were defeated by him.[3] In Bogdanov's conception, only a true, Communist revolution could forge a truly proletarian society. He attempted to cause such a change through the Prolekult (proletarian culture) movement, which was a template for the Cultural Revolution of 1966–1976 in the PRC.

Through the Cultural Revolution, Mao attempted to regain absolute power and purge the Party. Having been heavily marinated in Bolshevism since the CCP's foundation, there is no doubt that Mao was knowledgeable of Bogdanov's and the left-wing Communists' pioneering effort in this regard. The Cultural Revolution was heavily colored by Prolekult in every way, including its language and objectives. One objective was the removal of urban academics to rural areas to serve as farmworkers. In that environment, they would learn the "cleansing" value of hard work for those who had never known it.

Hence, the Bolsheviks were responsible for both of Mao's achievements, as Mao himself identified those feats to posterity. Fundamentally, the Bolsheviks and Mao shared Russian poet and Bolshevik supporter Alexander Blok's summation of the Bolshevik Revolution as this: "To *remake* everything: to organize things so that everything should be new, so

---

3 This included the cultural and educational movement Proletkult (proletarian culture), which sought to elevate proletarian art, cinema, theater, literature, and proletarians to positions within the Party, as well as tangible and immediate proletarian consciousness among the Bolsheviks, who were dominated by the intelligentsia. This served as a precursor to Mao's Cultural Revolution.

that our false, filthy, boring, hideous life should become a just, pure, merry, and beautiful life."[4] They did, indeed, remake their societies, although the end, in each case, was totalitarianism, precisely the opposite of what Blok envisioned.

At the same time, however, the importance of Mao and Chinese Communism does not depend on the intellectual sophistication of its dogmas. Mao was one of the greatest—if not the greatest—manipulators of large masses of people in the twentieth century. The ideology he used for the purpose is significant because of its effectiveness, not only in the PRC but in other parts of the Third World.

Communism was imposed upon China via the Comintern. That was Soviet imperialism, pure and simple. Communism should be considered intellectual colonialism—an artificial substitute for a discredited Confucian political tradition left in tatters by Qing misrule and European and Japanese domination. It was not an organic outgrowth of indigenous political development and culture. Yet, while not organic, it was effective at maintaining control because of the Comintern's and Stalin's efforts and later, sustained by Mao's Stalinism. The durability of the CCP, when contrasted with the collapse of the Soviet Union and its allies in Central and Eastern Europe, demonstrates its skill and determination to remain in power. The Leninist ideology remains in force and has enjoyed a renaissance under Xi. This alien import has become accepted as "Chinese" by the Party, due to Deng Xiaoping's effort to generate "socialism with Chinese characteristics" and Xi's forceful and sustained efforts to keep Communism at the center of the PRC's ideology.

The CCP stayed in power while the Soviet Union fell because the international political environment remained benign for the CCP due to the U.S. response. The U.S. did not push for regime change in the PRC, as it might have after the Tiananmen Square massacre or in the years

---

4 As quoted in Avril Pyman, *The Life of Alexander Blok*, Vol. 2 (Oxford: Clarendon Press, 1980), p. 282. Emphasis original.

afterward when the regime was unstable. Indeed, the administration of President George H. W. Bush worked to reassure Deng of the U.S.'s desire to sustain and improve relations in its wake. Subsequent U.S. administrations only compounded this mistake by allowing the PRC to enter the West's economic ecosystem.

In essence, the central issue is not what is Chinese about the CCP, but what is Communist about it. The answer is that most of it is Communist. Not much is Chinese, a balance that would please Lenin, Stalin, Zinoviev, and Borodin. This polity has lasted, carried on the backs of the Chinese people since 1949, despite the grave injuries inflicted on them by Mao, the Gang of Four, and Deng, and continued under Xi today.

The CCP could not have survived without the help it received first from the Soviet Union and then from the United States and the liberal international order that Washington created, which permitted the PRC's prodigious growth. That mistake enabled the rise of a great enemy, which now compels the U.S. to address the threat with urgency.

II. Xi Jinping's Ideology

The PRC threat today is existential because the CCP is doing its utmost to achieve domination of international politics as Leninism dictates. This intent has remained the same from Mao to Xi, or more accurately from Lenin to Xi. Of course, what has changed is the PRC's power. Mao was motivated to dominate global politics but could not because of the PRC's relative weakness compared to the superpowers, and their resistance, which checked his global ambitions. That is, the U.S. and the Soviet Union held respect for the PRC's power. The PRC fought the U.S. to a standstill in the Korean War and hindered Washington's prosecution of the Vietnam War. This was due to President Lyndon Johnson's concern over greater PRC involvement in it if the U.S. escalated the conflict.

The Soviets found the PRC to be a wily and determined foe in ideological and diplomatic realms, as well as a source of conflict during their border war in 1968 and 1969, and the sustained tension they faced through the 1970s and 1980s. This caused the Soviets in the 1970s and 1980s to deploy about forty-four divisions on its border with the PRC.

Of course, today the PRC is far more powerful and is able to advance its aims and ambitions in ways unavailable to Mao. The world is witness to the expansion of the PRC's diplomatic, technological—including in AI, cyber, space and planetary exploration—and economic achievements, such as the Belt and Road Initiative (BRI). Beijing's growing conventional and nuclear capabilities and nuclear infrastructure are impressive by any standard. Although the PRC's economy is faltering, that has not diminished its frenetic activity. The PRC is taking a prominent position in scientific and technological achievements, expanding intelligence abilities, and now challenges the U.S. for global leadership. It has come a long way from Mao's PRC, to say nothing of the fragmented and colonized Qing and republican China. The PRC now may credibly challenge the U.S. globally. It is doing so in a manner the U.S. has not witnessed since the long struggle with the Soviet Union.

Xi remains heavily influenced by Communist ideology and Maoism, as he frequently notes. His references to Mao and his dependence on Maoism mean that Xi is dependent on the Bolsheviks and the Comintern. The CCP learned well. Its past is even bloodier than Lenin's or Stalin's brutality. Civil war, wars against outside powers, and extensive war against their own people were definitive of the CPSU and the CCP. Likewise, famine was even more of a problem in the PRC than in Soviet Russia from 1918 to 1922, or Stalin's engineered famine known as the Holodomor.[5]

---

5 Frank Dikötter, *Mao's Great Famine: The History of China's Most Devastating Catastrophe, 1958–52* (New York: Bloomsbury, 2010). Dikötter estimates that 45 million people in the PRC died of starvation between 1958 and 1962. This is based on his careful analysis of the famine, which was caused by Mao's catastrophic Great Leap Forward. Traditionally, estimates had between 20 million and 40 million, but Dikötter's research demonstrates the famine was much worse. By comparison, approximately three million people died in the

Reflecting on this history, U.S. national security leadership, and more broadly the American people, must understand the CCP's Leninist ideology. In essence, if the American people as well as the Department of State and the Department of War civilian and military leadership can "think like a Communist," they may understand why the CCP fights and why they will continue to do so. The CCP seeks confrontation in order to achieve its conception of victory—fulfilling the CCP's ideological goals and replacing the U.S. with the PRC as the hegemon, or the dominant power, in international politics.

By its Communist logic, the PRC will fight the United States because it is the single major impediment to the PRC's strategic objectives. The U.S. model of political liberalism, capitalism, and a society and future defined by freedom, remains the most significant threat to the regime's existence and its justification for perpetual one-party rule. Beijing expects the "China model," anchored on Xi's rule, to replace it as the global economic-cum-political template for development. With the U.S. removed, there would be no single power, or constellation of powers such as Australia, Japan, and India, that could prevent Beijing from achieving its aims. Lenin's vision of Communist triumph would be realized, just not by the state he anticipated.

Xi has boldly and transparently advanced these objectives in his conception of a hegemonic PRC. The United States obstructs the PRC from realizing its ambitions and remains its principal ideological opponent. As discussed, Communist ideology is inherently aggressive and thus the CCP is the instigator of conflict with the U.S. Intense security competition, and maybe war, is possible as long as China's government remains Communist.

Bengal famine of 1943, the worst natural disaster experienced by India in the twentieth century. Of course, Mao never admitted that the Great Leap Forward was a failure, but he took a step back from leadership in the early 1960s. In fact, he made only one public appearance in all of 1962.

The 2019 declaration of "People's War" signaled the CCP's intent to mobilize and prepare the Chinese people for war against the U.S. and its allies and partners. Moreover, Xi's critical address in October 2022 at the CCP's Twentieth Party Congress was momentous, providing key insights into his leadership and impact upon the Party. In historical perspective, this congress was a significant development with lasting implications for the CCP, the PRC, and for the risk of war in international politics.

In his address Xi proclaimed that the CCP has achieved its first centenary goal—building a moderately prosperous society—and has moved on to achieving the second centenary goal of building the PRC into a modern socialist country in all respects and advancing the rejuvenation of the Chinese nation. This message was Xi conveying to domestic and international audiences that the PRC has reached a new standard and should be judged by different metrics.

This is an indication that the PRC now perceives itself as capable of achieving its aim of supplanting the United States and replacing the liberal international order and that it considers these actions will be legitimate by that order's standards. The "modern socialist country" Xi seeks is one in which the PRC sets the rules. Xi stated that the PRC will cause institutions to "open up" their rules, regulations, management, and standards. The "opening up" of institutions, in fact, means that they will bend to the will of the CCP. An example of this occurred with the World Health Organization (WHO) at the dawn of the Covid-19 pandemic, when the WHO cooperated with the CCP to deflect investigations into the pandemic's origins.

Xi has been steadfast that CCP ideology must remain firmly anchored in Leninism. A staunch believer in Communist ideology, Xi seeks to strengthen the CCP's ideological purity while strengthening its control over the PRC and influence in the world.

Belligerence was the order of the day in Xi's speech and in others the world has witnessed thereafter—in March 2023, for example, Xi delivered a series of major speeches and pronouncements. He directed his aggressive discourse against the U.S., with its denunciations of hegemonism, and implicitly its allies, like Japan, and partners, like India. Most explicitly, Xi's aggressive intent was directed against Taiwan. Xi stated that resolving the question of Taiwan's political status is a matter for the Chinese and that, in the matter of Taiwan or in other disputes, the CCP will never renounce the use of force. The implication is that coercive measures against Taiwan are likely. Xi has expressed his determination to resolve this issue and is certain to want to accomplish this while he remains in relatively good health.

Thus, the Twentieth Party Congress revealed that Xi has secured his place as one of the dominant CCP rulers in the Party's history, second only to Mao. Xi is indeed "thinking like a Communist" because he is a fervent Leninist. His image of the PRC—that the Party is now able to lead the world—his ideology, as a true believer in Communism and its consequences, his belligerence expressed against the U.S., its allies, and Taiwan, mean that Xi and the CCP will seek to cause the change they want ever more forcefully.

Like Stalin at the outset of the Cold War, Xi has provided the world with his vision for the CCP, the PRC, and international politics. He has explained his reasoning of why the CCP is at war with the U.S. and its allies and partners. Now these states are compelled to recognize the gravity of the threat and respond with far greater alacrity than they have.

Also like Lenin and Stalin, the PRC's grand strategic vision is one of primacy—the hegemony of the PRC in global politics. Realizing this vision is intended and will require supplanting the United States as the dominant power in international politics. The PRC's quest for greater resources, and its expanding diplomatic, economic, and military capabilities, are oriented toward achieving this grand strategic objective.

Linked to the growth of the PRC's power are the territorial demands the PRC has made in the East and South China Seas, as well as with its border with India. These demands are empirical, real-world indications that the PRC is not a status quo power but intends to overthrow the international order. Beijing's actions are strong indicators that it seeks to replace the United States as the dominant state. The CCP seeks to establish—as Xi has implied—that the PRC can and should lead the world.[6]

Communist ideology has always been essential to the CCP and its rule, and this is especially so under Xi.[7] Of all political parties the world has witnessed, the CCP is at the forefront for understanding the role that ideology plays in gaining and sustaining power; in grasping the relationship between ideology and material power; in legitimizing political power; and in creating a front in warfare: Political warfare is to be waged against the enemy as surely as kinetic measures are.

As argued, all states have ideologies that heavily affect their domestic and international behavior. For the CCP, Leninist ideology is extremely significant. Ideology provides the legitimacy of the CCP: a Communist Party, with the Leninist "scientific" understanding of society, ruling in the name of the workers-peasants alliance, which provides it with self-justified authority to rule over 1.4 billion people. It explains why the Chinese people must support the CCP—it mobilizes the masses—and why they should sacrifice for it. Ideology explicates which states are allies and which are foes, and thus the ultimate reason for the struggle with other states: Communism is superior to democracy or other forms of government and must be defended against its inevitable class enemies. Ideology is the force that unifies and provides cohesion for the Party and like-minded people around the world. As a corollary, it defines the domestic enemy, as well as the enemy abroad. It is also a weapon the CCP should use to expand its

---

6 Xi Jinping, *The Governance of China*, 2nd ed., 2 Vols. (Beijing: Foreign Language Press, 2018), Vol. 1, pp. 360–367.

7 Key studies documenting the importance of Communist ideology for the CCP are Chalmers A. Johnson, *Peasant Nationalism and Communist Power: The Emergence of Revolutionary China 1937–1945* (Stanford: Stanford University Press, 1962); Julia Lovell, *Maoism: A Global History* (New York: Knopf, 2019); Robert C. North, *Moscow and the Chinese Communists*, 2nd ed. (Stanford: Stanford University Press, 1963); and Benjamin I. Schwartz, *Chinese Communism and the Rise of Mao* (Cambridge, Mass.: Harvard University Press, 1951).

influence, as well as to deny and negate the legitimacy of liberal democracy and traditional imperial rule in the minds of the Chinese people, their allies, and worldwide.

The trinity of Marxism-Leninism-Maoism has long been enshrined as the official guiding ideology for the CCP—the largest and most powerful political party in the world with about 100 million members. But just as important as the ideology is its interpretation by major leaders. After the foundational "Mao Zedong Thought," which the Eighth Party Congress added in 1945, the PRC has witnessed a cavalcade of ideological guidelines for the CCP, the state, and the Chinese people: "Deng Xiaoping Theory," "The Three Represents," "The Scientific Outlook of Development," and, most recently, "Xi Jinping Thought on Socialism with Chinese Characteristics for a New Era."

There is a note of caution here for the U.S. Washington must never dismiss the ideological component of the PRC's grand strategy as a platitude, formulaic, or philosophical musings because it is gravely serious and heavily informs the CCP's decision-making. Beginning with Mao Zedong's "catch up with the British and surpass the Americans" (赶英超美) and Mao's advocacy of "Third World Solidarity," with China inherently understood to be at the forefront of the Third World movement, to Deng Xiaoping's "realization of four modernizations" (实现四个现代化) and, finally, to Xi Jinping's "China Dream" (中国梦), all should be considered ideological narratives for a consistent grand strategy of achieving the PRC's hegemony in global politics—while simultaneously denying and disavowing that objective.

Historically, all major CCP leaders have denied that they seek hegemony or, indeed, that the PRC should be one. "Never seeking hegemony" originated with Mao Zedong in the late 1960s and early 1970s, when Mao issued one of his highest directives: "Dig deep underground holes, accumulate grain widely, and do not seek hegemony in the world" (深挖洞、广积粮、不称霸).

In using this terminology, Mao paraphrased Zhu Sheng, a great strategist in the Ming Dynasty (1368–1644). Zhu advised Zhu Yuanzhang, the founder of the Ming Dynasty, "to raise the city wall high, collect more grain, but delay to the declaration of hegemony" (高筑墙,广积粮,缓称王). Zhu Sheng's fundamental point was that if Zhu Yuanzhang were enthroned too early, he would be the primary target for all warlords' opposition to the regime and thus lose the opportunity to build an empire. It was far wiser to bide time and make the attempt when the time was propitious.

Six centuries later, Mao was in the throes of a fierce competition with the Soviets for leadership of the Communist world, he echoed Zhu Sheng's anti-hegemonic rhetoric. Therefore, the real meaning of Mao's "not seeking hegemony" is to oppose the Kremlin's hegemony of the Communist world, while biding his time to make his own attempt, with the aim of being greater than Stalin or even Lenin.

Mao's principal successor, Deng Xiaoping, continued this theme with his "24-Character Strategy." In a series of talks with the CCP leaders in the wake of Tiananmen, Deng instructed them to "keep calm, handle well our own affairs, and do not stick our head out." In April 1992, when he talked with his staff about China's development issues, he first used the phrase "hide our capabilities and bide our time" (韬光养晦). Deng wanted the CCP to maintain a low profile and hide its real intentions.

Deng's talks were later synthesized and expanded into the "28-Character Strategy" to guide China's foreign relations: "Calmly observe, stabilize our own position, quietly handle affairs, hide our intentions, be good at pretending to be clumsy, never stick our head out, and achieve more" (冷静观察、稳住阵脚、沉着应付、韬光养晦、善于守拙、决不当头、有所作为).

The cause of Deng's strategic narrative was clear—a weak PRC confronted a precarious situation. With the conclusion of the Cold War, and the absence of the Soviet threat, the PRC became vulnerable to U.S. pressure to reform significantly the CCP and to democratize. Beijing needed favorable conditions for its economic development. A confrontational approach was not an option because China was not yet a great power. It was still largely an agrarian state. The PRC had to avoid being a target while Deng laid the foundation for a challenge to the United States.[8] His strategic narrative contributed to the West's inability to identify the PRC as a threat.

The PRC's behavior post-Mao and pre-Xi can be seen as the "period of strategic opportunity." While avoiding military entanglements in the region and, especially, with the United States, the PRC eagerly pursued—free from any serious challenger—the political and economic opportunities available to a rising power, particularly increasing its comprehensive national strength and international competitiveness.[9]

Under Xi's rule, a heavy emphasis on Communist ideology has returned to a prominence matched only by Mao's leadership. Xi has stayed in power beyond the traditional two terms since Deng's retirement and is likely to remain in power for many years, as Mao and Deng did, unless his health fails him or he is overthrown.[10] Xi has moved the pendulum from oligarchic rule of the last two decades to increasingly totalitarian rule by a "great leader" as modeled by Mao's experience. Moreover, for a CCP leader, Xi is extraordinarily open regarding his explanation—to both domestic and international audiences—of why the PRC should dominate.

---

8 These remarks were echoed by his successor, Jiang Zemin, who made the promise that China would never seek hegemony in a speech at Cambridge University in 1999. Hu Jintao, Jiang's successor, not only repeated the rhetoric of not seeking hegemony but also added "never engage in expansion," in a keynote speech at China's 2008 Boao Forum for Asia Annual Conference.

9 Xu Jian, "Rethinking China's Period of Strategic Opportunity," *China International Studies* (March/April 2014), pp. 51–70. At: <http://www.ciis.org.cn/english/2014-05/28/content_6942258.htm>. Accessed April 11, 2026.

10 Nan Li, "Party Congress Reshuffle Strengthens Xi's Hold on Central Military Commission," *The China Brief*, Vol. 18, No. 3, February 26, 2018. At: <https://jamestown.org/program/party-congress-reshuffle-strengthens-xis-hold-central-military-commission/?mc_cid=3132e01c7f&mc_eid=7bf8bdbc8d>. Accessed April 11, 2026.

Xi has stated that ideology decides the Party's future and existence, as well as long-term stability of the country and national cohesiveness. Thus, he has challenged the Party to be indefatigable and steadfast in its ideological focus. Upon coming to power, Xi immediately tightened his grip on the Party's ideology, which is a major pillar supporting his leadership.[11]

As a fifth-generation CCP leader, Xi does not enjoy the authority of Deng, not to mention Mao. Xi has no military achievements, no bureaucratic merits, nor any notable achievement. To strengthen his position, Xi draws on Mao's playbook—after all, Mao started as an assistant librarian. The parallels Xi seeks to make to Mao are transparent. Xi is employing every tactic of the Yan'an Rectification Movement of 1942–1945, when Mao established his dominance in the Party. Like Mao, he also launched an offensive war to defend and expand CCP ideology.[12] As a consequence, in villages and factories throughout the country, as well as within the CCP

---

11 In early 2013, a few months after Xi became the Party chief, he issued "Document 9" (the Central Committee's Ninth Report that year), in which he ordered a serious crackdown on competing ideologies. He labeled seven political "perils," which must be completely banned in China. These include the following so called "false ideological trends, positions, and activities:" promoting Western constitutional democracy in order to supplant the current leadership and socialism with Chinese characteristics governance; advancing "universal values" in an attempt to weaken the theoretical foundations of the Party's leadership; encouraging civil society in an attempt to dismantle the ruling party's social foundation; promoting neoliberalism, attempting to change China's Basic Economic System; advancing the West's idea of journalism, challenging the CCPs principle that the media and publishing system should be subject to Party discipline; supporting historical nihilism, trying to undermine the history of the CCP and of New China; and questioning "socialism with Chinese characteristics."

12 Estimates are that the PRC distributed 4.6 million copies of Mao's work in twenty-five languages to 148 countries and regions in the world. This history is significant because Xi Jinping is following Mao's playbook in this as well. Xi's two volume book encapsulating "Xi Jinping Thought," *The Governance of China*, has had over 40 million copies published and distributed to more than 160 countries.

and government, the Party has held numerous study sessions of turgid and stultifying "Xi Jinping Thought" to enforce unity and control of the Party.[13] Xi wages a constant ideological war to ensure control of the Party.

Similarly, Xi continues to establish his authority in international politics as a leader of a superpower. The PRC's economic success has enabled it to accumulate power, and to do so in a remarkably short time by historical standards. In turn, the PRC's economic power allows it to export its ideology to the world and influence international politics. But those halcyon days of rapid and consistent economic growth may be over forever because of the PRC's decline in its economic conditions. In these circumstances, Leninist ideology becomes even more important to sustain Xi's hold on power and advance the PRC's strategic objectives while Beijing finds itself in a more complicated international political environment.

III. How Xi Employs Ideology

Like Mao, a characteristic of Xi's rule is his employment of ideological offensives to secure his vision within the CCP and for the state and people of the PRC, but also to fend off Western ideology.[14] Under Xi, the CCP has warned that Western anti-PRC forces and internal "dissidents" are still actively trying to infiltrate the PRC's ideological sphere and subvert its ideology and cohesion. The CCP perpetually demands that Party members strengthen their resistance to foreign ideas, renew their commitment to

---

13 *Xinhua*, "Senior CPC Official Stresses Deeper Study of Xi Jinping Thought among Officials," November 16, 2019. At: <http://www.xinhuanet.com/english/2019-11/16c_138560537.htm>. Accessed May 11, 2025.

14 Xi has explicitly targeted the West in his "Five Principles of Peaceful Coexistence," which are: (1) all countries are equal; (2) mutual non-aggression; (3) no interference in other countries' internal affairs; (4) opposing hegemonism; and (5) peaceful coexistence. Xi has touted this as the cultural soft power of China, which is offered as grounding principles for China's relations with the world, in contrast to those advocated by the West, and as a mechanism to resist the penetration of Western values into Chinese society.

work "in the ideological sphere," and have renewed vigilance regarding all ideas, institutions, and people deemed threatening to the CCP's rule.

Foremost in Xi's ideological assault is the "China Dream" strategic narrative. Xi's attempt to move the PRC toward a confident and greatly elevated position is clear in Xi's statements on the "China Dream," particularly its emphasis on "the great rejuvenation of the Chinese nation" and developing "socialism with Chinese characteristics."[15]

The core of Xi's message is the belief that the Chinese model of global governance is superior to the status quo the West established, particularly the Anglo-Americans after World War II. Xi suggests that the PRC is the only country that can usher in this new world order. "Rejuvenation" implies the return to a status quo ante, which, it is reasonable to suspect, is PRC domination. According to Xi, this "new era" that the "China Dream" describes is characterized by "Chinese wisdom and a Chinese approach to solving the problems facing mankind."[16]

Xi's "thought" is important to examine, particularly the components that define the cynosure of his Communist ideology. As a Leninist Party, the CCP is the central actor of life in the PRC, as it leads the people and purportedly rules in their name. The CCP has reasserted its control over state, academic, and private-sector institutions. This comprehensive approach to governance integrates Party leadership at every level of society, ensuring that the Party's directives and ideology influence all aspects of governance and daily operations. By embedding its presence deeply within these sectors, the CCP aims to maintain ideological consistency and reinforce its

15 Xi, "Achieving Rejuvenation is the Dream of the Chinese People," *The Governance of China*, Vol. 1, pp. 37–39; "A Bright Future for Socialism with Chinese Characteristics," and "The Chinese Dream is the People's Dream," *The Governance of China*, Vol. 2, pp. 3–17.

16 "Opening ceremony of the 19th CPC National Congress," China.org.cn, October 17, 2017. At: <http://live.china.org.cn/2017/10/17/ opening-ceremony-of-the-19th-cpc-national-congress/>. Accessed May 11, 2025.

authoritative role, effectively centralizing power and establishing a uniform policy execution across the PRC.

Xi is deepening reforms that cement his control over the Party. His assertion that only Communism can save China, and only reform and opening up can develop China underscores his commitment to that ideology. Since 2012, Xi has championed reforms to fortify Party-State control over China's economy, society, and military. These reforms aim to enhance governance, boost economic efficiency, and ensure social stability. By integrating Communism with pragmatic reforms, Xi seeks to modernize China while maintaining the ideological foundation of the Communist Party, thereby reinforcing its authority and guiding the nation's trajectory and power in global politics.

Xi's demand is that the CCP must follow Communism, or "Xi Jinping Thought on Socialism with Chinese Characteristics for a New Era." Xi frequently emphasizes that state development should not take precedence over the people's livelihood. Under this guiding principle, the CCP allegedly aims to balance state-led modernization with the well-being of its citizens. By advocating for "socialism with Chinese characteristics," Xi stresses the importance of prioritizing social welfare, public services, and improved living standards. This approach provides an attractive public face: The state's economic and social policies are aligned with the people's needs and aspirations, reinforcing the notion that the people are the true masters of the country.

Xi has emphasized consistently that confidence in the PRC's political culture is a profound driving force for the nation's modernization. By promoting the core values of Communism, Xi aims to strengthen ideological commitment and strengthen support for the CCP. This confidence in political culture serves as a foundation for social unity and resilience, supporting the Party's vision of a prosperous, stable, and progressive society. Through these values, the CCP seeks to inspire and guide the PRC's path.

As a good Communist, Xi contends that strengthening national security is essential. The major principles of national safety include coordinating development and security, strengthening awareness, and preparing for crises in times of peace. This strategic approach is reflected in the People's Liberation Army's (PLA) focus on combat readiness. Xi emphasizes the importance of integrating national security into all aspects of governance, ensuring that the PRC is well-prepared to defeat both internal and external threats.

As dictated by Leninism, the CCP maintains absolute control over the PLA. Xi's reforms have reinforced the Party's control over the military through comprehensive political education, continuous reforms, and advancements in science and technology. By enhancing legal management within the PLA, these reforms ensure that Party authority remains unchallenged. The focus on ideological indoctrination and modernization of military capabilities aligns the PLA closely with the Party's objectives, maintaining its loyalty and readiness to serve the state under the absolute command of the Communist Party. That Leninist vision is coupled with Xi's Stalinist purges of the military.

In March 2026, Xi said that "the military must have no room for people disloyal to the party, nor any place for corrupt elements to hide."[17] Xi's longstanding and effective anti-corruption campaign is the most visible sign of his Leninist belief in maintaining his total control, the importance of the Communist Party's discipline, internal supervision, and political purity. Xi has emphasized that the Party must uphold strict discipline to maintain its legitimacy and effectiveness. By targeting "unhealthy tendencies" and corruption, the campaign seeks to strengthen the Party's internal culture and ensure that its members adhere to high moral and ethical standards. This focus on discipline and integrity is essential for reinforcing public trust and achieving the Party's long-term goals. In truth, its intent is to keep Xi in power.

---

17 Chun Han Wong, "Next Task for Xi Jinping: Rebuild the Military He Wiped Out," *Wall Street Journal*, March 7, 2026. At: <https://www.wsj.com/world/china/china-xi-jinping-military-command-4b0c6338?mod=hp_lead_pos6>. Accessed March 7, 2026.

Xi's actions against the PLA underscore this, such as with the announcement in June 2025 that PLA Central Military Commission (CMC) Member and Director of the Political Department Maio Hua had been purged and arrested on corruption charges, as people widely suspected. CMC Vice Chairman He Weidong was arrested in March 2025, also on corruption charges. Former Defense Minister Li Shangfu was purged and arrested on the same broad charge.

Moreover, the announcement, also in June 2025, of the arrest of General Xu Xisheng, the Political Commissar of the Strategic Rocket Force, who in July 2023 replaced another purged general, Xu Zhongbo; the arrest of Lt. Gen. Qiao Xiangji, the deputy commander of the Southern Theater Command and commander of its Air Force; and the purge of Li Hanjun, the chief of staff of the People's Liberation Army Navy (PLAN), demonstrate that Xi is in control and will purge those who potentially resist his rule.

Xi is consolidating his control over the CMC and military. By January 2026, more than seventy-five senior officers and defense industry executives have been placed under investigation or removed from office since 2023. Also in January 2026, Xi placed Gen. Zhang Youxia, his most senior general, the senior of two Vice Chairmen of the CMC, and Politburo member, under investigation for allegedly violating Party discipline and state laws. Zhang was a close ally of Xi. Another high-ranking officer, Gen. Liu Zhenli, chairman of the PLA's Joint Staff Department that handles war planning and operations, is also being investigated for similar charges. The probes into two of the PLA's most senior generals, both of whom are advocates of modernizing the PLA, demonstrates Xi's dominance. In bold actions not seen since Mao, Xi has dismissed five of the six uniformed officers serving under him on the CMC.

Xi has identified these enduring priorities as he seeks to maintain the CCP's monopoly on political power at home and avoid the always-possible specter of a Soviet-style collapse. Themes that come to the fore include the pervasiveness of CCP control in broader Chinese society, the populist need to frame Party activities as "serving the needs of the masses," and the importance of maintaining "ideological rigor" and "internal unity" within the Party and military, the better to secure the loyalty of the latter for the former. "Xi Jinping Thought on Socialism with Chinese Characteristics for a New Era" likewise provides a template for the type of authoritarian governance model to export abroad, the better to nurture a group of like-minded nations to help "make the world safe" for CCP-style tyranny.

The PRC's ambition is just as revolutionary as Lenin's was because Xi's "thought" is Leninist. A partial review of the evidence is the PRC's territorial expansion in the East and South China Seas, increasing coercion against Taiwan, pressure against India along their common border, the use of "debt trap diplomacy" to exploit less-developed states, gross human rights abuses against the Tibetan people and its Muslim minority in Xinjiang, and accelerated conventional and nuclear military expansion. Hence, the PRC is not a status quo great power. It is truly a Leninist revolutionary great power that seeks fundamental and permanent changes to the contemporary international order and to supplant the U.S. position in international politics.

Achieving that strategic objective was a major theme of Xi's meetings with President Joe Biden. Xi demanded that the U.S. accept what Xi himself has termed the "Four Red Lines" or the "Four Nos." These are actions that the U.S. must not support or undertake. Xi most recently advanced the "Four Red Lines" at the 31st APEC Economic Leaders' Meeting held in November 2024 in Lima, Peru. They are: the Taiwan question, democracy and human rights, the PRC's path and system, and the PRC's development rights. Xi demands that the U.S. must not: (1) support an independent Taiwan; (2) interfere in Chinese democracy and human rights; (3) support the overthrow of the CCP; or (4) interfere with the PRC's "rights" for advancement and development.

In addition, Xi stated in Lima that "words must be trustworthy, and actions must be fruitful. A person cannot stand without credibility. The PRC always follows through on its word, but the U.S. side always says one thing and does another. It is very detrimental to America's image and damages mutual trust."[18] He has said that Washington must not challenge these demands and that "they are the most important guardrails and safety nets for China-U.S. relations."[19] Moreover, Washington must abide by them if it wishes to avoid a "new Cold War."[20]

The correct response to Xi's "Four Red Lines" is total rejection. Notably, Xi has not repeated these demands since the second Trump administration took office. Still, the U.S. must take several measures to refute them completely. The United States, not Xi, sets U.S. policy toward Taiwan. With a new administration, it is an opportune time to revisit U.S. policy regarding Taiwan to reflect the strategic realities of the twenty-first century. While all Communist dictatorships abuse the human rights of their captive populations, the rest of the world must not accept this. The Chinese diaspora, people of goodwill around the world, and U.S. policymakers will speak for those oppressed by the CCP.

Even as President Donald Trump's administration recasts national security policy toward the PRC, it is evident the U.S. already is in a cold war—one started by the CCP. The many tens of thousands of Americans killed by the CCP's export of fentanyl and other narcotics each year alone shows that the CCP is at war with the United States and has no qualms about killing Americans.

The current cold war with the CCP is multifaceted and has been fought thus far short of kinetic war, but in all other domains—including the economic, diplomatic, and political realms. The similarities between this cold war and the one with the Soviet Union are important to comprehend. The most salient similarity is that the motivation for aggression remains the

---

18 Quoted in Bradley A. Thayer, "Just Say No to Xi's 'Four Red Lines,'" *WarRoom*, November 23, 2024. At: <https://warroom.org/just-say-no-to-xis-four-red-lines/>. Accessed December 20, 2025.
19 Quoted in Thayer, "Just Say No to Xi's 'Four Red Lines,'"
20 Quoted in Thayer, "Just Say No to Xi's 'Four Red Lines,'"

same: Leninist ideology. It is essential for Americans to comprehend the impact of Communist ideology and its role in driving the PRC's aggression.

Communism is a Western ideology imported into China and not a part of earlier Chinese civilization, political culture, or political history. But its effect on the PRC has been profound, creating a swath of destruction through the country. Communism has intentionally destroyed the traditional pillars of Chinese culture, society, and civilization and killed many millions of Chinese. Leninism seeks to force societies like the PRC's into an ideological Procrustean bed that it defines. In addition, Leninism requires, by definition, aggression, including unrestricted warfare, against non-Communist states. The effect on U.S. national security interests could not be more significant because this explains the CCP's aggression against the U.S. In the CCP's worldview, the U.S. is the fundamental enemy it must annihilate.

Understanding Leninism allows the American people to grasp Xi's motivation and the CCP's "center of gravity"—its leaders are terrified of being overthrown because they know deep down that they have no right, no legitimacy, to rule China. They are illegitimate because the CCP is a product of Soviet imperialism and the ideology imposed has no consent of the governed. The Soviets played a dominant role in organizing, instructing, and, in almost every sense that matters, *de facto* leading the CCP.

The CCP is illegitimate precisely because the Soviet Union and its tool, the Communist International, formed and nurtured the Party. The CCP's claim to rule, as all Communists contend, is based upon "a scientific understanding of society." That is absurd, political billingsgate.

Stalin, the Red Army, and U.S. mistakes made possible the CCP's seizure of power in 1949. Today, the CCP seeks to sustain the tyranny of the failed ideology of Communism on the Chinese people. This ideology should be considered for what it is: an illegitimate polity for China and the last surviving form of Western colonialism. The CCP cannot hide the fact that it is the product of Soviet imperialism and is, in truth, precisely that: a colonial government. Moreover, the CCP's abhorrent leadership has accelerated under Xi's misrule. Seventy years of the CCP's tyranny have led the Chinese people to recognize that the odious, corrupt, and illegitimate regime rules for itself, not for its people.

Given their august past, the Chinese people naturally possess a profound sense of pride in their civilization and its accomplishments. They rightfully perceive themselves to occupy a unique place in the world that has excelled in every aspect, including literature, philosophy, art, religion, and technology. Accordingly, the Chinese people have their own ideas about how to govern China based on a glorious and exalted history. Rule by a Soviet colonial government with a Soviet "knockoff" ideology is at odds with China's political history and culture.

Recognizing this introduces a tremendous vulnerability for the CCP, as it did for the Soviet Union, because its ideology remains dependent upon Leninism. For the Chinese people to move to a better future begins by recognizing that the CCP is illegitimate and has no right to rule them.

Xi knows that his government is illegitimate and tyrannical, and so the Trump administration might revisit every aspect of its policies toward the regime. It is certainly appropriate for the world's population to ask whether the CCP is a legitimate government and should be allowed to continue to oppress the Chinese people. Xi is asking that the U.S. not impede the PRC's power and to accept its position while the CCP seeks to supplant the U.S. For too long, the U.S. elite have supported the CCP because that stance profited them. It was only the first Trump administration (2017–2021) that turned the rudder and challenged the CCP. Xi's effort to define the boundaries of PRC-U.S. relations with the new Trump administration is certain to fail.

In fact, this is a time of great peril for Xi. The PRC's economy is always under strain because of CCP misrule. It is as close to the law of politics as you can get that Communists have always mucked up any economy with which they came in contact. But with a weakening domestic economy—and the indication from the CCP's Third Plenum in July 2024 that the CCP leadership has no idea how to improve their economy—the decline will continue. Moreover, foreigners are investing far less than they once did in the PRC—although that is still too much investment, particularly for U.S. entities—and firms are looking for ways to exit the PRC in favor of investing in India, Vietnam, or other more stable and secure countries. In addition to the escalating global tensions from PRC threats against the Philippines and Taiwan, the Russo-Ukrainian war and war in the Middle East, other major uncertainties multiply for Xi with President Donald Trump in the White House.

This occurs as the PRC's economy is in free fall for domestic reasons, too. Consumer demand lags because most Chinese are savers, not spenders. Many Chinese lost their savings during the country's lengthy Covid-19 lockdowns, and so their wealth lies in their property. However, the property market, which is also essential for local government spending, has collapsed. There have been warnings that the real estate market's bubble is collapsing.

The scope of the problem was illuminated by Evergrande Group's bankruptcy in January 2024. In 2018, Evergrande was listed as the world's most valuable real estate company, but just three years later, it was on the cusp of bankruptcy before its demise in 2024–2025 with over $300 billion in debt. The PRC invests between 20 percent and 30 percent of Gross Domestic Product (GDP) annually in the country's property and infrastructure sectors, and so that would be more damaging to the PRC's economy than the U.S. financial crisis of 2008—with adverse impacts for the global economy as well. Evergrande's collapse has become symbolic of a PRC economy that faces major and immediate obstacles: a collapsing property market, slowing growth, increasing debt, and a shrinking workforce.

Now the PRC's exports are weakening because of U.S. tariffs, declining investment, and the stalling economy, and its imports are rising sharply. This signals that export-led economic growth, the mainstay of the PRC's economy for more than a generation, may be over. Xi has expressed his intention to lift productivity through advanced technology investments, manufacturing, and innovation—an effort to wrest control of the "commanding heights" of global technology away from the United States, Japan, South Korea, and Taiwan. Nominally, Xi is attempting to shift the PRC's economy from exports to a greater reliance on domestic growth. This is likely to fail due to the limits of domestic growth, which will only worsen the PRC's economic and social malaise. Of course, the ultimate reason it will not succeed is that Communist governments inevitably distort and destroy the economy.

Faced with bad economic news on every front, Xi is advancing an economic model aimed at strengthening the PRC's resilience and self-sufficiency—this is not an economic plan to save the PRC's economy but, rather, a campaign that has ominous and bellicose undertones.

At a time of economic pain for the PRC, Xi's latest policy indicates his intentions: Xi is planning for war. The genesis of this new economic model is to fortify the PRC's economy from "extreme situations," including a protracted war, another pandemic, or other external shocks. What Xi is attempting is a new iteration of autarky. The Soviets, the Nazis, and North Korea have all tried policies of economic isolation. As these examples suggest, states adopt autarky as they move to a war footing to insulate their economies and populations from the effects of a war, and to allow the military to sustain conflict in the face of embargo, sanctions, and other tools of economic warfare such blockades, as employed during Epic Fury against Iranian oil shipments. Xi's policies are telling because they center on food and energy security, supply-chain robustness, civil defense mobilization, and the development of strategic reserve infrastructure. These are efforts to harden the PRC's economy and prepare the country for "extreme-case" scenarios, so that the PRC remains strong in the face of potential crises—which it may provoke through aggression against Taiwan, the Philippines, Japan, or the United States.

A slowing PRC economy adversely impacts the global economy, and Xi is likely trying to ensure that the rest of the world's economy slows as the PRC's does. Xi will do his best to manipulate macroeconomic forces to ensure that fiscal chaos is segueing into economic chaos. Chaos does yield propitious opportunities for Xi because he wants the U.S. to be hurt as well. There is much fodder that Xi can manipulate to hurt the major Western economies such as the U.S. and Japan—rare earths is just one area. Therefore, the American people and U.S. government should expect that Xi will do his utmost to sow economic and political chaos in the U.S. He is hardening his economy as he prepares for war, while seeking to weaken the U.S. economy such as through restrictions on rare earth minerals, their processing, and the products for which they are necessary components.

Trump understands that the threat from the PRC is the greatest danger to America. The menu of policies the president has introduced is designed to meet that threat without kinetic war. Trump is employing economic warfare to win without fighting. His administration is rewriting the rules on trade in large measure because those rules have aided the PRC's rise. He has imposed tariffs on all goods and advanced the necessary steps to decouple U.S. investment and trade from the PRC. He is considering limiting PRC investment in the U.S. These measures are targeted to weaken the CCP by denying the PRC's military and economic capital, trade, and technology. They place Xi's regime in danger. Starved of U.S. investment, and weakened by declining trade, Xi's regime could be hard-pressed to continue his policies of aggression against U.S. interests. Xi faces a legitimacy crisis at home amid a shrinking economy.

This is critical for the American people to understand because the PRC is providing insight into the type of world it seeks to create in place of the liberal international order. In the struggle for power, the Bolshevik strategic narrative promised "Peace, Land, and Bread," to win over supporters and legitimize their control after the Bolshevik Revolution.

Like the Bolsheviks, the words and phrases the CCP chooses as a strategic narrative are designed to legitimize its dominance. However, Beijing's effort to provide a palliative phrase to win the "hearts and minds" of the world cannot mask its form of neo-imperialism or the CCP's illegitimacy.

From Africa to Southeast Asia, its efforts are increasingly being checked and thwarted as more states question its ambition and encounter the truth about its behavior. The U.S. and its allies can augment this realization if they call attention to the true nature of the CCP regime and its strategic ambitions. By so doing, the truth about the CCP will be known to more audiences within the U.S. and globally.

IV. The Future of the CCP and Conflict with the U.S.

The future of the CCP is important to consider as it directly impacts the likelihood of kinetic war with the U.S. and the ability of the CCP to aid neo-Bolshevik progressive organizations in the U.S. This section explains the three Leninist scenarios for the CCP and their implications for the possibility of conflict with the U.S.: a new NEP, the status quo, or Leninism yielding to a neo-Stalinism. Of the three, a modern, efficient Stalinism is the most likely outcome and the one most likely to result in aggression.[21] These

21 Of course, there is the possibility that the CCP collapses. The U.S. must prepare for this. China may act in an unanticipated manner as it is both susceptible to immediate aggression as well as to the risks of imploding. A precedent is the Manchu-led Qing dynasty (1644–1911) suffered a profound loss of civilizational confidence in the nineteenth century due to its struggles with European great powers, Japan, and the United States. The loss of that confidence led to profound instability within China that reverberates today. The Qing were overthrown ultimately by republican forces that embraced Western ideologies and nationalism ("Mr. Democracy") for political organization, as well as for science and social organization ("Mr. Science"). The Nationalist government was overthrown by another Western movement, the CCP, that remains in power. As the study has emphasized, the legacy of China's civilizational confidence is that the CCP is illegitimate and therefore unstable as a polity.

There are relevant historical cases that support a variety of outcomes. For example, the loss of civilizational confidence by the Ottomans led to the "Young Turk" revolution of 1908, and to the modernization of the Ottoman Empire by dismantling sultan Abdul Hamid II's regime and scenarios assume that the CCP remains in power and is not overthrown by the Chinese people.

The threat from the PRC today is and will remain intense in the coming decades. This threat is existential for the U.S. because the PRC is doing its utmost to supplant the U.S. in world politics and destroy its society. This intent has been consistent from Lenin to Xi. Of course, what has changed is the PRC's economic and military power. Mao was motivated to dominate global politics but could not because of the PRC's relative weakness in comparison to the superpowers, which checked his global ambitions.[22]

As discussed in chapter 2, whether in the Soviet Union or the PRC, Leninism is defined by a strong, centralized Party, ruling without legitimacy but with the self-justification of possessing a "scientific understanding" of society. The Party is defined by an iron discipline and loyalty of its members

---

adopting Western multiparty politics and military reforms. This contributed to a bellicose outcome: the Ottoman decision to join World War I in October 1914 on the side of Germany and Austro-Hungary. In contrast, Japan's shock at the superiority of Western military power with Commodore Perry's visits to Japan, led to the Meiji Restoration (1868), a period of intense reform and adoption of Western institutions, technologies, and practices. During this time, Japan focused on its transformation before emerging a potent great power in the First Sino-Japanese War (1894–1895) and Russo-Japanese War (1904–1905). In the contemporary context with China, this would be a situation in which China receives an external shock, turns inwardly for at least a generation to execute a revolutionary change to its politics and society before returning to as a supremely confident great power determined to impose its interests on other states. Thus, there is considerable variation in outcome (the Qing implosion, aggression as with the "Young Turk" Revolution, or studied detachment and emulation of great power rivals as with the Meiji Restoration) for great powers undergoing a crisis in civilizational confidence.

22 That is, the U.S. and the Soviet Union had respect for the PRC's power. The PRC fought the U.S. to a standstill in the Korean War and hindered Washington's prosecution of the Vietnam War due to President Lyndon Johnson's concern over greater PRC involvement in it if the U.S. escalated.

with dire consequences for deviation or failure. Leninism also requires that the Party always operate on the offense and act with an urgency and immediacy to advance its revolutionary goals. Leninism is ruthless in sustaining power by crushing resistance, which became a defining component of subsequent Leninist regimes from 1917 onward.

As Table Two illustrates, based on Leninism, the strategic priorities for any Leninist polity like the CCP are: first, the survival of the leader of the Party, the General Secretary of the Communist Party; second, and then the Party's Political Bureau, or Politburo; third, the survival of the Party; and fourth, the coercive elements, the secret police and military, to defend the leader and Party from internal and external foes. The well-being of the population and economic growth are ancillary to these priorities.

Table Two: The Principles of Leninist/CCP Governance

The Principles of the Leninist Polity
1. Survival of the leader is paramount
2. Survival of the Politburo of the Communist Party
3. Survival of the Party
4. Coercive state components upon which the leader and Party depend: The secret police and military
5. The well-being of the population and economy are ancillary, even irrelevant, and wholly subordinate to the survival of the leader and of the Communist Party

As a Leninist party, the CCP seeks confrontation to achieve its conception of victory—that is, fulfilling the CCP's ideological goals, and replacing the U.S. by the PRC as the dominant power in international politics. The logic of Leninism compels the PRC to fight the United States because it is the single major impediment to the PRC's strategic objectives. The U.S. model of political liberalism, capitalism, and a society and future defined by freedom remains the most significant threat to the regime's existence and its justification for perpetual one-party rule.

This book argues that the PRC is not a status quo great power. It is truly a Leninist revolutionary great power that seeks fundamental and permanent changes to the contemporary international order. It is an existential threat to the U.S. position in international politics. Xi has identified these enduring priorities as he seeks to maintain the CCP's monopoly on political power at home and avoid the specter of a Soviet-style collapse.

For the purposes of this book, the external threat environment varies for each scenario. This variation occurs due to differences in economic growth. The larger the economy, the more wealth the CCP can devote to military technology and capabilities, making it a greater threat. In addition, in each scenario, while aggressive intent remains consistent, its immediacy and certainty vary. Leninist ideology is inherently aggressive, but war against other states is more likely when the leader firmly controls a Party that also dominates the country. This makes the last scenario of hard Leninism the most dangerous for the U.S.

The response of other great powers is relevant. They will balance against the PRC because it is a threat given its military capabilities and hostile intent. While there will be differences in response by the great powers, the threat posed by the PRC will be consistent. India, Japan, Russia, and the U.S. will be threatened by the PRC's power and ambition. Therefore, security competition in the Indo-Pacific will remain intense, even if there is no kinetic war in the decade to come.

Table Three summarizes the logic of each scenario, its impact on the Party and the economy, and the implications for the U.S.

Table Three: Three Scenarios Regarding the CCP's Future and Their Implications for the U.S.

Scenario	Party Control	Economy	Implications for the U.S.
1. Soft Leninism A Modern Form of Lenin's and Deng's NEP	Weak	Potentially Strongest if NEP Works	If NEP Successful, Greatest Economic Growth and So Military Power Maximized Negative Outcome for the U.S. If NEP Fails, as Is Likely, CCP Most Vulnerable to Loss of Power Positive Outcome for the U.S.
2. Leninism as Brezhnevism	High	Weak, PRC's Relative Decline Continues	Weak PRC Positive Outcome for the U.S.
3. Hard Leninism (Stalinism)	Absolute	Of Secondary Importance for the Leader, Absolute Political Control Is Paramount	Strong Leader in Absolute Control of Party Will Aggress against U.S. Interests Most Probable Outcome and Cause of PRC's Aggression Negative Outcome for the U.S.

IV.A. First Scenario: Soft Leninism—A Modern Form of Lenin's and Deng's NEP

The first scenario is that the CCP returns to an NEP-like policy to restore economic growth. This should be thought of as relatively weak or soft Leninism.[23] As mentioned, Lenin argued that the NEP was taking a step backward to take two steps forward. In this case, however, the CCP's NEP would take one step backward—the CCP's control of the economy is reduced to promote economic growth—without the promise of ever taking

23 Weak or soft in relative terms, of course, because all Leninism is ruthless.

two steps forward. Loosening the Party's control over the economy is a great risk for a Leninist party and might result in the Party's overthrow.

In this scenario, the CCP attempts to restore the economic growth of Deng's opening of the PRC, which was his *de facto* NEP policy. The reasoning for this decision would be to rescue the CCP from economic failure. In the decades that followed, the openness to U.S. and other Western trade and investment caused economic growth without parallel.

The leadership of the CCP prepared the ideological battlespace with genius. Under Deng, the PRC expertly, even perfectly, concealed its intent and capabilities while manipulating the stronger state. To his great credit, Deng's strategic principles, captured in the 24-Character and 28-Character strategic aphorisms, were realistic: China was weak and confronted a precarious situation.

With the conclusion of the Cold War and the end of the Soviet threat, the PRC was vulnerable to U.S. pressure for significant reform of the CCP and pressure to democratize. Beijing needed favorable conditions for its development. A confrontational approach was not an option. Because the PRC was not yet a great power, it had to avoid becoming a target while Deng laid the foundation for a peer-competitive challenge to the United States. His strategic narrative—that the PRC was weak and would remain so for a long time—contributed to the U.S.'s threat deflation, that is, a deliberate CCP political warfare strategy to shape U.S. perception which resulted in a sustained unwillingness to identify the PRC as a threat despite overwhelming evidence to the contrary.[24] While avoiding military entanglements in the region and, especially, with the United States, the PRC eagerly pursued—free from any serious balancing against it—the political and economic opportunities available to a rising power within the international system created by the United States.

---

24 This is analyzed in detail in James E. Fanell and Bradley A. Thayer, *Embracing Communist China: America's Greatest Strategic Failure* (New York: Skyhorse Publishing, 2024), pp. 16–18.

Thus, the attractiveness of an NEP is clear for a CCP that presently has a moribund economy. The GDP economic growth rates of the 1990s (exceeded 10.5 percent per year, on average, in that decade), 2000s (approximately 10 percent), and 2010s (6–8 percent) were historic. As the PRC's economy is a mix of State-Owned Enterprises (SOEs) and free-market sectors operating under the rubric of the CCP, there are the concomitant Leninist misdirection, inefficiencies, and corruption inherent in any economy under Communist control. A new NEP would change the balance between SOEs and relative free-market sectors strongly in favor of the latter.

The CCP reasonably might expect that artificial intelligence fuels new free-market energy, driving growth, followed by a slower growing state-owned sector. Indeed, it is clear from Xi's remarks and those of other officials that the PRC views artificial intelligence with great promise. Xi and Party officials often speak of "the active deployment of a systemic strategy" centered on "new quality production forces to reshape the global competitive landscape" (以"新质生产力"为核心来重塑全球竞争格局). AI must be the principal "new quality production force."

The possibility of widespread economic growth that converts immediately to military might and population surveillance would clearly be attractive to the Party as a solution to political vulnerabilities arising from low economic growth.

The first of those vulnerabilities is popular unrest due to declining living standards. This danger would be particularly acute in the PRC because today's living standards are the best in memory for most of the Chinese people. Substantial negative change would cause social and political turmoil, which may threaten the CCP.

Second, the PRC's vulnerability is great because of relative power. International politics is defined by competition over power, which is necessary to advance a state's interest and to compel its will upon its enemies. Although power is essential, a key principle of great power politics is the distinction between absolute and relative power. A state's absolute power is significant, but more important is the relative power of the state—how it ranks in terms of power against other states.[25]

Great powers that do not carefully sustain their power are condemned to lose their position. How relative power is distributed in international politics is of central importance. In that light, trade factors into the equation with respect to its strategic impact. The free-market economists' emphasis on absolute gains from trade must be supplanted by the strategists' emphasis on the distribution of relative power: Which state will gain more power from economic exchange must be the metric. The question is not "will both trading partners gain" but "who will gain more." Inevitably, one side will, and for decades the PRC gained more from trade and investment than did the U.S., with the result that the PRC gained in relative power year after year.

Accordingly, the CCP would be aware of the changing relative balance of power against it in a competitive international political system. In relative terms, the PRC would become weaker in relation to the U.S., India, Japan, and Russia. Consequently, there is a great danger for the PRC as its relative power would decline while its peer rivals' relative power would increase. The external threat environment may cause the CCP to turn to a New Economic Policy to save the PRC's position in the relative balance of power.

Only rapid economic growth through AI offers the PRC a chance to grow at rates approximating its economic expansion after 1992, when Deng implemented his New Economic Policy by opening the PRC to investment and manufacturing. Yet the promise of AI is a multifaceted issue that depends upon continued development and implementation of technology.

---

25 The example of Great Britain underscores this point. In absolute terms, Great Britain is far more powerful than it was a hundred years ago. However, in relative terms, Great Britain is much weaker than it was then. The rise of Germany, Japan, the Soviet Union/Russia and the United States mean that Britain is weaker in comparison. London is worse off than it was a century ago when it ruled the waves and its empire was arguably the world's greatest military power.

If the PRC successfully harnesses AI to be the locomotive of economic growth, then it would realize this scenario's promise of a new NEP.

However, the CCP's need to sustain control of technology, lest it weaken Party control, is a powerful consideration that would defeat the PRC's effort to lead in this technology. Based on the history of the PRC's economic growth, the most probable outcome would be AI success in another country that Beijing emulates. This issue merits detailed analysis to discern how the PRC's employment of AI would be unlike its history of economic growth. At this point, it is unclear whether AI will aid the CCP's control or weaken it.

In this scenario, the Party leadership would welcome an NEP to rescue the CCP from its colossal mistakes, even if it came at the cost of ceding greater economic control to private actors. The example of Jack Ma of Alibaba is perhaps the most famous—a businessman who grew too powerful and required chastisement by the CCP. The surveillance state that is the PRC means that the CCP does not have to make the hard trade-off that historically Leninist states have had to—greater autonomy for economic growth at the cost of Party control, which may lead to its overthrow.

The effect on the future security environment would be profound if that happened. The hostility of the Leninist CCP would be constant, because of the principles of that ideology. Hence, expect intense security competition if this scenario occurs.

The logic of this scenario is that a successful NEP fueled by AI would result in the rapid growth of the PRC, which the CCP would then convert to military power, as one of Xi's "new quality production forces" that will reshape the global competitive landscape. Consequently, the cold war with the PRC would intensify as the PRC's wealth converts to military and diplomatic might, and technological advancement. Indeed, the PRC might overtake the U.S. in sustained relative economic growth, as the PRC did from 1992 until the Covid-19 pandemic.

The result for the future U.S. security environment would be dire. A rebirth of the PRC's bustling economy would convert to diplomatic and military power, and so a change in the relative balance of power in Beijing's favor. The stalled economy of the mature Xi period would give way to an echo of the economic dynamism of decades past. From greater wealth comes the ability to project power. Growth also would permit greater trade for the PRC. Equally, it would permit more investment and aid for states and enhance the attractiveness of the PRC model of governance.

This suggests that U.S. national security planners should ensure that their economic models used for strategic assessments anticipate periods of stasis in the PRC's economy due to its profound economic problems, punctuated by periods of rapid economic growth in which the PRC is able to close the relative power gap with the U.S. Moreover, the U.S. should work with allied governments and partners to ensure that no future NEP would be successful. An NEP would be valuable for U.S. national security if it fails and if it generates Party vulnerability.

At the same time, absent tremendous growth made possible by AI, the pace of the PRC's economic growth would not be the equal to what occurred in the wake of Deng's NEP because of reduced marginal returns alone. But the growth would be positive and still greater than the current moribund PRC economy.

Despite the success of NEP policies for rescuing Leninist states from the economic, social, and political implosion that Leninist policies inevitably cause, there is cause for doubt that an NEP would realize the CCP's objectives. Three problems could prevent this scenario from happening.

First, the paucity of historical evidence for adopting NEP policies is notable. In the history of the major Communist states, the Soviet Union and the PRC, there have been only two NEPs—that of Lenin from 1921 to 1928, and Deng's from 1992 until Xi moved away from Deng's direction by 2019. Both followed economic and social disasters. Lenin's NEP was a bitter pill for the Bolsheviks to swallow after War Communism destroyed the economy of Soviet Russia. Deng's NEP was a desperate measure to save the CCP in the near term at a time when the CCP was vulnerable to overthrow by the U.S., while in the long term, his reforms would allow the CCP to defeat the U.S.

While NEPs are rare events, there are lesser reforms in the history of Leninist states. These include General Secretary Mikhail Gorbachev's economic restructuring (*perestroika*) twinned with a purported "openness" (*glasnost*) in expression, which were failures due to the unwillingness of the CPSU to open the Soviet economy to capitalism, in favor of tinkering at the margins of the Soviet economy, as Nikita Khrushchev had done and as Yuri Andropov was planning to do before his death in 1984. All failed. Similar reforms would be no more likely to save the PRC's economy than they were able to save the Soviet economy.

Leninists turn to NEPs when they are in dire circumstances: The continued rule of the leader and Party are threatened. Inherently, they are a gamble for regime survival. But they worked both times they were applied. Once NEPs have served their purpose of saving the states, Leninists like Stalin, after Lenin's death, and now Xi, push hard in the opposite direction.

Second, it is more than being ideologically unacceptable for Leninist states—it is heresy for Communist states because it is an admission that its economic policies cannot sustain the economy. Of course, that heresy did not stop Lenin. After all, Lenin was willing to make any accommodation to advance Communism—even to take the "one step back" by reintroducing the free market to Russia. However, this admission is damaging to the economic model that the PRC seeks to portray to the rest of the world as part of its political warfare strategy of undermining the U.S. global position. It compels the recognition that Communism is unable to serve the economic needs of a state.

Third, compared to 1992, the conditions of the global economy are radically different today. The PRC is not the only source of inexpensive labor. There are many alternative sources of manufacturing, including India, Indonesia, Vietnam, and onshoring back to the U.S. and other Western states.

There is "CCP fatigue" among Western businesses and governments given the hand-over-fist intellectual property theft that causes most businesses in the PRC to generate their own PRC competitor in a short period of time, and the endemic corruption of the CCP, as well as the heavy-handed tactics of the PRC's intelligence and police services. Other states may be corrupt, but they do not steal in such a flagrant fashion, through illegal means, the intellectual and physical property of firms. Moreover, they do not require their entities to cooperate in every respect with the government security services. As noted, AI's wildcard effect on economic growth is multifaceted but probably will not return the PRC to those growth rates.

Trump's tariffs and other forms of economic warfare with the PRC are certain to hinder its economy, perhaps permanently. The Sino-American economic relationship will never be as unrestrictive as it was in the early 1990s, and even after Trump's presidency, it is probable that some form of U.S. trade and investment restrictions will remain.

Hence, the CCP may turn to NEP-like policies to generate growth but will likely fail in the effort. The marginal gains from a complete free market—that is, the absolute removal of the CCP from the economy—will not generate the economic growth needed to rescue the economy from Xi's doldrums. Moreover, the weakening of the Party might lead to a Cromwell-like or Bonaparte-like challenge from the military, a challenge from a Party rival like Lin Biao or a Boris Yeltsin-like politician, or a Jack Ma-type business figure rising to seize control or to overthrow the Party. That is too great a risk unless the leader is, like Lenin or Deng, supremely confident in his control of the Party. Thus far, Xi has had that degree of control but being a Communist dictator has certain occupational hazards. These include the possibility of overthrow or falling into ill health. Of course, death is the one hazard he cannot avoid.

At root, the CCP can have control and little economic growth or growth at the cost of loss of control. That violates Leninist principles of power and the CCP has never tolerated loss of control. In turn, while AI remains a wildcard, that is positive for U.S. strategic planning and U.S.

national security because it necessitates political control over economic growth and diminishes the PRC's relative power.

IV.B. Scenario Two: Leninism Becomes Brezhnevism—The Continuation of the Status Quo

The second scenario considers the effect on the future security environment if the PRC's present strategic direction continues. The PRC under Xi's rule is defined by two elements.

The first is a stalled economy. The PRC's economy has plateaued and is in decline and AI, or any other technological *deus ex machina*, cannot save it. For this scenario, the PRC will remain in similar circumstances—not in collapse but in stasis or gradual decline. The economy of the PRC is always under strain because of CCP misrule, but has worsened because of Trump's tariffs, with the threat of higher tariffs to come, restrictions on U.S. investment and technology transfers, and efforts to stop legal and illegal technology transfers, whether by cyber means or via the presence of Chinese students at U.S. universities. But with a weakening domestic economy—and the indication from the CCP's Third Plenum in July 2024 and Fourth Plenum in October 2025 that Party leaders have no idea how to improve their economy—the decline will continue.

Moreover, foreigners are investing far less than they once did in the PRC—although that is still too much U.S. and other Western investment—and firms are looking for ways to exit the PRC in favor of investing in India, Indonesia, Vietnam, or other more stable and secure countries. In addition to the escalating global tensions from PRC threats against the Philippines and Taiwan, the Russo-Ukrainian war and turmoil in the Middle East, other major uncertainties multiply for Xi as Trump is in the White House.

This occurs as the PRC's economy is in free fall for domestic reasons, too. Consumer demand lags because most Chinese are savers, not spenders. Many lost their savings during the country's lengthy Covid-19 lockdowns, and so their wealth lies in their property. However, the property market and broader real estate market, which are also essential to local government spending, have collapsed.

The second element is ideology. Xi remains heavily influenced by Communist ideology, as he often notes. Under Xi's rule, ideology has returned to a prominence matched only by Mao's tenure. His frequent references to Mao and dependence on Maoism mean that Xi utilizes Bolshevik thought for his ideology and his objectives. Xi has boldly and transparently advanced the aim of a hegemonic PRC. The United States obstructs the PRC's ambitions and is its principal ideological opponent. Thus, it is the focus of the PRC's enmity.

Xi has stayed in power beyond the traditional two terms since Deng's retirement and is likely to remain in power for many years, as Mao and Deng did, unless his health fails him, or he is overthrown. Xi has moved the pendulum from oligarchic rule of the last two decades to increasingly totalitarian rule by a "great leader" as modeled by Mao's experience. Moreover, for a CCP leader, Xi is extraordinarily open regarding his explanation—to both domestic and international audiences—of why the PRC should dominate world politics. This ensures that the cold war with the U.S. will endure.

The declaration of "People's War" that Xi made in 2019 was an unambiguous signal of the CCP's intent to mobilize and prepare the Chinese people for war against the U.S. and its allies and partners. Moreover, as argued above, Xi's momentous address at the CCP's Twentieth Party Congress provided key insights into his leadership and impact upon the Party. In historical perspective, this congress was a significant development with lasting implications for the CCP, the PRC—and for the risk of war in international politics. Xi has been steadfast in demanding that CCP ideology remains firmly anchored in Leninism and its guiding role for the Party. Xi seeks to strengthen the ideological purity of the CCP while also strengthening its control over the PRC and influence in the world.

The direction for the CCP that Xi illuminated at the Twentieth Party Congress underscores its path of the CCP under this scenario's logic—that is, a stalled economy and a tightening ideological grip on the society and in enforcement of ideology and rectitude to police Party members who may anticipate opposing him. With a moribund economy, and with an ideology that no longer can inspire Communists, it nonetheless remains essential for the Party's self-justification of its rule. At the same time, it serves as a dead weight on the Party and is an intellectual *cul de sac* preventing necessary political, economic, or social change.

The great danger of a "Brezhnevism" afflicting the CCP is that the PRC loses relative power in relation to its great power adversaries. The Soviet Union's economy and society were greatly damaged by its period under Soviet leader Leonid Brezhnev, who ruled from 1964 to 1982, and its relative decline with the U.S. occurred precisely when the U.S. was its only peer competitor. The PRC will undergo this decline when it faces India, Japan, Russia, and the U.S. as formidable rivals. Beijing will feel the stress of power imbalances with great power rivals far more than Moscow did during the Cold War. No doubt, there will be economic, social, and political perturbations that affect India, Japan, Russia, and the U.S. But it is likely that the relative balance of power will favor the PRC's foes—India, Japan, Russia, and the U.S.—over Beijing in the coming decades.

Should this scenario occur, the PRC's decline may be precipitous and certainly CCP leadership would recognize it. This recognition might mean that this scenario would devolve into either the NEP-type throw-of-the-dice to rescue the economy, or hard Leninism to ensure the CCP's grip on power.

If it does transpire, the security environment for the PRC would be dire. As a result of prolonged decline, the global attractiveness of the PRC model will suffer. A stagnant economy will not entice states seeking economic growth and the PRC will have a reduced amount of aid to provide them. But with respect to ideology, despite its gross limitations and inability to generate economic growth, the CCP would remain a model of governance for authoritarian states because of its strength in preserving the leader and the Party's political power.

The implications of the future security environment are that, because there is no change in the PRC's ambition and strategic objectives, there will be intense security competition. However, the PRC will have reduced relative power.

This scenario is the closest of the three considered to the present status quo in the Sino-American relationship. The greatest difference is that, while there will be an economic relationship with the PRC, U.S. trade and investment will continue to decline and the PRC's leverage over the U.S., such as in providing rare earth minerals, will be reduced. In the realm of economic warfare, the PRC's economic weapons will be lessened.

So, the environment that the U.S. will face will be one of intense security competition caused by the PRC. The CCP will remain dependent upon ideology to provide coherence and self-justification for its rule, in an economy that failed to generate sufficient development because of a Leninist government and endemic corruption.[26]

---

26 Corruption is severe in the military. As noted expert on the CCP Lianchao Han writes, "In the CCP's rigidly hierarchical party-state system, every corruption case is a nested case. The higher the official's rank, the more people involved in the graft, growing exponentially. Its essence is akin to a Ponzi scheme—sustained by a chain of interests involving layer upon layer of bribery and corruption." He continues, "Take the military as an example: a Vice Chairman of the Central Military Commission controls hundreds of generals, lieutenant generals, and major generals, who in turn command tens of thousands of colonels and officers. They all need to extract more benefits from lower levels and resources within their jurisdiction—not only to recoup the costs of their bribes but also to accumulate funds for further bribes to superiors, while pocketing profits for themselves." Moreover, "military ranks come with clearly marked prices, a poorly kept secret long known in the open." Finally, "As long as this rigidly hierarchical system, devoid of any checks on power, remains unchanged, the soil for corruption will not disappear. Anti-corruption campaigns merely suppress the overt manifestations of corruption through political high-pressure tactics for the time being, without touching the structural roots of power-seeking rents. The result is that anti-corruption becomes the new normal of treating symptoms without addressing the root cause, and the party-state's systemic corruption will thus

Like Brezhnev's Soviet Union, the Chinese Communist Party will be strong, but the country's economy will be weak, with little chance of improvement. "Brezhnevism" will lead to the PRC's gradual relative decline.

From the perspective of U.S. national security, this is the best scenario. There is little that the U.S. can do to shape the ideology of the CCP and its ideological struggles. That is a given in the context of this scenario. An economy that has stalled and cannot generate technological advancement or serve as a threat to overturn U.S. economic dominance hobbles the PRC as a great power—assuming it does not employ the AI wild card more effectively. As noted, this is not likely but must be considered.

A poorer PRC means that its power projection capabilities in the region and globally will be stressed to meet the military demands of intense competition with the U.S. and other great powers. The PRC faces a multiple-threat war problem with Russia to the north, India to the south, Japan to the east, and with all supported as allies or partners of the U.S.—or potentially supported by the U.S., as Russia might be if there is a rapprochement in the relationship.

Hence, the distribution of global power is not in Beijing's favor, but far from it. In addition, an ideology that clearly cannot provide economic growth, and in which none of the leadership or members truly believes, is not an attractive model for other states that seek economic growth. Nonetheless, it will remain attractive for authoritarian states for whom this is an ideal polity for ensuring the leadership and its class remain in power.

In this scenario, the PRC is not a U.S. peer challenger, but it remains a great power threat. It is a great power akin to Brezhnev's Soviet Union, a threat to the American people, the U.S. homeland, and international

persist in an endless cycle." Lianchao Han, post on X, October 19, 2025. At: <https://x.com/lianchaohan/status/1979865610629546336?s=46&t=MWvVaFwWHHbqRtfknqZUlA>. Accessed October 19, 2025.

interests that should not be underestimated, and one which can generate strategic surprises and setbacks for U.S. national security, including the Department of War's strategy, planning, and force structure.

The PRC is a great power in gradual decline, with no solution to its demise. Leninism is a substantial brake on the economy, as historically it always is. Moreover, as in Brezhnev's Soviet Union, neither the people nor the Party believes the ideology any longer, in an economy that is weakening with no chance of revival.

The consequence is the PRC's continued relative decline, and its abandonment of pretensions defining the rules, norms, and values of international politics, while it faces stark, multiple-front war security competition from its great power rivals. Therefore, this is the best outcome for U.S. national security interests among the three scenarios considered in this book.

IV.C. Scenario Three: Hard Leninism—The Return of Stalinism

The third scenario evaluates a hard Leninism that easily may segue into Stalinism, where a single ruler controls the Party, the military, and the country, and sustains his power through a cult of personality and omnipresent mass terror. This should be considered a hard Leninism in comparison with the other scenarios.

Within Leninism there is the proclivity to its hardening to what the world knows as Stalinism. Lenin was an absolute dictator with a cult of personality who tolerated token opposition within the Party and, on occasion, would even lose Politburo votes on noncritical matters. Lenin was an obsessive-compulsive personality with a vindictive and supremely calculating mind—a political genius at the strategic and tactical levels of politics. With the exception of the NEP economy, Lenin's rule over the Party and society was already tightening by the time of his first stroke in May 1922. Party leadership removed him from day-to-day affairs even before his second stroke in December 1922 and kept him from all but the most serious issues before his death in January 1924.

Stalin built upon what Lenin created. Even more than Lenin, Stalin was an absolute dictator with a cult of personality who tolerated no opposition within the Party. Indeed, his rule is defined by the perfection of the cult of personality and ruthless terror that defined totalitarianism. He became the model of Communist rule for Mao and Kim Il-sung in Asia and the dictators of Soviet puppet states in Central and Eastern Europe.

The CCP experienced the hard Leninism of Stalinism under Mao's rule. A return to Stalinism would be far more effective and efficient because of the surveillance state it has constructed. The path to a hard Leninist CCP is clear and direct. Ever-increasing concentrations of power and more draconian policing of the Party and population lead to that outcome.

For the CCP, this would bring the advantage of a totalitarian leader with a strong cult of personality directing policy and ruling by fear. The two consequences of Leninist leadership—survival of the leader and of the Party—are realized. All aspects of the economy inevitably would fall under that control, with negative consequences.

Also in this scenario, the CCP would not turn inward, but there would be greater constraints on economic investment. The CCP's iron grip on the totality of the economy—state-owned enterprises and the open-market businesses—would tighten with the balance shifting to state control. Economic growth would slow and, thus, the PRC's wealth would be reduced. How great that reduction would be is uncertain. While reduced foreign investment would hurt, as would a return to a planned economy, this might be offset to a degree, at least, by targeted growth policies and AI.

For the Party, overt factionalism would disappear due to the cult of personality and terror, but factionalism within the cult of personality would be profound as lieutenants vied for the leader's support, generated their own fiefdoms, and undercut their rivals.[27] While terrifying for those

27 Milovan Djilas' *Conversations with Stalin* (New York: Harcourt, Brace, and World, 1962), is a useful reminder of the terror omnipresent at one of Stalin's dinners, how Stalin undermined allied leaders, and how his lieutenants demonstrated their loyalty while undermining their rivals.

caught within the Party, for the outside world there would be a certainty of diplomatic and military approach.

The Soviet Union under Stalin was defined by fear, terror, and the other odious attributes of Stalinism, but an often-overlooked aspect of his rule was the successful expansion of Soviet influence. This occurred in two forms.

The first was the war Stalin waged against the CPSU, the Red Army, and the Soviet people. Stalin expanded Soviet might internally against the Party, military, and Soviet citizens so that no aspect of Party or Soviet life was free from his influence. He finished Lenin's project of converting Russia from "the freest country in the world," as Lenin himself identified Russia under Alexander Kerensky's government (March–November 1917), into a totalitarian state. This was Stalin's most successful war.

The second form of expansion was of the influence and territory of the Soviet Union at the expense of other states. This occurred indirectly through the Comintern and Soviet aid, as happened during the Spanish Civil War (1936–1939). It also did directly through Stalin's expansionism in Europe before 1941 with invasions of Poland, Finland, all three of the Baltic states (Lithuania was in the German sphere of influence under the Molotov-Ribbentrop Pact of August 23, 1939, but was demanded by Stalin in 1940, a demand to which Adolf Hitler yielded), Bessarabia, and northern Bukovina. After World War II, of course, Stalin had control of all of Eastern Europe and most of Central Europe.

In Asia, Stalin's aggression occurred first against the Chinese in Manchuria in the war of 1929, then in 1938 at Lake Khasan and 1939 at Khalkhin Gol (Nomonhan) against the Japanese, and finally through his victories over Winston Churchill and Franklin Roosevelt at Tehran, Yalta, and Potsdam regarding Soviet territorial gains in Kurilcs, Sakhalin, Manchuria, and Dalian (Port Arthur), support for Mao and Kim Il-sung in North Korea, and occupation of Iranian Azerbaijan until 1946.[28]

28 Labour Party leader Clement Attlee replaced Churchill at Potsdam on July 27, 1945, due to the Conservative Party's defeat in the national election. The Potsdam conference occurred between July 17 and August 2, 1945.

A hard Leninist CCP would result in a bolder, more aggressive PRC than the other two scenarios for territorial aggression. This is the most dangerous scenario considered for U.S. national security interests and for the Chinese people.

There are stark implications for the possibility of war with the U.S. Washington would be challenged not just through ubiquitous political warfare but by the need to anticipate and deter the PRC's territorial expansion. This aggression would be generated by a leader confident of his control over the Party, military, and society. That would allow the PRC to aggress with confidence against U.S. national security interests—and to do so globally.

The PRC would execute this if the U.S. gave any indication of weakness in its force posture or in declaratory statements. The U.S. must meet such aggression with a strong U.S. conventional presence in the Indo-Pacific, supported by nuclear and missile defense capabilities that possess escalation dominance at the tactical, theater, and strategic level to deter PRC aggression. Those requirements are not yet present in the region. They are onerous and that force posture will require support by future administrations to achieve. Moreover, they must match the prodigious growth of PRC conventional and nuclear capabilities.

Therefore, U.S. national security planning and posturing of the joint force for this scenario must anticipate a high probability of aggression by the PRC, whose military capabilities will remain formidable. While the deterrence mission of conventional and nuclear forces is critical, the U.S. must anticipate that deterrence can fail, and so it must augment defenses of the homeland, allies, and partners in the region. In these circumstances, the U.S. must create sustained offensive strike capabilities against PRC leadership, command and control, nuclear forces, and other military targets as bulwark for the credibility of the U.S. conventional and nuclear deterrent, but also to defeat the CCP if deterrence fails.

As part of this force posture, the U.S. will require close cooperation with allies like Japan and partners like India and Taiwan will be needed to base U.S. forces in order to strengthen deterrence.

A Stalinist CCP's aggression will be precisely like Stalin's and Mao's. While, arguably, Stalin was more calculating with aggression aimed at other states, Mao was not. Mao's PRC was weaker than Stalin's Soviet Union and yet Mao conquered Tibet just as the Chinese Civil War ended—even as the CCP feared that Chiang Kai-shek would return to the mainland. Almost at the same time, Mao invaded Korea to support the North Korean army against United Nations forces. In addition, he faced two nuclear crises with the U.S. over Taiwan, aided North Vietnam with PLA units during the Vietnam War, fought a limited war with India, and clashed with the Soviet Union during the quarter century he was in power. He accomplished all that when the PRC was a poor, agrarian state, with a military that was, in essence, only a mass army with a weak air force and navy. CCP aggression will occur when the leader is fully in control of the Party. Belligerence will define the future security environment.

The likelihood of this scenario is complicated by the fact that Xi, who was born June 15, 1953, probably will be dead, and his death will spark a leadership struggle in no small measure because he has not named a successor. That turmoil will result in a leader bound by the coalition norms that governed Jiang Zemin's and Hu Jintao's leadership—that is, a CCP camarilla with one man first among equals, or a strong ruler like Xi. The latter is more likely, since Xi has busted the norms that Deng sought to impose and it is difficult to foresee how those would be reconstructed even if there were willingness to do so.

This leadership struggle will pose significant vulnerability to the CCP if it is a long one, generated by the battles between competing factions. Xi is leading the PRC to such an outcome because of the absence of a successor. Deng set the rules of succession and Xi has destroyed these, so there should be no expectation that the struggle will be short, with a strong leader imposed quickly, as happened with the transition from Deng to Jiang to Hu to Xi. The outcome of this leadership struggle will be akin to the Gang of Four-Deng struggle, in which a single, more adroit, leader triumphed over committee leadership.

Hence, there is little danger a leadership struggle will lead to the collapse of the CCP, and so interesting ancillary questions—such as, whether the CCP collapse will be peaceful, as with the Soviet Union at the end of the Cold War, or will generate conflict—are moot. This scenario compels the U.S. to prepare for an environment where the PRC is even more aggressive.

Variations in Leninism of the CCP will impact the future of the Party and the security environment for the United States. First, there will be the continuation of the Leninist NEP that Deng started, which has contributed to the PRC's rapid growth. This is the PRC as an NEP-state scenario. Second, there will be the continuation of the status quo. This will witness a tightening of the CCP political control and accompanying ideological purity, which is already evinced in Xi's policies, but that leads to economic stasis, or the equivalent of Brezhnev's Soviet Union. Third, Leninism worsens further than in scenario two and devolves into a modern form of a hard Leninism, or Stalinism, with a single leader's cult of personality and complete control through terror—domination of the CCP, military, economy, and society. This is the return of the PRC to a Stalinist scenario, as it was under Mao.

The first scenario contains danger for the U.S. if the NEP succeeds because it would mean great growth in the PRC's economy. The likelihood of confrontation with the U.S. would remain possible because of the PRC's Leninist ideology and military power, which might be considerably greater if the NEP is successful. It is supremely important that the U.S. ensures that the PRC does not win an AI-arms race. This scenario is Janus-faced, however, and it entails the possibility of the CCP's loss of control due to competing centers of power within the Party, and within the PRC, and the fact that a new NEP will not generate the returns it did a half-century before. If the NEP fails, the CCP would be vulnerable and that would open opportunities for the population.

Second, there will be the Leninism of the status quo under Xi. Within the Party, political control and accompanying ideological purity will tighten, which is already evident in Xi's policies, but the PRC's economy will plateau. This scenario will be largely a continuation of the status quo. From the standpoint of U.S. national security interests, this is the best scenario—although it is the least likely.

The third scenario foresees a hard Leninist government with purges and totalitarian control of the CCP and society. The result of totalitarian control by a single leader would be an outwardly focused, aggressive PRC.

From the standpoint of U.S. national security interests, the third scenario is the worst scenario for the future security environment—but it is the most likely due to the natural evolution and direction of Leninism, which seeks a strong leader in absolute control of a unified, subservient, and disciplined Party.

Importantly, U.S. national security policy will have little impact upon these scenarios with the exception of hindering the CCP's efforts to return to an NEP. The U.S., as the world's dominant economy, would have a role to play to prevent a successful NEP. In turn, this underscores that the AI fight is critical for shaping the future security environment, and the Departments of State and War, acting with government partners, must prevent PRC access.

Finally, U.S. national security policy must anticipate that the third scenario, the most aggressive scenario of a hard Leninism—Stalinism—is Leninism's natural evolution. The strong leader in firm control of the CCP is a condition that invites the PRC's territorial aggression in the East and South China Seas, in South Asia, and perhaps against Russia. It also encourages the continuation of the CCP's political warfare campaigns against the U.S. to undermine the U.S. homeland and its position in world politics. U.S. national security planning and policy must anticipate a belligerent and territorially expansive PRC, which defines its Leninist ideology.

Chapter 4

American Identity Is Defined by the American Trinity: The American Spirit, Political Liberalism, and Western Civilization

Time for a welcome break from thinking about the poison of Leninism and the CCP to discuss their antidote: American identity and the greatness of America. There are many reasons why America is extraordinary, but I argue that it is the American trinity. The core of American identity is the American trinity: American spirit, the ideology of political liberalism, and Western civilization. Each of those is a necessary pillar of American identity that has sustained the country from 1776. But it is threatened today as it never has been. What Americans now face is an existential struggle, a fight between the doctrines of Lenin and Madison, for the survival of the American identity in the United States and the survival of the Western civilization.

Here I explain American identity and why it is the antithesis of Communism. The core of American identity provided the U.S. with strength in the past to resist Communism, and this must be sustained to ensure that Leninism does not succeed in conquering America, as it did Russia and later China.

The bulwark is the American people and their identity, which is composed of the American trinity. It remained strong and implacable until neo-Bolshevism began to surface overtly and show its muscle in social changes during the 1960s and after. The good news for Americans is that as long as American identity remains grounded in the American trinity the country will be safe from Communism. The bad news is that the Communists know this and have targeted each pillar of the American trinity assiduously for many decades. They have seriously undermined the American trinity to the point where the country is now in a period in which American identity is consistently attacked and Americans are in the worst period of ideological upheaval in their history. Defenders of American identity must protect that identity from advancing Communism. In essence, the stronger American identity, the weaker Communism in America. The weaker American identity, the stronger Communism. Everything depends upon American identity defeating Communism.

I. The American Spirit

For most of U.S. history—until, it seems, the last ten minutes—American identity was a product of the American spirit, political liberalism, and Western civilization. The American spirit is the entelechy or spirit of the nation held by the Founding Fathers and the "Spirit of 1776" held by the Revolutionary generation and provided to their progeny. Subsequent generations of Americans have held that spirit very close to them because it informed their history and identity as Americans. It was inherent in American politics and culture and was a prodigious strength of the country.

The American spirit is the American people's inheritance bequeathed to them by the Founding Fathers and Western civilization and the natural environment. That is an important point. The inheritance was not only from the Founding Fathers, not only from the British or, more broadly Europeans, and not only of the eighteenth and nineteenth centuries, but the whole of Western civilization. These served as the foundations for the basic institutions of American life, the state, church, and family, which

Americans have maintained, as well as the fundamental values and culture which they have cherished.

Americans today must recognize that the American spirit was achieved with a speed unprecedented in history. It took centuries for the people of Britain, France, Germany, or Italy to establish national monarchies and governments and establish a common identity. But Americans brought forth a new nation in a single generation. As Thomas Paine (1737–1809) wrote: "Our citizenship in the United States is our national character.... Our great title is, AMERICANS."[1]

Moreover, it was gained without an established church, or by a monarch, or by the power of the ruling class. Americans should pause a moment to appreciate that fact. The American spirit did not result from a national past or its strength from a traditional enemy.

The American spirit came from the people and the founding ideology of the country. Americans understood that their country was not Europe, but something new in history. The repudiation of Europe was not just political, economic, or social. It was all that, but even more—it was an embrace of a new beginning, realized by a Revolution of 1776 that was the most powerful instrument, the most potent single event that created a sense of common destiny and national identity for Americans.

The natural environment mattered as well—Americans should ask whether the American people made the land, or did the land make the people? The American continent contained a multiformity comparable to all of Europe. The America into which men and women of Europe entered was new not only in the sense of being an alternative to Europe. It was new in its unrivaled natural beauty and spaciousness—with room enough, as Jefferson said in his Inaugural Address in 1801, "for our descendants to

---

1 Thomas Paine, *The Crisis Papers*, No. XIII, April 19, 1783, in *Thomas Paine: Collected Writings* (New York: The Library of America, 1995), pp. 348–354, 352–353. Emphasis original.

the thousandth and thousandth generation."[2] The environment got a vote, too, on what made Americans "American." The American environment's impact helped to produce an amalgam that was distinctively American. As a result, the differences between a Mainer, a Kansan, or Californian were insignificant compared to an Italian, German, or Frenchman.

Yet, it was not the particular environment—or the many environments that are America—that created the American spirit but the whole of the American space. The tremendous beauty of America, the invitation to mobility, the belief in independence, and encouragement for practical solutions to problems, enterprise, good humor, and optimism nurtured the American spirit. The American people, who have thrived in all the climates and soils of America, have achieved a coherent, distinctive, and remarkably stable national identity for most of the country's history with an ease that confounded not only the expectations of America's critics but all of history.

The 1803 Louisiana Purchase is now seen as evidence of Jefferson's genius, and indeed it was, as was Secretary of State William Seward's 1867 purchase of Alaska, but all too often forgotten today is the wisdom of the 1787 Northwest Ordinance. It resulted in extensive roadbuilding and took advantage of America's rivers, which made it easy to unite the seaboard and the interior. Soon canals and steamboats made this extensive territory an asset rather than a liability. That allowed Americans to move in great numbers from the coast and piedmont into the depth of the country to make America truly a continental power.

Nothing in history has succeeded like America, and Americans knew it. Nowhere else on the globe has nature been at once so rich and so generous, and available to all who have the enterprise to take from that bounty. Nature and experience justified optimism, and so early Americans certainly were. Collectively, these Americans had never known defeat, or oppression,

2 Thomas Jefferson, First Inaugural Address (1801). At: <https://constitutioncenter.org/the-constitution/historic-document-library/detail/thomas-jefferson-first-inaugural-address-1801>. Accessed September 10, 2025.

or grinding poverty in America, and they believed those characteristics defined Europe. Progress was not a Hegelian concept but the reality of American experience and of the American work ethic. Americans saw progress daily due to sweat of their brow in the transformation of wilderness into farmland, towns into cities, and the steady rise of community and country to great power and wealth.

American power could accomplish anything, with little concern for the past or its limitations, and the ethos of American labor: Know your job, do your job, never quit, never make excuses, and simply get the job done. For these Americans, Europeans lived in the past, while they lived in the future. Americans planned ambitiously from the Erie Canal to the transcontinental railroad to the Apollo program. There was no "iron cage" of bureaucracy, as German sociologist Max Weber wrote, that governed modern life to constrain American dynamism. Even the recent past quickly became legendary. The American spirit lived in a practical present, with an eye to the wondrous future. The American future was certain to be brighter for coming generations than it was in the past. That certainty was fuel for justifying and enduring the hard sacrifices that generations of Americans made.

That stupendous optimism contained a sense of power and of vast reserves of energy. To carve from the wilderness a farm, to educate millions of children, to feed the Western world with America's surfeit of meat, soybeans, wheat, and corn, to be followed by its abundance of hard ciders, bourbon, and rye whiskey, did not seem remarkable. It seemed naturally American. Even American folklore was on a grand scale—Paul Bunyan, Mike Fink, the "king of the keelboaters," and John Henry—and the empire builders from Daniel Boone, Davy Crockett, Sam Houston, Andrew Carnegie, Thomas Edison, George Westinghouse, Henry Ford, Alfred Sloan, Thomas J. Watson, Theodore Roosevelt and his Panama Canal, Henry Kaiser, Walt Disney, Bill Hewlett and David Packard, to Steve Jobs.

It created great literature and theater, insightful poets, fearless astronauts, soldiers, sailors, athletes, entrepreneurs, explorers, farmers, miners, pastors, and woodsmen, an inventive nature, a love of sport, baseball at first and later football, and of animals.

In their collective personality, Americans were largely wholesome, good-natured, generous, hospitable, and sociable. They valued equality and nothing was more fatal to political success than the appearance of superiority or ostentatious wealth. Presidential candidates had better drink hard cider from a jug than fine wines from crystal glasses. Inauthenticity was also damaging. The posting on social media of Hillary Clinton pretending to enjoy beer and whiskey at a bar during her 2008 campaign for the Democratic nomination for president was painful to watch for all audiences—her supporters and opponents. It served every ambitious politician well to have been born in a log cabin, and to know how to enjoy a beer.

For America's defense, the militia was its principal instrument. There was no military class dominating the remarkably small army and even smaller navy, and except in time of war, no social advantage was attached to the uniform. Except in the antebellum South, leading families did not earmark one son for the law, one for the church, and one for the army or navy. Not possessing a strong military caste as the major European states, France, Germany, and Russia did helped America maintain republican government and the American spirit, and allowed it to thrive, particularly in the country's early years when it was weak and therefore vulnerable to the depredations of Great Britain or France.[3]

If Americans did not always get it right, they mostly did. What might have become a military caste, for example, the Society of the Cincinnati, founded in 1783, was limited to Revolutionary War officers and their descendants, became instead a museum piece as years passed. Today it focuses on preserving the values of American independence. In contrast, the

3 As both Otto Hintze and J. G. A. Pocock recognized in their respective great works. See Felix Gilbert, ed., *The Historical Essays of Otto Hintze* (Oxford: Oxford University Press, 1975); and J. G. A. Pocock, *The Machiavellian Moment: Florentine Political Thought and the Atlantic Republican Tradition* (Princeton, N.J.: Princeton University Press, 1975).

Grand Army of the Republic, a fraternal organization founded in 1866 for veterans of the Union Army, Navy, and Marines, embraced privates and generals, sailors and Marines, alike. It was a broad and powerful organization due to the devotion that bound the men. Such was the fealty of its members that, in 1885, they guarded President Ulysses S. Grant as he lay dying from throat cancer at an estate on Mount McGregor in New York. His funeral procession included 60,000 people, most of whom were Civil War veterans.[4]

Certainly, American culture was material, but it had no use for caste or class. The American materialism was both democratic and equalitarian. Every barefooted boy could be a president or millionaire, but that boy's democracy was social and political, rather than economic. The "self-made man," not the first-born son as the aristocratic heir, was the hero. If Americans had not yet attained the luxury of the European aristocracy, they had achieved a way of life higher than the rest of the world could only dream. In no other country did the workingman's or farmer's table have such abundance or his family better nourished.

Hard work was the answer to most questions and to most problems. Americans met hardship with courage and fortitude because both, together with industry, shrewdness, and a little luck, were bound to be rewarded in the end. The work ethic of Americans surpassed all others. Americans preached the gospel of hard work and regarded shiftlessness as a vice more pernicious than immorality. In the American approach to business, whatever promised to increase wealth was regarded as good. Consequently, the American was tolerant of speculation, advertising, deforestation, and the exploitation of natural resources. They endured the worst manifestations of industrialization from the mills of New England and North Carolina and the hellish heat of the steelworks of Pittsburgh and Gary, Indiana, to the copper mines of Bisbee, Arizona, and the coal mines of Harlan County, Kentucky.

---

4 See Charles Bracelen Flood, *Grant's Final Victory: Ulysses S. Grant's Heroic Last Year* (Boston: Da Capo Press, 2011).

These beliefs and approach to life were uniquely American. They tended to give a quantitative cast to Americans' thinking and directed them to place a quantitative valuation on most things. The French political philosopher Alexis de Tocqueville (1805–1859), perhaps the most insightful observer of Americans, the American spirit, and American political life, understood this when he wrote: "As one digs deeper into the national character of the Americans, one sees that they have sought the value of everything in world only in the answer to this single question: how much money will it bring in?"[5] Hence, when an American was asked what a man was worth, he meant material worth. His solution for most problems was therefore quantitative—in education, industry, democracy, and war.

Europeans who too often viewed Americans as bumpkins who just fell off a turnip wagon thought this vulgar, had no conception of its origin or its connection with the realities of American life, nor could they conceive of power and quantity in American terms. It is no accident that America was the arsenal of democracy. At the same time, all the muses of the fine arts were known to Americans and each flourished in Columbia's soil.

This quantitative worldview was also an indication of an intense practicality. Americans were practical about politics, religion, culture, and science. The American was ingenious and resourceful, and always ready to improvise. The American borrowed from the Native Americans or immigrants and was willing to try anything to see if their ways worked. The American reaction to most situations was straightforward, and he was happiest when he could find a mechanical or, later, an electronic solution to the problems he faced. The American spirit animated the creators of the cotton gin, the steamboat, the harvester, the six-shooter, the sewing machine, vulcanized rubber, the telegraph and telephone, barbed wire, the typewriter, the airplane, the atomic and hydrogen bombs, the lunar

5 Alexis de Tocqueville, "To Ernest de Chabrol, 9 June 1831," in Roger Boesche, ed., *Selected Letters on Politics and Society* (Berkeley: University of California Press, 1985), p. 39.

module, the microchip, the home computer, the application of the internet, AI and countless other inventions.

Yet when Americans consider their past, they may proudly state that they were born politically mature. The American had longer and larger experience with government than the average Englishman, Frenchman, or German. In fact, Americans displayed a natural talent for politics. The American's political instruments were as ingenious as his mechanical inventions: the Declaration of Independence, federalism, the Articles of Confederation, and later, the constitutional convention and Constitution, the peaceful transfer of power from one political party to another as first occurred in 1801 between John Adams and Thomas Jefferson after the vituperative election of 1800, and judicial review were products of great sophistication and masterful art. Statesmen and political philosophers of all countries could read *The Federalist Papers* with profit. They still can.

II. The Ideology of Political Liberalism

The American spirit was twinned inextricably with the political ideology of liberalism, the second element of the American trinity. Each supported the other. Political liberalism is an individualistic political theory and employs the concepts of inalienable rights and individual freedoms. It is constituted of three components.

The first of these are its assumptions. For political theorist John Locke (1632–1704), liberalism's starting point is an assumption of atomized individuals, in a "state of perfect freedom," equal to all others and endowed with a set of inalienable rights. Individualism is thus the core of the ideology and serves as a sharp break with earlier political thought, including that of Plato, Aristotle, St. Augustine, and Machiavelli, all of whom argued that humans are naturally social beings.

As Tocqueville argued: "Our ancestors had no word for *individualism*, a word we have coined for our own use because, in their time, there was no individual who did not belong to a group or who considered himself to be entirely alone."[6] Additionally, liberalism is anchored upon an assumption of the human ability to reason, which includes the ability to discern what is best for human political organization.

Second, from this foundation, liberals argue that humans possess inalienable rights including the right to life, understood as not only survival but also the freedom to live a good life as one sees fit. A person is able to choose whatever lifestyle he wants as long as it does not infringe on the rights of others. This includes the freedom of conscience to live according to one's religious beliefs, and the freedom of economic exchange, to produce goods and services and exchange them in a marketplace minimally policed by government—free-market or laissez faire economics. Rights are designed to maximize the amount of freedom individuals have in their daily lives, which allows them to lead the best and most fulfilling life possible. This concern for rights is the basis of its individualism—everyone on the planet has the same inherent set of rights.

Freedom means the ability to act without fear of government intrusion. This entails freedom of speech, freedom of the press, the right to hold property. Liberalism also assumes that individuals differ intensely regarding political, economic, and social issues. These differences necessitate a state. But the government exists to protect freedoms from threats that might emanate from within the society or outside of it.

The necessity of toleration also stems from liberalism's bedrock assumptions. People have the right to pursue their own way of life, which others must recognize. They accept that others sometimes will disagree with them about core principles. However, even if we strongly dislike or despair over what others say, we may not punish them for their opinions. Instead, all should adopt a live-and-let-live approach, resolve their conflicts peacefully, and maintain a respect for their shared political principles.

---

6 Alexis de Tocqueville, *The Ancien Régime and the French Revolution*, trans. and ed. Gerald Bevan (New York: Penguin, 2008 [1856]), p. 102. Emphasis original.

Of course, not all accept or value a difference of opinion and the right of others to hold and express their beliefs. This is a principal cause of historical difficulty for liberalism, but has been resolved traditionally by requiring the population to understand and accept that differences will be resolved in what John Stuart Mill famously described in 1859 as the need for vigorous debate arising out of a free intellectual exchange.[7] Often called the "marketplace of ideas," good—or at least better—ideas will win, that is, be accepted by the majority, over bad ones. Those possessing the bad ideas must accept that they lost, and while they are free to hold them, and continue to persuade others, they must accept that most fellow citizens do not hold their beliefs.

Third, advancing and protecting the freedom of individuals is the principal political problem of the polity—all government is limited in its powers and exists only with the consent of the governed.[8] Government power and ability to restrain liberty is necessary only to the degree that it may protect individuals from being harmed by others. As Paine wrote in 1776 at the dawn of the American Revolution, government is "a necessary evil" to serve this objective.[9]

For liberalism, the government may be controlled by several measures. The first of these is the separation of powers, which Montesquieu (1689–1755) advocated in 1748, into what we now term an executive

7 John Stuart Mill, *On Liberty*, ed. David Bromwich and George Kateb (New Haven: Yale University Press, 2003 [1859]), pp. 88–84. It is important to note that while Mill advanced its argument, he did not use the term in his writings.

8 This was first advanced most compellingly by Locke in 1690 in the second of his two treatises. John Locke, *Two Treatises of Government* (Cambridge: Cambridge University Press, 1960 [1689]). For interpretation and exposition of modern liberalism see John Gray, *Liberalism* (Milton Keynes: Open University Press, 1984); and Gray, *Enlightenment's Wake* (London: Routledge, 1995); and Alan Ryan, *The Making of Modern Liberalism* (Princeton, N.J.: Princeton University Press, 2012), p. 26.

9 Thomas Paine, *Common Sense* (New York: Peter Eckler Publishing, 1918 [1776]), p. 1.

branch, legislature, and judiciary as separate and co-equal divisions of government.[10] The unwritten Constitution of the United Kingdom or the U.S. Constitution and the Bill of Rights and other, subsequent amendments is the second.[11] Federalism offers a third avenue to check the concentration of power in a central authority by dividing political power with lower branches of government. Periodic popular elections also serve as a check on governmental power. Finally, the rule of law contains the government. The rule of law is the authority and influence of law in society. It is the principle that all members of a society, including those in government, are equally subjected to publicly disclosed legal codes and legal processes. Thus, the rule of law serves as a constraint on individuals and the state, including the state's lawmakers, police, and judiciary.

Significantly, the trajectory of liberalism in America is unlike Europe's. This is because a central characteristic of American liberal society is that it has lacked a genuine revolutionary tradition. That tradition was strong in Europe and had been linked with the Puritan Revolution, which caused the English Civil War in the 1640s and Oliver Cromwell's Lord Protectorship—a dictatorship in all but name—in the 1650s, as well as the French Revolution of 1789. The United States had no related historical experience. The reason is that America was "born equal," as Tocqueville famously observed in his 1835 classic, *Democracy in America*: "The great advantage of the Americans is that they have arrived at a state of democracy without having to endure a democratic revolution; and that they are born equal, instead of becoming so."[12] For Tocqueville, the great advantages

10 Charles-Louis de Secondat, Baron de Montesquieu, *The Spirit of the Laws* (Cambridge: Cambridge University Press, 1989 [1748]), Bk. XI, chapter 6.

11 The Constitution was signed by its drafters in Philadelphia on September 17, 1787, ratified in 1788, and came into effect on March 9, 1789.

12 Alexis de Tocqueville, *Democracy in America*, 2 Vols., ed. F. Bowen (Boston: J. Allyn, 1873 [1835]), Vol. 2, p. 123. As there was no revolution, there was no reaction. Thus, no Algernon Sydney (1623–1683), one of the major theorists of the English Civil War and one of the first proponents of liberalism and

of the United States were its equality, its pluralism, and the strength of its civil society.

Louis Hartz, a foremost theorist of American political thought, expanded Tocqueville's argument. Hartz wrote, "For a society that begins with Locke . . . stays with Locke, by virtue of an absolute and irrational attachment it develops for him, and becomes as indifferent to the challenge of socials in the later era as it was unfamiliar with the heritage of feudalism in the earlier one."[13] Hartz argued it was the liberalism that anchored the political system of America and made it immune to its ideological challengers and thus ideological unrest.

For Hartz, in the American context, Karl Marx was wrong "in his historical analysis, attributing as he did the emergence of the socialist ideology to the objective movement of economic forces."[14] Hartz identified socialism as arising out of philosophical principles, ideology, and experiences that were alien to the American experience. "Socialism is largely an ideological phenomenon, arising out of the principles of class and the revolutionary liberal revolt against them which the old European order inspired," and, thus, "[I]t is not accidental that the America which has uniquely lacked a feudal tradition has uniquely lacked a socialist tradition."[15] British political and economic historian Sir William Ashley captured the point well when he identified the importance of the lack of a feudal experience: "As feudalism

---

republican government, meant no Charles II, who, upon the restoration of the monarchy, attaindered many of those who questioned the divine right of kings. In the French context, no revolutionary firebrand and liberal theorist Maximilien Robespierre meant no Joseph de Maistre, one of the foremost philosophers of the counter-Enlightenment and of unabashed support for aristocratic social hierarchies and monarchical rule.

13 Louis Hartz, *The Liberal Tradition in America* (New York: Harcourt, Brace and World, 1955), p. 6.

14 Hartz, *The Liberal Tradition in America*, p. 6.

15 Hartz, *The Liberal Tradition in America*, p. 6.

was not transplanted to the New World, there was no need for the strong arm of a central power to destroy it."[16]

Hence, the American and European experiences caused very different political traditions and variation in the strength of liberalism on the two continents. Despite regional influences, even the American antebellum South was the component of America closest to Old World Europe but was not really Europe—as the author and poet of the American South, John Crowe Ransom, described.[17]

To be sure, there were other factors that assisted America's rise and growth. As argued, the abundance of land on the frontier aided the building of the American spirit and a liberal system, and in that sense, the people did not make America, but America made the people. Yet it was the political ideology of liberalism that unified Americans, later immigrants, and framed and explained what Americans sought in their society and fought for in their wars, and what they must do to assimilate.

But possessing a single political ideology came at a cost. The American problem is subtle, for the psychic heritage of a nation "born equal" is what Hartz termed a colossal "liberal absolutism."[18] By "liberal absolutism," Hartz meant that America was an absolutist state—it has and always had

---

16 W. J. Ashley, *Surveys Historic and Economic* (London: Longmans, Green, and Co., 1900), p. 406.

17 Hartz, *The Liberal Tradition in America*, p. 8. The antebellum South, for both Ransom and Hartz, "has been an alien child in a liberal family, tortured and confused, driven to a fantasy life which, instead of disproving the power of Locke in America, portrays more poignantly than anything else the tyranny he has had." Ransom, along with Donald Davidson and Allen Tate, was one of the leading Southern Agrarians of the 1920s and 1930s who argued that the South was a unique culture, and that Southern principles, practices, and lifestyle—defined as agrarianism, conservativism, and Protestant religious belief—should be maintained in the South in the face of change from industrialization, critiques from Northern Liberals, and a nascent civil rights movement.

18 Hartz, *The Liberal Tradition in America*, p. 285.

possessed a single ideology. For Hartz, America is a liberal absolutist state possessed of a sober faith "that its norms are self-evident," and the spirit of liberalism "arose out of contact with an opposing way of life," was held without doubt, and "so sure of itself that it hardly needed to become articulate."[19]

The American liberal faith, the mechanism of American liberal absolutism, can be seen clearly, preparing for the responses to the Bolshevik Revolution.[20] To Hartz, if the Great Depression of the 1930s suggested anything, "it was that the failure of socialism in America stemmed from the ideological power of . . . liberalism, rather than from economic circumstances."[21] Rather than turning to Marxism-Leninism in the depths of a prolonged economic crisis, "what emerged to deal with the economic problem was a movement within the framework of the liberal faith," that is, "a movement which belonged to the genre of Western Liberal Reform . . . which sought to extend the sphere of the states and at the same time retain the basic principles of Locke."[22]

In all of its wars and struggles, the United States has faced an ideological challenge. Meeting them has proved formative conceptually, and pivotal

---

19 Hartz, *The Liberal Tradition in America*, pp. 58–59. The American never doubts "his general principles, this is also the reason he is able to dismiss his critics with a fine and crushing ease." But liberalism has its own rare violent moments of doubt and hysteria when it rises to the surface with a vengeance, when civil liberties collapse. "Anyone who watches it then can hardly fail to have a healthy respect for the dynamite which normally lies concealed beneath the free and easy atmosphere of the American liberal community." Hartz, *The Liberal Tradition in America*, p. 59. Another negative consequence of "liberal absolutism" is that it leads to the death by atrophy of the philosophic impulse as there was only one ideology. Hartz, *The Liberal Tradition in America*, p. 285. Unfortunately, the Communists were undermining the dominance of liberalism precisely at the time Hartz was writing. Far from being "absolute," liberalism has been tested by Communism and may well be defeated by it.

20 Hartz, *The Liberal Tradition in America*, p. 286.

21 Hartz, *The Liberal Tradition in America*, p. 259.

22 Hartz, *The Liberal Tradition in America*, p. 259.

strategically. The Revolutionary War was prototypical. That ideological conflict defined the essence of the political principles of the United States. Its outcome established that individuals possess political liberty, free-market economics, rule of law, and societal openness as exemplified by the right of dissent.

Americans' principles have expanded with those borders, formal and informal. Throughout his presidency, Jefferson declared that the United States was "an empire for liberty," describing it as "a chosen country," and a "rising nation" that was already "advancing rapidly to destinies beyond the reach of the mortal eye."[23]

The American spirit and the ideas Jefferson expressed were commonplace in his day and were already motivating the exploration and—by means both seemly and ignoble—the acquisition of territory once held by Native Americans and by European empires and their former subjects. The growth of material power and territorial wealth made ideology grow, too, feeding on its own success. As argued, it was fundamentally Lockean: America's ideology was quite robust, but it was also demanding. It required constant vigilance to guarantee individual liberty, due process, market freedom, and at times, orderly immigration and assimilation. As its credited successes mounted, "Americanism" forced open its own traditions. Such was the American spirit, "We, the People" came to admit most everyone who was formerly subordinated or unfairly excluded.

---

23 For a comprehensive discussion of Jefferson's view of the United States in the world see Robert W. Tucker and David C. Hendrickson, *Empire of Liberty: The Statecraft of Thomas Jefferson* (New York: Oxford University Press, 1990). On September 19, 1803, Jefferson characterized the United States as an "empire for liberty," in a missive to Andrew Jackson. See Adrienne Koch, *Jefferson and Madison: The Great Collaboration* (New York: Alfred A. Knopf, 1950), p. 244. Jefferson's 1805 remarks about the United States as "a chosen country" and "rising nation" are quoted in Anders Stephanson, *Manifest Destiny: American Expansion and the Empire of Right* (New York: Hill and Wang, 1995), p. 21.

That ideology served as the structure into which flowed the tremendous material growth of the United States through individual liberty, free-market beliefs, the rule of law, a careful and guarded receptivity to European immigration, and the enforcement of assimilation.[24] In turn, the growth of the material power of the United States helped to ensure that the American spirit and Americans' liberal ideology remain dominant, despite the challenges from the New England Federalists, Southern aristocracy, fascism, socialism, or Communism.

Considering the sweep of American history, a mix of material and ideological motivations came to characterize American behavior throughout the modern era. This mix compelled the United States to intervene in World War I. Woodrow Wilson's motivations were to prevent a hegemon on the European continent when it looked like Germany might win, and to eliminate German militarism—a threat to Germany itself, to Europe, to the United States, and to all seafaring peoples.

With Germany's defeat, the threat of militarism was gone, the balance of power restored, and the United States returned to its shores. The direction of the United States, torn between two contending visions of American foreign policy, so well identified by renowned historian of American foreign policy Michael Hunt, was still unresolved. The first of these foresaw "that the American pursuit of lofty ambitions abroad, far from imperiling liberty, would serve to invigorate it at home while creating conditions favorable to its spread in foreign lands."[25] The second vision foresaw the reverse. American security was best advanced by minimizing U.S. commitments because restraint was "essential for maintaining liberty

24 Capturing the complexities of immigration and assimilation in U.S. history are Roger Daniels, *Guarding the Golden Door: American Immigration Policy and Immigrants Since 1882* (New York: Hill and Wang, 2004); and Rogers M. Smith, *Civic Ideals: Conflicting Visions of Citizenship in U.S. History* (New Haven: Yale University Press, 1999).

25 Michael H. Hunt, *Ideology and U.S. Foreign Policy* (New Haven: Yale University Press, 1987), p. 42.

at home."[26] The second, and more proximal, vision proved more compelling, and the United States after World War I contentedly retrenched far from the front.

The rise of Fascist Italy, Imperial Japan, and Nazi Germany once again brought ideological and material threats to the fore, and the Roosevelt administration responded with vigor by 1940. The United States supported the British after the fall of France—over 1,300 American merchantmen, sailors, and Coast Guardsmen died in the North Atlantic fighting the Germans before December 1941. Also before Pearl Harbor, the U.S. also aided the Nationalists in China directly through the American Volunteer Group and indirectly by pressuring Japan diplomatically and economically.

With the demise of the Axis powers, the new and more potent threat of the Soviet Union emerged. President Harry Truman rapidly recognized that national security, as diplomatic historian Melvin Leffler argues, meant "more than defending territory," that is, the Soviet Union did not have to attack the United States to undermine its security.[27] National security requires "defending the nation's core values, its organizing ideology, and its free political and economic institutions."[28]

To combat the Soviet Union's material power, the United States strengthened its economy, military, and alliance relationships. To combat Soviet ideational power, the Truman administration turned to America's ideology. As in its previous wars, the role of ideology in this struggle

---

26 Hunt, *Ideology and U.S. Foreign Policy*, p. 43.

27 Melvin P. Leffler, *A Preponderance of Power: National Security, the Truman Administration, and the Cold War* (Stanford, Calif.: Stanford University Press, 1992), p. 13. Leffler's consideration of U.S. foreign policy is rivaled only by Hunt's. Leffler is sensitive to the role of the ideology of the United States throughout his analysis.

28 Leffler, *A Preponderance of Power* p. 13.

critically reinforced the material aspect, as prisoners in the Gulag like Natan Sharansky testified.[29]

There is a sense that the United States is in stasis or is lost. This is due in large part to the ideological upheaval in contemporary American politics between liberalism and the success of Communism in its guise as neo-Bolshevism, or the progressive politics of the American political left.[30] This is indeed the greatest challenge to political liberalism that the ideology has faced.

Of course, the U.S. faced difficulties before but none as grave as the challenge of Communism. The historical cases of major stresses on the American political system are three.[31] These were the War of 1812, the

---

29 Naturally, liberalism does generate enemies and has the proclivity of turning political conflict into a scientific and ethical conflict. For the liberal, has theorist of international politics, Hans Morgenthau, identified: "The political opponent becomes a scientific and ethnical opponent as well. . . . The liberal will feel the full measure of his superiority only when he can prove to the world and to himself the righteousness of his position and moral baseness of the enemy who must be punished for his crimes." Hans J. Morgenthau, *Scientific Man vs. Power Politics* (Chicago: University of Chicago Press, 1946), p. 36.

30 Montesquieu notes that the decline of states does not come as the result of defeat in a single battle but for deeper and far more profound causes when he wrote in his *Reflections on the Causes of the Rise and Fall of the Roman Empire* (1758): "It is not fate that rules the world. Ask the Romans who experienced a continual series of prosperity as long as they governed themselves in a certain way; but they suffered an uninterrupted flow of calamities, when they acted upon different principles." Charles-Louis de Secondat, Baron de Montesquieu, *Reflections on the Causes of the Rise and Fall of the Roman Empire* (Glasgow: Robert Urie, 1758), chapter xviii, p. 182.

31 There are other examples that might be considered, such as Shays's Rebellion (1786–1787), the Whiskey Rebellion (1791–1794), the Mormon Rebellion (1857–1858), or the threat of Bolshevism or anarchism in the wake of World War I (the first Red Scare of 1919–1920) and their successful suppression by the Palmer raids, during which about 6,000 suspected Communist aliens and American citizens were arrested without warrants in twenty-three states. However, they do not equal in gravity the cases considered as they were

battle over states' rights and chattel slavery before the Civil War, and the Vietnam War during the Cold War. There was a significant ideological upheaval and thus challenge to the political institutions of the United States during the War of 1812 when the New England Federalists undermined the U.S. government's war effort against the formidable threat that Great Britain posed, but even more significantly, debated secession before the abrupt end of the war stemmed the flowering of such a movement.

In the decade before the Civil War, growing cleavages over the correct interpretation of the American Revolution of 1776 and the Constitution, the relationship between the federal government and the states, and the institution of slavery in the American South, led to the greatest break in America's political institutions and the temporary bifurcation of the country. In 1861–1862, there was the danger of British intervention on the side of the Confederacy during the *Trent* Affair, but the North's acceptance of British demands led to a de-escalation of the crisis. The North more easily parried efforts by Imperial France and Spain to intervene on behalf of the Confederacy.

Finally, in the Cold War, while the external threat from the Soviet Union was formidable, the ideological challenge to the U.S. was significant

---

localized disputes. Of these, Shays's was certainly the most significant as it contributed to the calling of the Constitutional Convention (May–September 1787, ratified in 1788, and in effect in 1789). On Shays's Rebellion, see Leonard L. Richards, *Shays's Rebellion: The American Revolution's Final Battle* (Philadelphia: University of Pennsylvania Press, 2003). An exceptional account of the Whiskey Rebellion is Thomas P. Slaughter, *The Whiskey Rebellion: Frontier Epilogue to the American Revolution* (New York: Oxford University Press, 1988). For an excellent analysis of the Mormon Rebellion see David L. Bigler and Will Bagley, *The Mormon Rebellion: America's First Civil War 1857–1858* (Norman: University of Oklahoma Press, 2011). On the Palmer Raids, see Melvyn P. Leffler, *The Specter of Communism: The United States and the Origins of the Cold War, 1917–1953* (New York: Hill and Wang, 1994), pp. 14–15; and John Maxwell Hamilton, *Manipulating the Masses: Woodrow Wilson and the Birth of American Propaganda* (Baton Rouge: Louisiana State University Press, 2020), p. 385.

but defeated by liberal ideology. The ideological upheaval the United States faced in the waning days of the Vietnam War was significant. The war's aftermath affected the ability of the U.S. Department of Defense, now Department of War, to recruit and employ the force for much of the 1970s.

However, in each historical case, the American spirit, the ideology of liberalism, and Western civilization were still dominant, and overwhelmingly so. Indeed, the American political system was stable and confident enough to reform itself from the mid-1960s to permit equal rights for racial minorities through the civil rights movement and subsequent ones for women and, in time, sexual minorities. The Soviets had considerable success in intelligence collection, based on ideological and other means, but were never able to generate a mass movement to support their objective of undermining the United States from within.

As I will discuss in the next chapter, a challenge that did exist came from the neo-Bolshevik thought of the "New Left," which favored ideational and cultural approaches to revolution rather than a workers' revolution originating on the factory floor. But the "New Left" was never powerful enough during the Cold War to cause the change it sought in the Cold War's time frame. The American trinity was far too powerful at that time and the neo-Bolshevik control over the educational system, the media, and much of civil society had only started to take hold.

Nevertheless, the Vietnam War and the years following provided the opportunity for the neo-Bolshevik left to undermine the anti-Communist consensus that had governed American foreign and domestic policy and provided an opening to change America's ideology and political institutions, which would happen after the Cold War's end.

III. Western Civilization

Grounded in Judeo-Christianity, Western civilization's contribution is the third pillar of American identity. This section considers civilizational confidence employed in the fight against Communism at home and abroad, providing an explanation of Western civilization, explaining civilizational confidence, and offering an examination of the role and consequences of civilizational confidence in the struggle for America and the West.

For this analysis, civilizations encompass shared descent, language, religion, and way of life. Civilizations are comprehensive—that is, their component parts cannot be fully understood without reference to the encompassing civilization. They are not permanent but may be very long-lived and serve as a point of reference and identification long after they are consigned to the pages of history, as classical Greek and Roman civilizations have for Western civilization from the Middle Ages onward. They evolve, adapt, and are the most enduring of human associations. Civilizations are cultural, rather than political, entities as a rule of thumb, although in some cases, such as with China and Japan, a civilization and a polity may coincide.[32]

Western civilization is defined by ideas, principles, religious beliefs, societies, art, languages, and cultures that date to ancient Greece. Western civilization exists in a specific geographic space that was transplanted to the Americas, Australia, and New Zealand. Although there are important differences between the ancient world and the modern, and many discrete periods—Greece, Rome, Dark Ages, Christendom, the Renaissance, the Reformation, the Enlightenment and post-Enlightenment—the core beliefs are clear. They are the understanding and value of the individual, of faith, and an appreciation of philosophy, medicine, justice and beauty—as

32 Samuel Huntington's discussion of civilization is relevant. See Samuel P. Huntington, *The Clash of Civilizations and the Remaking of World Order* (New York: Simon & Schuster, 1996), pp. 40–44. For Huntington, there are seven civilizations: Sinic, Japanese, Hindu, Islamic, Western, Orthodox, Latin American, and possibly African. Huntington, *The Clash of Civilizations and the Remaking of World Order*, pp. 45–48. Also see Samuel P. Huntington, "Foreword: Cultures Count," in Lawrence E. Harrison and Samuel P. Huntington, eds., *Culture Matters: How Values Shape Human Progress* (New York: Basic Books, 2000), pp. xiii–xvi. Following Huntington, this study employs Han rather than Sinic to describe China's civilization.

expressed in all the arts, the dominant religion of Christianity, and science and logical examination—is prized.

III.A. Western Civilizational Confidence

Civilizational confidence is defined by this book as the belief that one sees one's civilization as unique, more meaningful and cherished, and more valuable to oneself and one's country than other civilizations. The definitive political ideas and principles, the shared history of triumphs and struggles, common philosophies and ways of reasoning, and standards for justified arguments, are all part of the conception of what is "a good society." Moreover, it entails religion, which encompasses one's and one's society's relationship to the Divine, an understanding of the role of men, women, children, and religious, ethnic, and sexual minorities, the relationship of the self to the community, standards and heritage of art and beauty, and how one's civilization contributes to one's values.

Additionally, civilizational confidence explains how members of the civilization perceive and appreciate these values, and whether they consider it better than alternative civilizations. When one possesses civilizational confidence, one perceives alternative civilizations as meaningful and deserving of respect and consideration because of their value to their members. However, they are not seen as definitive regarding the right form or standard of living, or of being meaningful concerning how one should live one's life and the values and beliefs one should hold.

The civilizational confidence of the West has provided its strength in previous struggles. Civilizational confidence has provided members with a community consisting of those who belong together. How that is determined is a consequence of the possession of some or all of the following ties. They may be genetic, geographic—that is, one is a denizen of a designated territory or land—or they may be environmental. This would be through an inherited language, culture, religion, beliefs, ideas, and shared memories and myths, and a popular culture.[33] Historically, these ties have provided the foundation of membership in Western civilization. Ultimately, the institutions and members of Western civilization "get a vote" to determine if a newcomer belongs to it or another.

In times of war, all Western governments have made appeals to Western civilization to mobilize their populations and sustain that mobilization and sacrifice through conflicts and national tribulations. As most of Europe's wars and those of the United States have been intra-civilizational, there has been a common appeal to the shared beliefs and values of the civilization, while usually accompanied by the demonization of others, based on nationalist considerations—the Germans were the Huns for the Anglo-Americans during World War I, while Berlin called for their shared Christian God to punish England (*Gott strafe England*) for her perfidy and other sins.[34] While mobilization is maximized in war, it also must be maintained in periods of intense security competition.

Yet, no matter how significant their differences, and how willing Europeans were to kill one another by the millions in internecine wars throughout the centuries, they appealed to the same ideas and art anchored in Greek and Roman histories, and shared the Christian religion, always Latin, French, or English as the *lingua franca*, although with important sectarian differences. At a macro scale, the Europeans possessed the same sense of identity that defined them as members of Western civilization. That identity was transplanted around the globe by all of Europe's great empires. There was certainly uneven success in the effort to transplant

33 Benedict Anderson, *Imagined Communities: Reflections on the Origins and Spread of Nationalism* (New York: Verso, 1991), pp. 1–7; John Dunn, ed., *Contemporary Crisis of the Nation State* (Oxford: Blackwell, 1995), p. 3; and Anthony D. Smith, *Nations and Nationalism in a Global Era* (Malden, Mass.: Polity Press, 1995), pp. 56–57.

34 "May God punish England," famously a line in Ernst Lissauer's World War I poem *Hassgesang gegen England* (Hate Song against England, or Hymn of Hate against England).

Western civilization. It found its lasting home in the United States, as well as the major Anglophone Dominions of the British Empire, Canada, Australia, and New Zealand. One could argue convincingly that it did in Latin America as well.

In contrast, it failed in today's Zimbabwe (formerly Rhodesia) and South Africa, and clearly found only limited success in Indochina, the Middle East, South Asia, or Africa among their elite populations, but only for a limited time among them as colonial empires waned, and indigenous rule returned. Even in these instances, the legacy of Western civilization due to the colonial encounters left a telling and lasting imprint on these civilizations.

Western civilization matters in competition with Communism because it heavily informs the core national identity—for what its members should fight and what they should defend.[35] Western civilization is defined by the set of principles and beliefs identified above, and its achievements that impact its states. That civilization must be supported. It is a source, indeed, the principal source, that explains why alternative civilizations and political, cultural, social, and economic organizations are different, and inferior to the achievements of the pantheon of the West.

---

35 There can, of course, be multiple identities operating at the same time. One may belong to Western civilization, while being an American, with racial, national, gender, religious, and sports identities. To a great degree, they may be overlapping, and also but never completely defined by the self. Which is most relevant depends upon context or is a consequence of the empirical issue at hand. Within the U.S., Americans may not think of themselves as Yanks but will be defined as such abroad. Of course, individuals possess multiple identities, which they may learn to emphasize or suppress in a given context. The audience members watching England v. Ireland in Six Nations rugby at the Temple Bar in Dublin share a common identity as lovers of the sport, but in this context England supporters may suppress this aspect of their identity. A military officer may identify simultaneously with his company, division, and service. Thus, narrower identities do not necessarily conflict with broader ones, and the multiple identities individuals possess run the gambit from the sacred to the profane, the profound to the trivial.

Importantly, from the civilizational perspective, the fight against Communism is both an inter- and intra-civilizational conflict. It is inter-civilizational because in Western countries, the importation of Muslims means that an increasingly vocal and forceful Muslim minority confronts native Western populations. The fight is also intra-civilizational because the Western elites support neo-Bolshevik ideas of progressivism and endless immigration and clash with those who support political liberalism, individual freedom, and Western civilization. The future of America and Western civilization depends upon the outcome of that struggle.

Accordingly, and in contrast to intra-civilizational conflicts, in inter-civilizational conflicts, the differences will be transparent and serve as points of direct opposition for the civilizations. Significant differences define inter-civilizational conflicts apart from intra-civilizational.

Inter-civilizational conflicts will involve a greater civilizational emphasis on how populations and governments define national identity and national interest. The shared civilizational components of the identity will come to the fore and be employed in the fight. During the Cold War, the United States appealed to its allied governments to stand with the West or Western Bloc against the East. The threat from the Soviet Union and its Eastern Bloc allies compelled the West to conceive of itself as a bloc with civilizational identity. The U.S. made appeals regarding the unity of history, culture, political values and institutions—the glory that was Greece and the grandeur that was Rome, Christianity, the Renaissance, the Reformation, the Enlightenment, the French and Industrial Revolutions, representative democracy, the rule of law, and the market economy. This helped to define the alliance coalition of many states unified against the Eastern Bloc threat and by Western civilization.

These appeals were made to overcome the centrifugal forces in the West. Not all Western states and political parties viewed Moscow as a threat, and indeed, on the political left, Washington was often seen as negatively as the Soviets, especially during the Vietnam War and its immediate aftermath. West German Chancellor Willy Brandt and French President Charles de Gaulle evinced favorable opinions about the Soviet Union and supported *Ostpolitik*, or the Third Way, a Europe that was independent of Washington or Moscow.

Appeals to Western civilization helped to undercut fissiparous tendencies, especially as they helped to welcome West Germany into the Western fold after Naziism and needed for West Germany to redefine German identity. They reminded the world of France's great contributions to Western civilization and so weakened de Gaulle's message.

The reverse was also the case, and is evinced in Mao Zedong's famous November 17, 1957, statement to Chinese students in Moscow that it was not "the west wind prevailing over the east wind, but the east wind prevailing over the west wind." As Mao stated, of the 2.7 billion people at that time, 600 million were in the socialist camp and 400 million in capitalist states, and so the correlation of forces favored the East.

Yet, despite Mao's aspirations, the Eastern Bloc was at a major disadvantage because there was no Eastern civilization to which Mao or Soviet leaders could appeal. The poly-civilizational Eastern Bloc was incoherent and held together by an illegitimate Western ideology. It was composed of Western civilizational states in Czechoslovakia, East Germany, Hungary, Poland, or Cuba, the Orthodox in Russia, the Han in China, and Buddhists in North Vietnam. Other states like North Korea were an amalgam with multiple major influences. The centrifugal forces operating in the Eastern Bloc were tremendous. In fact, they were so formidable that the united front lasted only as long as Stalin was alive. Once Khrushchev denounced Stalin in his "secret speech" of February 1956 and began his de-Stalinization campaign, Mao had to break with the Soviets, first, to prevent his own "Khrushchevs" from denouncing him and, second, because he perceived himself to be the leader of the bloc.[36] Neither was ideology sufficient to

36 On Mao's vision of himself as the leader of Eastern Bloc and worldwide Communist movement, and his interpretation of Khrushchev's de-Stalinization of the Soviet Union and Communist movement, see Han and Thayer, *Understanding the China Threat*, pp. 52–54.

sustain such a coalition, particularly as that ideology was flawed and riven with almost innumerable tensions.

Inter-civilizational conflicts differ from conflicts within civilizations because they inspire individuals to make sacrifices, and so governments will mobilize more resources from across the civilization. One characteristic message that political and military leaders have used to inspire Western soldiers for centuries was General Dwight Eisenhower's D-Day proclamation on June 6, 1944. Eisenhower's message to all 175,000 soldiers, sailors, and airmen of the Allied Expeditionary Force was meant to inspire the invading forces on their tremendous undertaking. He wrote that they were about to "embark upon the Great Crusade," to resonate with the Christian conception of crusade against the heathen enemy and so place the Nazis beyond the boundaries of Western civilization, as did his appeal for the "blessings of almighty God."[37]

Another example is *al Qaeda's* creation to support the Afghani mujahideen, although one that also reveals help from civilizational allies may be deleterious due to their incompetence. An example of more effective aid was the unified civilizational front the European powers, Austro-Hungary, France, Germany, Great Britain, Italy, Russia, and the U.S. were able to generate to suppress the Boxer Rebellion and to sustain the coalition. Forty years later, during World War II in the fight against Japan, France, Great Britain and its empire, the Netherlands, and the United States advanced the same civilizational front against Tokyo, with Nationalist China included because it was a "Westernizing government" in the struggle against a barbarous Japan. The war in Asia and the Pacific and the war between the Germans and the Soviets had the overtone of clashing civilizations, with each identifying their own civilizational in-group as superior and the

37 Gen. Dwight D. Eisenhower, "D-Day Statement to Soldiers, Sailors, and Airmen of the Allied Expeditionary Force," Dwight D. Eisenhower Presidential Library, National Archives and Records Administration. At: <https://www.archives.gov/historical-docs/todays-doc/?dod-date=606 >. Accessed September 10, 2025.

out-group enemy as inferior "subhumans" or "demons."[38] This characterization aided states to mobilize resources to fight the enemy, which was rapacious and existential for the values and existence of the civilization itself.

But even between civilizations, common identity can assist a great power, even so if it is an imperial one. For much of the nineteenth century, Indian elites accepted British imperialism not only as a precursor to civilizational advancement but also as a country whose aims should be supported in the "Great Game" against Russia. The pamphlet, "Why Do Indians Prefer British to Russian Rule?," was circulated by the most important political associations of the era.[39] The work expressed great admiration for the British, who were "the freest and most liberty-loving people in the world," and who despite defects in control over India, were "the friend and sympathizers" of subject nations like India, whom it was seeking to "elevate and educate," in contrast to Russia's "iron yoke."[40]

Inter-civilizational conflicts will generate great and intense hatred. They will be more intense because the enemy is alien, someone from a foreign and merciless civilization. Additionally, this is worsened as each civilization perceives itself to be superior, and so the pretense of the other civilization to be the equal or superior to one's own drives an intense hatred. The conflict between India and Pakistan is more than a traditional one over disputed territory or hegemony on the subcontinent. Its civilizational dimension provides fuel for the hatred held among the elite and populations

---

38 The classic analysis is John W. Dower, *War Without Mercy: Race and Power in the Pacific War* (New York: Pantheon, 1986). Also see Max Hastings, *Nemesis: The Battle for Japan, 1944–1945* (London: William Collins, 2016).

39 "Why Do Indians Prefer British to Russian Rule?" in Rahul Sagar, ed., *To Raise a Fallen People: The Nineteenth-Century Origins of Indian Views on International Politics* (New York: Columbia University Press, 2022), pp. 126–128.

40 "Why Do Indians Prefer British to Russian Rule?" in Sagar, ed., *To Raise a Fallen People*, p. 127.

of both as the other inferior, loathsome, dangerous, and barbarous civilization seeks to impose its will.

These will be long-lived conflicts that will reverberate beyond immediate tribulations. Intra-civilizational conflicts will continue as civilizations themselves are long lived. So-called frozen conflicts, such as between Armenia and Azerbaijan, Georgia and Ossetia, India and Pakistan, and Russia and Chechnya are long-lived in no small part because of the civilizational differences between the participants. But this is so not only for these states. Viewed through a civilizational lens, the Sino-American, or the West's dispute with Russia, or Russia's fundamental difficulties with China, are great power civilizational conflicts. As political scientist Samuel Huntington argued, these conflicts often occur along the "fault lines" of civilizations, where one meets another, as along the Indo-Pakistani border or Sino-Russian border.[41] However, these faultline territorial conflicts are symptoms of deeper civilizational causes, which explains why they are intractable.

Civilizational cleavages and tensions will be revealed in inter-civilizational struggles—for example, among the Han civilization in contrast to the West. A long struggle will exacerbate old tensions or contradictions within civilizations, such as grafting the Western ideology of Marx, Engels, and Lenin onto the Han civilization. They will also create new tensions and divisions that the civilizational enemy may exploit. An example would be demographic change in the major states of Western civilization and its consequences for the coherence of the West, as discussed below.

III.B. The Consequences of Civilizational Confidence for Amcrica and the West

There are four consequences of a high degree of civilizational confidence for the West. First, if there is a high degree of civilizational confidence,

41 Huntington, *The Clash of Civilizations and the Remaking of World Order*, pp. 207–208, 246–265.

then there will be great unity and the impermeability of Western societies to civilizational attacks. This will define the interest of the state and permit it to engage in peer competitive competition. At the same time, there is the risk that the conception of the United States, as held by its citizens, greatly changes how someone who is not Western perceives the United States and U.S. identity. Certainly, Western civilizational identity is likely to be a significant source of identification for many Americans, but it will be eroded by other, competing civilizations.

This competition is already having major consequences in Western civilization due to the importation of large numbers of migrants from non-Western societies, beginning with a trickle in the 1960s into their own, a trend that has accelerated after German Chancellor Angela Merkel's 2015 decision to void the Dublin Regulation and permit migrants to settle in Germany, a decision that was amplified by other EU-member states. The result of this multi-decade introduction of non-Western populations, with much greater and sustained numbers after 2015, has at minimum uncertain implications for the political, social, and civilizational stability of those states, and at a maximum could tip these states into sustained sectarian violence like Northern Ireland, or civil war.

There is a weakening or loss of civilizational confidence, then the ability to pose a coherent response to Communism is fragmented, as is the ability to face the consequences of rapid demographic change. As Huntington identified, far more significant than economics and demography "are problems of moral decline, cultural suicide, and political disunity in the West."[42] For Huntington, manifestations of the moral or civilizational decline include the following elements. There are increases in antisocial behavior, such as crime, drug use, and societal violence in increasing intensity and scope. There is family decay, including increased rates of divorce, increased rates of crime and drug addiction, illegitimacy, and single-parent families. There

42 Huntington, *The Clash of Civilizations and the Remaking of World Order*, p. 304.

is the decline of "social capital," that is, membership in voluntary associations, and a decline in interpersonal trust and confidence in institutions. There is a weakening of the work ethic and rise of entitlement and personal indulgency. There is decreasing commitment to learning and intellectual activity, manifested in the United States as lower levels of academic achievement and discrimination against those who do perform well, such as the discrimination against East Asian or white applicants to elite universities like Harvard University.

The second consequence of civilizational confidence for the West is that the coherence of Western civilization is necessary to keep modern representative democracy viable, credible for its citizens, and to provide them with the identification of what Western civilization has accomplished. This is to provide its denizens with the best and most rewarding civilization for all of its members, rather than only a priestly caste or an imperial court. Moreover, the members should be proud that its riches have been shared with the rest of the world. Fundamentally, its future health will be determined by its ability to address these challenges.

The challenge to Western civilization stems from other civilizations such as the Han and Islamic, but also by groups within Western civilization made possible and amplified by Communists. One challenge comes from immigrants from other civilizations who reject assimilations and continue to adhere to and to propagate the values, customs, and cultures of their original civilization. This is most evident among Muslims in Europe, even those who immigrated there in the 1960s and after. It seems particularly acute among more recent immigrants, those who came after 2015. Similarly, in the United States and Canada, assimilation has weakened in the case of the former and has been explicitly rejected in the latter. Therefore, both states face the risk of these cleavages, including greater internal strife and disunion.

The third consequence of civilizational confidence for Americans and the West is that confidence has lessened because Communists targeted it deliberately. As Christianity and historic national identity fade as a salient force for people in the West due to the sledgehammer blows of the Communists, and as representative government transitions into a force for the erosion of Western civilizational identity through multiculturalism or woke ideologies, the internal support for Western civilization weakens. It is not clear what will replace it. It might be that representative governments promote an alternative civilizational hybrid, or they explicitly advance an identity that rejects Western civilization. The consequences of either will be that Western civilizational identity fades and its unifying bond weakens.

A useful comparison comes from international politics where Western civilization was hegemonic within Western states. There was no viable alternative. Neither did Western populations seek one. Even serious disagreements, such over the Reformation and Counter-Reformation, or between the Enlightenment and counter-Enlightenment, occurred within the confines of Western civilization. No ideology or movement sought to overthrow it or remove it from the guiding and underlying principles of Western societies.

Today, Western civilization faces peer competition within its traditional confines. Alternative civilizations, most prominently Islam, are present in substantial numbers. They are now a political force within Western states. This presence often includes openly proselytizing against Western civilization. That would be bad enough. But this is coupled with the advance of Communism. As a result of its successful penetration, the West faces the disastrous situation where Western governments weaken their support for the tenets of Western civilization through the removal of Christianity from the public sphere, restrict heretofore celebrated individual rights like freedom of speech, and actively import people from non-Western civilizations.

The result is that the West has lost its hegemony. It faces peer competition from Han and Islamic civilizations. Within most Western states, there is bi- or multipolarity, where two or more civilizations are vying for power within the political dimension of once uniformly Western states. The "Red-Green" coalition, "Red" signifying Communists and "Green" Islam, is an illustration of how quickly Western societies may be undermined as a step toward their destruction.

This book sees immigration from non-Western societies as akin to Lenin calling in reinforcements to win the civil war in Western civilization. The Red-Green coalition shows acutely how the "Red" element weaponizes immigration deliberately and why they favor endless immigration from anywhere but the West.

This has never occurred before in American history. America and all other major Western states are in a real and immediate sense conducting an enormous social science experiment on their own societies. Of course, it is not an experiment but is a genuine change in societies, with untold consequences, many of which already may be seen.

The fourth consequence of civilizational confidence is, if this fight is not won, Western states will never again be homogenous but henceforth be multi-civilizational. A result is deliberate fragmentation and the acceleration of centrifugal forces. Traditional appeals made in Western societies regarding their own identity, the confidence and trust between government and population, that each class within the society is in the same position, perceives the same enemy, and they are unified for the same end, is now more complicated and diffuse. Appeals to Western civilization, once certain to resonate with nearly the totality of the population, as they were its product, will reach an ever-decreasing size of it.

In addition, sacrifice, mobilization of people and resources, and recruitment in war will be impacted. Appeals anchored on other grounds will have to be generated and will receive increasing salience. They will have to be tailored to specific populations, such as each racial, religious, or sexual minority group to explain their interest in supporting the government against the enemy. To a degree, the U.S. has done this before. For example, in World War I, the "Four Minute Men" from George Creel's Committee on Public Information were able to explain succinctly why the war effort should be supported to popular audiences, including German-Americans and Irish-Americans, whose loyalties were seen not to be the equal of other

Americans and to Midwesterners and Southerners, where isolationist sentiments were concentrated.[43]

However, with multi-civilizational identities, the task is clearly harder, and success is far from certain. The effort will be broader and more sustained, with no guarantee of success, particularly because Communists will wage countervailing messages to the same audiences, and employ their influence, including political warfare, to defeat the government's centripetal attempts to forge unity.

Moreover, the entreaties made thus far to Western allies will be affected, too. The "special relationship" with Great Britain will mean far less to people with no ties to American or British history, no legacy of sacrifice, and who, in fact, have shallow roots in the soil of either country. Indeed, members of other civilizations might find the U.S. or Great Britain guilty of supporting oppression or conflict within their civilization and so perceive these traditional allies as an enemy of their civilization. The Labour government in the UK is doing precisely this by allowing illegal immigrants by the tens of thousands to enter Great Britain.

Communist influence has intentionally made their lives far more complicated than what their predecessors faced, and these societies will have to thread the needle adroitly to sustain the unification and coherence of their societies. A great strength of Western civilization is that it is broad and flexible enough to permit other civilizations to be present in their countries, while still sustaining Western civilizational confidence. However, there rapidly will be a tipping point—many Western countries like Great Britain, Germany, Ireland, and Sweden, are there now—when there are too many adherents to non-Western civilizations as well as from traditional Western populations that are now anti-Western civilization to make the continuation of a Western identity possible. Precisely where that point is located is

---

43 Excellent accounts are Hamilton, *Manipulating the Masses*; and David M. Kennedy, *Over Here: The First World War and American Society* (New York: Oxford University Press, 1980).

uncertain, but it is not ineffable or unable to be identified. The answer is as much an ideational issue as it is one of numbers or demography.

Hence, the West may already be there. If the elites governing Western societies so intend or desire, they can take the steps to augment the civilizational confidence of the West. The 2022 death of Queen Elizabeth II and the ceremonial mourning, funeral, and outpouring of grief and expressions of loyalty in Great Britain, the Commonwealth, and even globally was a civilizational snapshot and an indication of how strong Western ties can be. The number of people worldwide who support its pillars or traditional symbols like the British monarchy remains substantial in contemporary Western societies, as well as in Japan, Hong Kong, and China.

There is a need for a rapid response. Among major Western states, only President Trump is moving in a positive direction. If other Western decision-makers seize upon the opportunity to advance civilizational confidence within their societies, it will be just in time given the intense threat that the West faces from internal centrifugal civilizational challenges, coupled with the CCP's external challenge to American national security. Of course, the CCP will employ measures to accelerate fissiparous cleavages within the U.S. to weaken it. This includes utilizing the United Front Work Department measures and what the PRC terms the "Three Warfares" (public opinion, psychological, and lawfare) to hurt the domestic stability of the U.S. The assault on Western civilization is an assault on American identity. All of those who have a stake in that order, including those who advance political freedom, the rule of law, and the rights of women and racial, religious, and sexual minorities, have an interest in sustaining America and defending it from domestic and international enemies.

All civilizations go through emergence, rise, and decline. Western civilization differs from others not in the way it has developed but in the distinctive character of its principles, values, and institutions, and the way they are able to adapt to new environments yet sustain these core attributes. Christianity, individualism, rule of law, and pluralism made it possible for the West to invent modernity, expand through the world, and become the envy of other civilizations. As Harvard University historian Arthur Schlesinger, Jr., argued in 1991 at the outset of the post–Cold War world, "the source—the *unique* source" of the "ideas of individual liberty, political democracy, the rule of law, human rights, and cultural freedom. . . . These are *European* ideas, not Asian, nor African, nor Middle Eastern ideas, except by adoption."[44] They make Western civilization unique, and Western civilization is valuable to its members and the world not because it is universal but because it is unique.

A danger that Schlesinger, and later Huntington, perceived was that ethnic conflict had destroyed empires and states in contemporary history, including in states of the former Soviet Union, Yugoslavia, and Rwanda.[45] Given this unfortunate and alarming recent history, "one cannot look with complacency at proposals to divide the United States into distinct and immutable ethnic and racial communities, each taught to cherish its own apartness from the rest."[46] In contrast, Western leaders have a responsibility to preserve, protect, and renew the unique qualities of Western civilization. So far, they have failed and will do so until they confront and defeat Communism in their countries.

---

44 Arthur M. Schlesinger, Jr., *The Disuniting of America: Reflections on a Multicultural Society* (New York: Norton, 1991), p. 127. Emphases original.

45 See Huntington, *Who Are We?*.

46 Schlesinger, *The Disuniting of America*, pp. 17–18. Schlesinger optimistically believed that the solution would soon come. "The situation in our universities, I am confident, will soon right itself once the great silent majority of professors cry 'enough' and challenge what they know to be voguish nonsense." Schlesinger, *The Disuniting of America*, p. 18. This view seriously underestimated the threat from Communism and the blinding speed with which it would transform America once it possessed the ideas industry. Sadly, he also did not foresee the degree to which Communists would so dominate that his fellow academics supported Communists, or would go along, or be intimidated into silence.

Chapter 5

The Internal Communist Threat: Communism in America—Bolshevism and Neo-Bolshevist Progressivism

Leninism was successful not only in Russia and China, of course, but it also made great inroads into America. To achieve its aim of destroying the West, it must destroy America. Whether it will be successful or whether freedom will be sustained is the dispositive question of our time—and one of immediate concern for all Americans because America is at a "1776 Moment." In this chapter, I explore how Communists penetrated the U.S. by employing Lenin's united front strategy and tactics through the Comintern—the Communist Party, the underground party, front organizations, fellow travelers to capture the ideas industry of the country—intellectuals, journalists, film, and popular culture—to advance the revolution. This chapter also addresses the neo-Bolshevik ideology of progressivism and how it successfully dominated American journalism, education, civil society, and generated the street muscle of Antifa.

I. Communism in America

Before the Bolsheviks, America had two revolutionary traditions—socialism and syndicalism—represented politically by the Socialist Labor Party, formed in 1877, the Socialist Party, founded in 1901, and the Industrial Workers of the World (IWW), created in 1905, that provided most of members and the intellectual perspective of many of the early American Communists. The 1917 revolution changed everything in the U.S. The American Communist movement would absorb the syndicalist energy of the IWW and neuter the socialist movement. The Comintern was instrumental in creating the Communist Party of the United States, as it did with the CCP.[1] The Comintern worked with American Bolsheviks to found two Communist Parties in 1919.[2] The Communist Party of America, led by Chares Ruthenberg, had about 24,000 members. The rival Communist Labor Party, led by John Reed, the author of *Ten Days That Shook the World*, and Benjamin Gitlow, had about 10,000. Fewer than 4,000 members of both parties spoke English.[3]

Journalist Eugene Lyons, who had lived in the Soviet Union in the 1920s, captured their disconnect from the American people, when he

1 Exceptional histories of the Communist Party of the United States of America are: Irving Howe and Lewis Coser, *The American Communist Party: A Critical History, 1929–1957* (Boston: Beacon Press, 1957); Theodore Draper, *The Roots of American Communism* (New York: Viking, 1957); Theodore Draper, *American Communism and Soviet Russia: The Formative Period* (New York: Viking, 1960); and Harvey Klehr, *The Heyday of American Communism: The Depression Decade* (New York: Basic Books, 1984).

2 "Extracts from a Letter from the ECCI to the Industrial Workers of the World," January 1920, in Jane Degras, ed., *The Communist International 1919–1943 Volume I 1919–1922* (London: Oxford University Press, 1956), pp. 71–74.

3 Reviewing the situation in the United States in February 1929, the Comintern recognized its weakness and that the Party was heavily influenced by immigrants rather than native-born American workers: "The Workers' (Communist) Party of America has been for many years an organization of foreign workers not much connected with the political life of the country." "Extracts from an ECCI to the Sixth Convention of the CP [Communist Party] of the USA," in Jane Degras, ed., *The Communist International 1919–1943: Documents, Volume III* (London: Oxford University Press, 1965), p. 10.

wrote: "They had not succeeded—nor really tried—to establish living contact with the larger American public."[4] Most of these Communists were immigrants from the former tsarist empire and not until the 1930s were a majority of American Communists English-speaking and native-born.[5]

Both were Leninist parties dedicated to the overthrow of the U.S. government and the imposition of Bolshevism in the U.S. The phrase that was popular among Communists in the 1920s was "boring from within."[6] As Lenin had advocated in *Left Wing Communism*, it was the duty of Communists to penetrate organizations. That meant Communists would enter an organization and capture it from inside instead of torpedoing it from outside as in the past. Employing the united front, Communists the world over were obligated to join everything from trade unions to the nation's military and begin to bore into those institutions and in time dominate them. That was a supremely successful strategy in the U.S. and allowed the Communists to dominate most areas of American life, including the media, the universities and educational system, and the Democratic Party.

Under Comintern pressure for unity, the two American Communist parities merged in 1921, and Charles Ruthenberg became the first leader of the Communist Party of the United States of America (CPUSA).[7] Comintern

---

4 Eugene Lyons, *The Red Decade: The Stalinist Penetration of America* (New York: Bobb-Merrill, 1941), p. 36.

5 Harvey Klehr, John Earl Haynes, and Fridrikh Igorevich Firsov, *The Secret World of American Communism* (New Haven: Yale University Press, 1995), p. 5. Also see Harvey Klehr, *The Heyday of American Communism: The Depression Decade* (New York: Basic Books, 1984); and Harvey Klehr, John Earl Haynes, and Kyrill M. Anderson, *The Soviet World of American Communism* (New Haven: Yale University Press, 1998).

6 Lyons, *The Red Decade*, p. 38. Also see Max M. Kampelman, *The Communist Party vs. the C.I.O.: A Study in Power Politics* (New York: Praeger, 1957), pp. 9–10.

7 "Extracts from a Letter from the ECCI to the Central Committee of the Communist Party of America and the Central Committee of the Communist Labour [*sic*] Party of America," June 1920, in Degras, ed., *The Communist International 1919–1943 Volume I 1919–1922*, pp. 101–102. In 1923 the

representatives ordered the Party to organize itself as an aboveground entity, while still maintaining a covert arm. As with all Communist parties, the Comintern was the final arbiter of Party disputes.

And few disputes escaped Moscow's gaze—no significant ones did. Their decisions were final and obedience was required. As William Z. Foster, who was a major figure in the Party, stated: "I am for the Comintern from start to finish . . . and if the Comintern finds itself criss-cross with my opinions, there is only one thing to do and that is to change my opinions to fit the policy of the Comintern."[8] In 1929, party leaders Jay Lovestone and Benjamin Gitlow were expelled on Stalin's orders after they defied Comintern instructions. Stalin accused Lovestone of being an ideological adherent of Bukharin and right-wing deviation.[9] Within a year, Earl Browder, a fresh-faced Kansan who had just returned from Comintern work in China, was placed in charge. Browder remained in charge of CPUSA until Moscow overthrew him for defying Soviet policy in 1945.

With the Great Depression, America seemed on the cusp of revolution. Of course, the Party fostered this. Moreover, the Party received considerable attention from the liberal press for a series of dramatic strikes and demonstrations against capitalism, evinced by mass and sustained unemployment during these years.[10] Many idealistic Americans were attracted to the Communist narrative of social justice and turned to the Party to

---

Communist Party changed its name to the Workers Party, so the name of the Communist Party was temporarily relinquished in the U.S., until 1929 when it once again became CPUSA. For simplicity, throughout this book refers to the Party as the CPUSA.

8 Quoted in Howe and Coser, *The American Communist Party*, p. 154.

9 Ruthenberg had died in 1927. Klehr, Haynes, and Firsov, *The Secret World of American Communism*, pp. 7–8.

10 These included violent strikes by textile workers in Gastonia, North Carolina, and by coal miners in Harlan County, Kentucky. It also included CPUSA leadership of the defense of the Scottsboro case, which became a symbol of Southern racial discrimination. Klehr, Haynes, and Firsov, *The Secret World of American Communism*, p. 8.

advance that agenda. Lyons wrote that the Comintern "penetrated more deeply than the general public ever realized. Frequently it was so beautifully masked that some of its most overworked dray horses [had] not yet realized who held the reins. Many of those who considered themselves leaders—in government posts, in the world of art and culture, in education and youth movements—are still smarting from the humiliating discovery that they were despised stooges of Communist masterminds."[11]

Even in the Depression, the appeal of Communism was limited, and far more Americans supported the two major political parties, especially Franklin Delano Roosevelt's New Deal, and its promise of the reform of capitalism within the liberal tradition. With the Comintern's approval, the CPUSA denounced Roosevelt as a reactionary seeking to save capitalism from its inevitable failure. The Communists labeled the New Deal the American embodiment of fascism.

Growing Nazi aggression changed Moscow's orientation, and thus the Comintern and the actions of the CPUSA. At the Seventh Congress of the Comintern in Moscow in 1935, the new Comintern leader, Georgi Dimitrov, a Bulgarian who gained fame as a defendant at the Reichstag fire trial in 1933, called for the Popular Front against fascism.[12] Communist parties now made alliances with the liberal and socialist parties, which previously they had condemned.

In the U.S., the CPUSA now welcomed the New Deal but did not stop its subversive activities. Not unexpectedly, Labor was going to be a key vehicle for that subversion. In the 1920s, the CPUSA created the Trade Union Unity League (TUUL) and other revolutionary unions as rivals to the AFL.[13] As part of the Popular Front, the CPUSA dissolved the TUUL and sent their experts at agitation, propaganda, and organization into

---

11 Lyons, *The Red Decade*, p. 27.

12 Kampelman, *The Communist Party vs. the C.I.O.*, p. 12.

13 Kampelman, *The Communist Party vs. the C.I.O.*, p. 10; and Klehr, Haynes, and Firsov, *The Secret World of American Communism*, p. 9

the mainstream labor unions. The principal beneficiary was the Congress of Industrial Organizations (CIO), led by John L. Lewis. Lewis was eager to organize mass production industries such as automobiles and he needed skilled organizers. He made use of Communist aid. The CIO grew rapidly and with its expansion so, too, did Communist influence—by the late 1930s, a quarter of the CIO members were in unions led by Communists.[14]

Aided by the Comintern's Popular Front direction, American Communists soon could be found in scores of organizations and found in every aspect of American life, from workers on the factory floor to scientists to writers to intellectuals. They flocked to Communist front organizations like the American Student Union, League of American Writers and the American League Against War and Fascism, and the American Youth Congress, a federation of the largest youth groups in the country.[15] A common slogan was "Communism is the Americanism of the Twentieth Century."

Communist penetration of Hollywood is well known, and it served as a source of great support, funds, and influence for Communist messages and for shaping the public image of Communism. State and local politics were affected as well. In Minnesota, a breeding ground for Communist support due to widespread immigration of socialists and Communists from Sweden and Finland, a Popular Front faction took control of the Farmer-Labor Party, which dominated Minnesota politics in the 1930s. When it merged with the Democratic Party in 1944, Communists retained their influence in the Democratic-Farmer-Labor (DFL) Party.[16] This influence remains today

14 On the myriad and complicated relationships between the Communists and the CIO, see Kampelman, *The Communist Party vs. the C.I.O.* Also see Klehr, Haynes, and Firsov, *The Secret World of American Communism*, p. 9.

15 Kampelman, *The Communist Party vs. the C.I.O.*, p. 13.

16 Klehr, Haynes, and Firsov, *The Secret World of American Communism*, pp. 9–10.

with Governor Tim Walz's fondness for the CCP, some of which came to light in the 2024 election.

As the CPUSA was controlled by the Comintern, the major change in 1939 in Soviet foreign policy caused the Party to make significant contortions. The Molotov-Ribbentrop Pact hurt the Party's membership rolls. But it did not stop the Party's influence. Hollywood made antiwar films and the novel *Johnny Got His Gun* by the Communist Dalton Trumbo received significant attention and radio adaptation by NBC. Communist-controlled labor unions staged strikes in the U.S. defense industry to hinder U.S. support for Britain and U.S. rearmament. Lyons wrote: "The epidemic of defense strikes was no surprise to those who had been watching the Communist penetration of American life. There was for them no mystery in the circumstance that those strikes developed particular virulence in plants whose products were essential for the operation of a large number of other industries."[17] The pattern was always the same: "Wage and other legitimate demands would be made . . . but always the pro-Soviet leadership would select and concentrate on some far-fetched issue not easily adjustable, and the strike protracted."[18]

In the first six months of 1941, some 2.5 million man-hours were lost in vital defense industries. Major strikes occurred at Vultee Aircraft in Downey, California, and at Allis-Chalmers, a vital navy defense plant in Milwaukee. In May 1941, 12,000 members of the International Woodworkers Association went on strike in logging camps and sawmills of the Puget Sound region. Other strikes impacted the aluminum industry. The most dramatic strike was at the Inglewood, California, plant of North American Aircraft. North American became famous for designing and manufacturing the P 51 Mustang fighter. In fact, by the time of the strike the fighter already had been designed. The plant was closed by a CIO strike

17 Lyons, *The Red Decade*, pp. 394–395.
18 Lyons, *The Red Decade*, p. 395.

on June 6, 1941, before President Roosevelt, weeks later, ordered the Army to take over the plant.[19]

The strike climate changed overnight, specifically over the night of June 22, 1941, when the Germans invaded the Soviet Union. Essentially, Adolf Hitler ended the strike. The penetration of the U.S. defense industry by Communist-led unions was significant and prevented U.S. rearmament and aid to Great Britain at a time when London stood alone against Germany and its ally, the Soviet Union.

After the German invasion of the Soviet Union, the Party dropped its peace program and demanded U.S. support for the Soviet Union and U.S. intervention. Browder was arrested in 1941 for using a false passport but was released by FDR in May 1942 as a gesture of goodwill toward the Soviet Union. Emboldened by Stalin's dissolution of the Comintern in 1943, Browder dissolved the CPUSA in 1944 and reformed it as the Communist Political Association, intending to make Communists the left wing of the Democratic Party.[20] That aim certainly has been achieved today. Vice President Kamala Harris replaced President Joe Biden at the top of the Democratic ticket in July 2024 without a single primary or caucus vote. Biden was ejected faster and more efficiently than any CPUSA, CPSU, or CCP leader, and Harris installed as a candidate more easily.

In the spring of 1945, Moscow signaled its disapproval and Browder's comrades expelled him and resurrected the CPUSA, choosing Eugene Dennis, a Comintern veteran with experience in China, South Africa, and the Philippines, as Party leader. At the dawn of the Cold War, CPUSA demanded that their liberal allies support Soviet foreign policy, resist and question U.S. foreign policy, and oppose President Truman's effort to confront the Soviet Union. CPUSA threw its might behind Henry Wallace's 1948 presidential campaign as the Progressive Party candidate. The failure of Wallace and increasing anti-Communism due to a greater

19 Kampelman, *The Communist Party vs. the C.I.O.*, pp. 25–27.
20 Klehr, Haynes, and Firsov, *The Secret World of American Communism*, p. 11.

comprehension of the Soviet threat led to major setbacks for the Party. CIO leaders like Philip Murray and Walter Reuther drove the Communists and Communist-controlled unions out of the CIO, which had been a great source of CPUSA strength.[21]

Overwhelmingly, Americans turned against the CPUSA. Fundamentally, this was because, as Lyons identified, "the simple truth . . . of American Bolshevism . . . was, in the final analysis, a foreign agency pulling off jobs for its employers [the Soviet Union], and not in the remotest sense an American social movement."[22] It was also due to a series of spectacular spy cases that convinced Americans that Communists were disloyal. The most visible symbols of Communist perfidy were Alger Hiss, Laurence Duggan, Harry White, and Julius and Ethel Rosenberg.[23]

Hiss, who was a former high-level governmental official convicted for perjury, fueled fears that Communists had penetrated the government. His treachery was revealed by Whittaker Chambers, a former-Communist and Soviet spy from 1932-1938, whose 1948 testimony before the House Un-American Affairs Committee (HUAC) was essential for revealing Communist infiltration of the government. Duggan was a senior diplomat in the State Department. White was an Assistant Secretary of the Treasury in the Roosevelt administration. The Rosenbergs' conviction for involvement in a Communist spy ring that had penetrated Los Alamos and stolen America's atomic secrets showed Communism had infiltrated the country's most sensitive military secrets.[24] After the Korean War started and

---

21 See Kampelman, *The Communist Party vs. the C.I.O.*

22 Lyons, *The Red Decade*, p. 46.

23 See Allen Weinstein and Alexander Vassiliev, *The Haunted Wood: Soviet Espionage in America—The Stalin Era* (New York: Random House, 1999).

24 Spies were numerous. They included William Perl, a brilliant young government aeronautical scientist who provided the Soviets with the results of secret tests and design experiments for jet engines and aircraft. Within the Manhattan Project, two physicists, Klaus Fuchs and Theodore Hall, and one technician, David Greenglass (Julius Rosenberg's brother-in-law), gave the Soviets the secrets of the atomic bomb and many of the technical plans

Americans were dying while fighting Communist troops, the CPUSA lost even more support.

Beginning in 1948, the U.S. Department of Justice used the Smith Act to imprison more than a hundred Communist leaders, including Eugene Dennis, for conspiring to teach and organize the overthrow of the government by force and violence. In 1951, the CPUSA ordered hundreds of its cadres into hiding in its underground organization. Yet, the CPUSA was never outlawed and continued to function openly. Khrushchev's "secret speech" in February 1956, in which he denounced Stalin and Stalinism and admitted Stalin's crimes, was another blow to the Party, as was the crushing of the Hungarian uprising in 1956. In fact, by the late 1950s, the American government had ended most of its legal attacks on the Party.

But the subversive activities of the Party never waned, as Klehr, Haynes, and Firsov write: "It is no longer possible to maintain the Soviet Union did not fund the American party, that the CPUSA did not maintain a covert

---

for production facilities. The Venona decryptions identified most of the Soviet spies uncovered by American counterintelligence between 1948 and the mid-1950s. These included Fuchs and Greenglass and led to Lauchlin Currie (former administrative assistant to FDR) and Donald Maclean as a major spy—one of the Cambridge Five—in the British embassy, as well as Guy Burgess. Also caught were Judith Coplon, Robert Soblen, and Jack Soble. Moreover, evidence gained by Venona helped to confirm the veracity of former Soviet spies Whittaker Chambers (regarding spymaster J. Peters and the "Ware group") and Elizabeth Bentley's (the Golos-Bentley network) accusations of Soviet spies in the U.S. government, including the "Silvermaster group" and the "Perlo group." Interestingly, incomplete Venona messages also pointed to additional spies in the Manhattan Project, including Quantum, an unidentified spy in 1943 and Fogel/Pers, an unidentified spy in 1944. See John Earl Haynes and Harvey Klehr, *Venona: Decoding Soviet Espionage in America* (New Haven: Yale University Press, 1999), pp. 7–22; and John Earl Haynes and Harvey Klehr, *Early Cold War Spies: The Espionage Trials that Shaped American Politics* (Cambridge: Cambridge University Press, 2006).

apparatus, and the key leaders and cadres were innocent of connection with Soviet espionage operations."[25] They continue: "But the Soviet Union and the American Communists regarded these activities as normal and proper. Their only concern was they not become public."[26]

In 1959, Gus Hall, a Soviet loyalist trained at the International Lenin School in Moscow, replaced Dennis as CPUSA General Secretary. Under Hall, the Party survived with its core membership and secret Soviet subsidies, but Browder's suggestion to become the left wing of the Democratic Party, and the Vietnam War, changed the Party's prospects for victory. Success would come not through the Party but indirectly. The CPUSA moved into the Democratic Party in all but name.

More than "McCarthyism," which has come to be defined as the reckless use of unverified charges and guilt by association, which conveyed political opprobrium, the Vietnam War and the rise of the New Left changed the position and fortunes of the Communist movement. The wake of the Vietnam War contributed heavily to the end of the anti-Communist consensus in American politics.

The anti–Vietnam War movement was the perfect vehicle for the Communists to unhinge the anti-Communist consensus and make possible the Communist goal of the "anti-anti-Communist" prevalent on the American left. The triumph of the neo-Bolshevik New Left movement ensured that Bolshevism would thrive under the guise of the New Left, later known as progressivism.

II. Neo-Bolshevism: Progressivism

Anchored in Bolshevik thought and tactics, the neo-Bolshevik ideology of progressivism is prominent in contemporary American left-wing politics.

---

25 Klehr, Haynes, and Firsov, *The Secret World of American Communism*, p. 18.

26 Klehr, Haynes, and Firsov, *The Secret World of American Communism*, p. 19.

That is an important development, which undermines Hartz's conception of American political thought as being inherently liberal. In the history of Western political thought, progressivism has a more truncated history than liberalism but clearly may become even more significant if it wins the ideological war and successfully becomes America's ideology.

As discussed in chapter 2, Marx and Engels argued that as technology changed so, too, did the economic means of production. The means of production causes specific economic classes. In each epoch—slavery, feudalism, and capitalism—the classes were perpetually and dialectically opposed to each other. Under capitalism, the bourgeoisie, or the middle class, owned the means of production and exploited the proletariat, the working class, by extracting surplus value from their labor. For Marx and Engels, the capitalists would always strive to maximize surplus value, which causes accumulation of capital and ever greater exploitation of the working class, until ultimately the working class would execute a revolution. This would then result in the common ownership of the means of production, and thus class would disappear, resulting in Communism, the abolition of private property, and the end of alienation. Under Communism, the state was no longer necessary and would wither away.[27]

This book has emphasized that Lenin's contributions were even more essential. His argument was capitalist imperialism allowed the capitalist to extract surplus value from colonial peoples, and the greater exploitation allows modest improvements in the conditions of the working class in the metropole states like Great Britain, France, Germany, and the United States, forestalling increasing levels of alienation and thus delaying the Communist revolution.

Also as analyzed in chapter 2, the responsibility of the Communist Party was to increase revolutionary consciousness among the working class

---

27 As Engels argued in his *Anti-Dühring*, formally known as *Herr Eugen Dühring's Revolution in Science*, 8th printing (Moscow: Progress Publishers, 1978 [1877]), Part 3, Chapter 2, pp. 341–342.

and make the revolution by seizing the control of the state—that is revolution from above via the Communist Party and through the Comintern, versus a revolution from below driven by the working class as Marx and Engels, and the Left-Wing Communists, envisioned. In order for the dictatorship of the proletariat to come to power, there must be a hard core of professional revolutionaries—a revolutionary elite—advancing the revolution through a centralized, organized, stable, and disciplined Communist Party, controlled by one man, or at most, a small number of men, to make decisions, while providing direction, instruction, and tutelage for the workers and peasants.

These ideas were not limited to Russian conditions that birthed the Soviet Union. In China, the Comintern applied Lenin's template to China, but given the weak proletariat, the Comintern working through the CCP could be the principal vehicle of revolution, which inspired additional Communist revolutions in the Third World during the Cold War.

In the West, Lenin's ideas and tactics advanced through the Comintern and respective Communist Parties of countries around the world. Two other Communist theoretical approaches to revolution are notable and were heavily influenced by Lenin's united front tactics. The first was Italian communist Antonio Gramsci. The second was the establishment of the Institute of Social Research, known as the Frankfurt School, in Germany. The Frankfurt School argued independently that culture would be the instrument of revolution in the West. As Lenin did, Gramsci and the Frankfurt School recognized that conditions for the working class were too good in the West for a revolution to be possible by "Russian conditions," that is, where a weakened state makes possible a revolutionary *coup*. However, by changing culture, from bourgeois culture to revolutionary socialist culture, a revolution could be executed over decades of gradual change.

Gramsci identified ideology as the key to social change and stable social order. The proletariat needed ideology to cause Communist revolution. The bourgeoisie used ideology to sustain and police social order.

For the proletariat to win over other exploited classes, especially the peasantry, required the emergence of a new stratum of intellectuals who would undermine and supplant the current bourgeois ideology. For Gramsci, the task was to create a new proletarian ideology which would penetrate the minds of the governed, undermine popular consent to the reigning point of view—the "hegemonic ideology"—and lay the foundation for the new state to be ruled by the proletariat.[28]

Importantly, Gramsci argued that the task for the philosophy of praxis (what he called Marxism-Leninism) was not violent revolution. In that assessment, Lenin would have agreed. The actual condition of the West has passed beyond this stage where a new order could be created by the Communist Party seizing control of the state in a dramatic revolution. What is required is a "war of positions"—that is, the battle for people's minds, in which the moral and intellectual legitimacy of the bourgeois is replaced in the popular mind with the moral and intellectual outlook of Communism.[29]

This will be accomplished only when Communist intellectuals win over traditional intellectuals to Communist ideas, not the ideology of Communism explicitly, which would be too much to expect. Instead, people would be won over to Communism indirectly, such as through euphemisms of Communist ideas and verbiage—progressivism rather than Communism. For example, Mayor Mamdani of New York City, his advisers, and other Democrats deny that they are Communists, but they will admit to being progressives or Democratic Socialists. Then the "fortress," ideological and cultural dominance, will pass into the hands of the proletariat, followed by the occupancy of the front line, or "trench" in Gramsci's description, that is, political domination.[30]

---

28 David Forgacs, ed., *The Antonio Gramsci Reader: Selected Writings, 1916–1935* (New York: New York University Press, 2000), pp. 112–119.

29 Forgacs, ed., *The Antonio Gramsci Reader*, pp. 222–230.

30 Antonio Gramsci, *Selections from Cultural Writings*, ed. David Forgacs and Geoffrey Nowell-Smith, trans. William Boelhower (Cambridge, Mass.:

Gramsci identified the need to change the "hegemonic ideology" of the state from monarchical government or from liberal democracy to Communism through gradual cultural change.[31] Western audiences were sophisticated. So, the messages had to be inserted slowly, targeting and undermining bourgeois ideology, religion, and civil society, and replacing them with messages at first undermining them and then offering ideas that would advance a Communist agenda without explicitly referencing Communist ideology.[32]

He argued that hegemony was not created in a final form by capitalists or their representatives but could be volatile and contested by the development of counter-hegemonic narratives. Bourgeois hegemony could be undermined by the media and educational system. Students could be educated by critically aware teachers to resist the hegemonic ideology and their narratives—for example, that capitalism is the best economic system, socialism is inferior to capitalism or "un-American," merit determines economic, political, and social success, America is not inherently racist, or that the "American Dream" is possible for all Americans. The American trinity had to be undermined to the point where the American youth rejected the American spirit, liberalism, and Western civilization.

Like the Bolsheviks, Gramsci saw that educational systems may be inherently reproductive for the hegemonic bourgeois ideology, but if they could be captured by Communists, they would be powerful centers for critiquing the bourgeois ideology, developing anti-bourgeois

---

Harvard University Press, 1985), pp. 88–80, 164–165, 172. Also see Giuseppe Fiori, *Antonio Gramsci: Life of a Revolutionary*, trans. by Tom Nairn (London: New Left Books, 1970), pp. 253–258.

31 Antonio Gramsci, *Selections from the Prison Notebooks*, trans. by Quintin Hoare and Geoffrey Nowell-Smith (New York: International Publishers, 1971), pp. 78–81; and Forgacs, ed., *The Antonio Gramsci Reader*, pp. 192–210.

32 This anticipates the Frankfurt School's attention to what they termed the "culture industry," and its role in marketing Communism in the West as one might any other commodity.

counternarratives, with the expectation that the bourgeois hegemonic ideology would be replaced by Communist hegemony.[33]

This would begin a "march through the institutions" by which Communists, over time, would penetrate and then control bourgeois institutions in civil society, education, and the church—as well as in government. The educational system was of central importance to shape subsequent generations' perceptions of the right and proper political and social system for Western states. Through these means, Western countries could become Communist states without the Bolshevik-style 1917 revolution. Thus, like Lenin, Gramsci was a realist. There would be no workers' revolution in the West. The path to Communism was different in the West. It would take longer, even happening over generations, and its tools largely would be cultural and ideological, but the end result would be the same.

Independently from Gramsci, the Frankfurt School—most significantly Theodor Adorno, Erich Fromm, Max Horkheimer, and Herbert Marcuse—put forth a similar message for advancing Communism in the West.[34] Theoretically, the Frankfurt School provided a modern Communist critique of bourgeois liberal ideology and society and advanced a theory of culture to provide revolutionary change.[35] This would evolve into a new social theory called "critical theory." Its tools were what they termed

---

33 In this sense, Gramsci and the Frankfurt School should be seen as applying Leninism to conditions in Western states. They are often seen as the fountainheads of Marxism in the West, and no doubt their contributions were considerable, but Lenin's work must be seen as the genesis of the Communist revolution as well as the instruction manual to realize it.

34 See Andrew Arato and Eike Gebhardt, eds., *The Essential Frankfurt School Reader* (New York: Continuum, 1982), pp. 3–11.

35 The Frankfurt School was officially established in 1923 and moved to Columbia University in the mid-1930s, first offering lectures there in 1936, before returning to Germany in 1949. The background and development of the Frankfurt School is insightfully provided in Rolf Wiggershaus, *The Frankfurt School: Its History, Theories, and Political Significance* (Cambridge, Mass.: MIT Press, 1994).

the "culture industry," by which they meant the tools and processes to manufacture culture—film, radio and television, literature, theater, and print—and that broadened to include psychology, journalism, educational systems and universities, and publishing houses.

In actuality, the "culture industry" should be conceived of as the "ideas industry" since the Frankfurt School, as the Bolsheviks did, sought to seize the universities, educational system, media, film, TV, civil society to overthrow liberal ideas with neo-Bolshevik ones. The tactics were the same as the Bolsheviks' and Gramsci's; first undermine the existing cultural, political, and social order by imposing and policing ideas, and then replace that order with radical ideas, if no longer Communist verbiage.[36]

Formally, critical theory seeks to examine and explain how bourgeois society functions and how it can be changed to realize ideals of equality and social betterment. The task of critical theory is to hasten the creation of a society without injustice. To accomplish this, the role of critical theory is to provide a criticism of the existing, bourgeois order. This required first questioning with the aim of destroying the heart of the Western Enlightenment and science, the scientific method, sometimes termed "positivism," which claimed that one can study natural and social worlds objectively and without bias. Enlightenment science rested on the importance of reason, principles of rational thought, the infallibility of observation, and the discovery of natural laws and principles governing society. Critical theory developed in part as a response to the goals of the Enlightenment and presumed infallibility of the scientific method, in favor of addressing questions about whose rationality and whose presumed objectivity underpinned science.[37]

---

36 These ideas influenced Saul Alinsky's thought regarding how to gain local political power through community organizing in the United States. See Saul D. Alinsky, *Rules for Radicals: A Practical Primer for Realistic Radicals* (New York: Vintage, 1989).

37 Independently of the Frankfurt School, French philosophers, principally, Jacques Derrida, Michel Foucault, Pierre Bourdieu, and Jacques Lacan, also studied related questions. This largely French "continental school" augmented

For Horkheimer, the failure of the proletariat in the West to fulfill its revolutionary potential assigned to it by Communism and the efforts of the Comintern, led the Frankfurt School to study the working class in the West.[38] In essence, he sought to discover why the proletariat were not behaving as Communist thought required. The answer was the bourgeois family. The Frankfurt School identified what Lenin had noted several decades before: that is, the socialization in the family and its role in generating authoritarian or antiauthoritarian perspectives. Critical theorists concluded that the role of the family in society was essential for comprehending the strength of bourgeois society and the inability of the working class to generate sufficient consciousness to effect revolutionary change.

In particular, to cause change, the role of the father and his authority needed to be undermined. This was necessary because of the indispensable education for authority that occurred in the patriarchal family. "The family was the 'germ cell' of bourgeois culture and it was, like the authority in it, a living reality" that could be undermined, destroyed, and reconstituted.[39] For Communists, the bourgeois family, a married father and mother, raising children in a stable community, supported by church, fraternal organizations, and other aspects of civil society, was a bourgeois institution that perpetuated oppression and was a barrier to progressive change. Accordingly, the family and civil society, everything from churches to the Boy Scouts and Girl Scouts, must be targeted, weakened, and transformed either into a progressive force or their traditional roles eliminated.

---

the work of the Frankfurt School and also influenced movements in the 1960s and subsequently, such as the antiwar, civil rights, Black Power, feminist, gay rights, environmental, and indigenous peoples' movements. See Patricia Hill Collins, *Intersectionality as Critical Social Theory* (Durham: Duke University Press, 2019), pp. 54–84.

38 Max Horkheimer, *Critical Theory: Selected Essays* (New York: Seabury Press, 1972). Also significant are Horkheimer, *Eclipse of Reason* (New York: Oxford University Press, 1947); and Theodor Adorno and Max Horkheimer, *Dialectic of Enlightenment* (New York: Seabury Press, 1972).

39 Horkheimer, *Critical Theory*, p. 128.

While Communists sought to change the status of the working classes and the family, a similar need was present in the modern arts. For critical theory, art is knowledge, elegance, and beauty, but more importantly it can be employed as a mechanism of progressive change. Indeed, they recognized that art, in all of its forms, could be more effective at changing political perceptions and ideology than any other tool of change because of the perceived absence of politics in art—including cinema, music, radio, television, or literature. In fact, the Frankfurt School recognized that art could advance a progressive agenda by conveying its ideas to a broad, popular audience and critiquing bourgeois life as being uninteresting, leaving no room for personal expression in favor of a strict conformity.

Thus, the common portrayal in art and media of 1950s America in popular culture, including film, television, and literature, as embodying these characteristics is a perfect and trenchant illustration of how potent the critique was. It has shaped the image of 1950s America as odious—a political and social order to be rejected—in contrast to the 1960s, which is celebrated, and the decade when critical theory began its march through the institutions.

Finally, Marcuse is significant for contemporary American politics because he advanced the idea of "liberating tolerance," also called "repressive tolerance."[40] This is a neo-Bolshevik term for crushing free speech. Marcuse argues that to achieve tolerance of progressive ideas and concepts requires intolerance toward prevailing policies, attitudes, and opinions. Moreover, the extension of tolerance toward prevailing polities, attitudes, and opinions must be made to encompass those which are outlawed or repressed. Thus, the concept of "liberating tolerance," which is intolerance of the political right for the advancement of the political left. As Marcuse

---

40 Robert Paul Wolff, Barrington Moore, Jr., and Herbert Marcuse, *A Critique of Pure Tolerance* (Boston: Beacon, 1965). The authors have discrete sections, and Marcuse's is titled "Repressive Tolerance," in *A Critique of Pure Tolerance*, pp. 109–111; and Marcuse, *Eros and Civilization: A Philosophic Inquiry into Freud* (Boston: Beacon, 1966), pp. 93–94.

writes: "Liberating tolerance, then, would mean intolerance against movements of the Right, and toleration of movements from the Left."[41]

For Marcuse, the scope of this tolerance and intolerance would be total: "It would extend to the stage of action as well as of discussion and propaganda, of deed as well as word."[42] He continues, "In past and different circumstances, the speeches of the Fascist and Nazi leaders were the immediate prologue to the massacre. The distance between the propaganda and the action, between the organization and its release on people, had become too short."[43] Marcuse argues the rise of fascism might have been prevented if the left could have prevented the fascists from communicating: "but the spreading of the word could have been stopped before it was too late: if democratic tolerance had been withdrawn when the future leaders had started their campaign," then "mankind would have had a chance of avoiding Auschwitz and a world war."[44]

Consequently, the advancement of a progressive agenda requires the withdrawal of tolerance before the deed—that is, at the stage of communication in word, print, picture, or social media post. Marcuse's logic may only be described as pure Bolshevik. That explains why the European Union (EU) and the Labour Party in the UK hate free speech and work to punish the social media platform X because it permits free speech. For Marcuse, and now progressivism in U.S. politics, and the EU, "'the marketplace of ideas' is organized and delimited by those who determine the national and the individual interest."[45] The "small and powerless minori-

41 Marcuse, "Repressive Tolerance," in Wolff, Moore, and Marcuse, *A Critique of Pure Tolerance*, p. 109.

42 Marcuse, "Repressive Tolerance," in Wolff, Moore, and Marcuse, *A Critique of Pure Tolerance*, p. 109.

43 Marcuse, "Repressive Tolerance," in Wolff, Moore, and Marcuse, *A Critique of Pure Tolerance*, p. 109.

44 Marcuse, "Repressive Tolerance," in Wolff, Moore, and Marcuse, *A Critique of Pure Tolerance*, p. 109.

45 Marcuse, "Repressive Tolerance," in Wolff, Moore, and Marcuse, *A Critique of Pure Tolerance*, p. 109.

ties which struggle against the false consciousness must be helped: Their continued existence is more important than the preservation of abused rights and liberties which grant constitutional power to those who oppress minorities."[46]

What Marcuse sought has been realized in U.S. politics. As he identified, what is necessary is the "withdrawal of tolerance from regressive movements *before* they can become active; intolerance even toward thought, opinion, and word" is necessary for the rejection of false consciousness and the realization of liberation.[47]

Hence, political opinions that are "suppressed" because they are made by minorities and women, or by other sectors of social or political life which traditionally have not possessed an equal voice in the public square, should be permitted. They should be given access to public expression, while those who traditionally have held power and whose voices were present must be suppressed.[48]

There is no "marketplace of ideas" for Communists. Politically progressive expression is permitted, and politically regressive expression is not and may be censored legitimately. Free speech as advocated by proponents of liberalism like J. S. Mill and giants of American jurisprudence like Louis Brandeis, Learned Hand, and Oliver Wendell Holmes, is rejected in favor of controlling expression.

Fundamentally, as Marcuse argued, not all speech is to be considered equal. Speech that is considered oppressive, supporting or justifying bourgeois ideology, values, and principles, is to be curtailed and then eliminated. Speech that is considered progressive, supporting or justifying Communist ideology, non-white racial identities, the variants of feminism that reject

46 Marcuse, "Repressive Tolerance," in Wolff, Moore, and Marcuse, *A Critique of Pure Tolerance*, p. 110.

47 Marcuse, "Repressive Tolerance," in Wolff, Moore, and Marcuse, *A Critique of Pure Tolerance*, p. 110. Emphasis original.

48 Marcuse, "Repressive Tolerance," in Wolff, Moore, and Marcuse, *A Critique of Pure Tolerance*, pp. 111–112.

bourgeois identity, multiple gender identity, sexual minorities, and immigration are to be advanced because they promote the liberation sought by critical theory—liberation of those who were once oppressed—and the destruction and replacement of liberalism and traditional American identity, values, and principles. Environmentalism may be employed as well to restrict political and economic freedoms in the name of environmental politics.[49]

This is the logic of why the EU and the British Labour Party hate Elon Musk's X. X permits free speech, and so is a fundamental danger to them as the truth about conditions in the EU and the UK, and facts and opinions that question their power, may be expressed. They seek to realize Marcuse's neo-Bolshevik goals and almost have. If X falls, that is the end of free speech in Europe and Britain. The battle lines have been drawn. Thankfully, the Trump administration is supporting X and laboring to end the EU's and Labour's efforts to crush free speech.

Lenin's ideas, those of Gramsci, and the Frankfurt School serve as the intellectual foundation of progressivism in contemporary U.S. politics. If neo-Bolshevik progressivism wins the "1776 Moment," then the U.S. will be on the path to totalitarianism. With respect to political power, progressive ideology seeks its concentration in the state. It rejects the separation of powers in favor of the concentration of political control in a single branch. Equally, progressive ideology would erase federalism because political power dictates central control, rather than permitting a state or local government to prevent progress.

The rule of law, as traditionally understood, is applicable to those who once held power—the state will deal with them harshly. But as critical legal studies advances, the law must take into account traditional American power structures. Ultimately for progressives, justice is wholly political and

---

49 See Giorgos Kallis, *In Defense of Degrowth: Opinions and Minifestos* (Brussels: Uneven Earth Press, 2017); and Serge Latouche, *Farewell to Growth*, trans. by David Macey (Cambridge: Polity, 2009).

whether you are entitled to receive it depends upon whether you support progressivism.

Those groups and identities that did not possess political power in the past must be a major factor, if not the determining factor, regarding how law applies to their circumstances. Thus, because bourgeois America traditionally oppressed racial and sexual minorities, women, non-Christian religions, minors, and immigrants from non-Western societies, the law must acknowledge this history of oppression and incorporate it into legal judgments.

Progressivism is totalizing in the sense that Marcuse sought—as did Lenin—which means that there can be no opposition or allowance of alternative political choices or political thought. The suppression and ultimate elimination of any alternative is a characteristic of all Communist governments. All opinions must be in accord with ideological precepts, what the Soviets termed political correctness, and which has become common in American political behavior as well.

Neo-Bolshevik progressivism employs threat deflation just as the CCP does, by minimizing or erasing the history of Communism almost from the totality of American life. Progressives today never discuss Lenin, the Comintern, or the history of Communism in America. By denying or ignoring their past, they seek to remove the threat of Communism from the American mind. Moreover, because neo-Bolshevik progressives control the ideas industry, they have created their own top cover. The history of Communism will not be discussed, not in schools, universities, film, media. An honest evaluation of Communism will not appear in textbooks. There is only one monument to the victims of Communism in Washington D.C., and it is not on the Mall but far from it. And that is it. Given the long war against Communism, Americans should expect a monument in every city, town, and village.

To deflate the very real threat of Communism, Communists have simply erased their ideology from history and public consciousness. Moreover, in a brilliant political warfare move, they have associated anti-Communism with McCarthyism, which is purportedly beyond the pale. Thus, just as Deng threat deflated the CCP threat, and made so many Americans complicit, American neo-Bolshevik progressives have done the same. Communism has all but disappeared and progressivism and Diversity, Equity, and Inclusion (DEI) allegedly have nothing to do with it. To raise the issue of the evils of Communism and neo-Bolshevism will be to invite opprobrium from them and the fellow travelers in politics, the media, and civil society, or be simply ignored. They own the "commanding heights" of the ideas industry—education systems, universities, think tanks, media, social media, law schools and law firms, so can choose which ideas to advance and which to bury.

Hence, the ideology has flowered throughout American society, including in the film industry, the advertising industry, social media, streaming services like Netflix, the U.S. military, but especially in journalism, education, civil society, and with the advocates of Critical Race Theory (CRT) and DEI in American politics, business, culture, and society. Table Four summarizes the Leninist and neo-Bolshevik progressive approach to revolution and tyrannical control.

Table Four: Lenin and His Children: Summary Comparison of Bolshevism and Neo-Bolshevik Progressivism

	Leninism and Bolshevik Thought	**Neo-Bolshevik Progressivism**
Motivation of leaders (Orwell's *why* question)	Incandescent hatred of established order, aristocratic (in Russia) or democratic Western societies, and Western civilization and desire to destroy all	Same, updated terminology is hatred of white, patriarchy, democratic capitalism, Western civilization, and desire to destroy all
Motivation of Followers	Mixed: Hatred, Idealism, Ignorance, Strategic Calculation	Same

	Leninism and Bolshevik Thought	Neo-Bolshevik Progressivism
Legitimacy	None, purported "scientific understanding" of society	None, especially given knowledge of consequences of Communist rule
How to execute revolution	Agitation, propaganda, organization, terror, and violence Through either through a *coup d'état* or through the united front to penetrate and take over all institutions in countries not vulnerable to direct *coup* Policing of thought, expression, and behavior	Agitation, propaganda, organization, terror, and violence Through united front strategy and tactics, particularly the seizure and control of the "ideas industry," which are the "commanding heights" of the revolution: the education system, universities, think tanks, journalism, film, entertainment, social media, law schools, law firms, and CCP support Policing of thought, expression, and behavior
Consequence of the revolution	Totalitarianism, so inevitable mass killings, starvation, destruction	Totalitarianism, so inevitable mass killings, starvation, destruction
How to spread the revolution	At first, through the Red Army and then the united front and Comintern Genius at political warfare	Through the support of the CCP and the modern, privatized Comintern—the NGO networks created by Soros, Singham, Jobs, and SPLC Genius at political warfare Use of immigration to destabilize and replace Western populations

(continued on next page)

	Leninism and Bolshevik Thought	Neo-Bolshevik Progressivism
Self-Identification	Communist	Avoidance of Communist at all costs in favor of progressivism or DEI
Effectiveness	Supremely effective, conquered first Russia and then China Penetrated U.S. and Western countries Large numbers of believers, fellow travelers, and spies	Supremely effective, almost completely conquered Western societies: intellectual elite, education, media, businesses, law, police, even military Large numbers of believers and fellow travelers

II.A. Journalism

Progressivism has remade many of the core institutions, professions, and civil society of the United States. It has had a transformative impact upon journalism, bringing about a dramatic evolution among journalists and the meaning of journalism. The dominant theory of journalism has changed toward public journalism or advocacy for progressive objectives.[50] In traditional American journalism, the journalist served the public by providing factual information: "who, what, where, when, and how" something occurred. This American conception of journalism has been replaced by progressive journalism, inspired and instructed by the ideas of critical theory. The most important of these theorists was Jürgen Habermas, who advocated the employment of narratives to promote a progressive agenda and undermine or ignore facts, beliefs, or opinions that contravene the favored narrative.[51] Media must conform, including social media like Facebook or X, and on search engines like Google. To modify Clemenceau,

---

50 Theodore L. Glasser, ed., *The Idea of Public Journalism* (New York: Guilford Press, 1999); and Jay Rosen, *What Are Journalists For?* (New Haven: Yale University Press, 1999).

51 Like Marcuse, Habermas advances the idea of a public sphere for debate which must be defined and policed. Jürgen Habermas, *The Structural*

for the Bolsheviks of the past or the neo-Bolsheviks of today, journalism was too important to be left to the journalists. Such power to influence and shape had to come under Communist control.

The idea that journalists should not select a side but be neutral, dispassionate seekers of factual information, has been replaced by the idea of journalism as a participant, a progressive force employing "repressive tolerance" to promote favored groups and ideas while undermining and de-platforming those that are not. Thus, for this ideology, free speech must be policed. "Hate speech," defined as "words that wound," is immoral and must be eliminated.[52] Those advocating such speech must not be allowed to express their arguments, beliefs, and opinions.

As a consequence of this decision by major media and principal journalism schools, like Columbia School of Journalism, trust in the U.S. media to convey factual information about political events, positions, politicians, and candidates is at a record low. While an imperfect but still insightful standard, during his presidency, numerous studies found that President Trump consistently had over 90 percent negative coverage in his first term.[53]

That has not changed in his second term. The Media Research Center finds that negative coverage of Trump is 92 percent.[54] The data revealed

---

Transformation of the Public Sphere: An Inquiry into a Category of Bourgeois Society, trans. by Thomas Burger (Cambridge, Mass.: MIT Press, 1989).

52 Richard Delgado and Jean Stefancic, *Must We Defend Nazis? Why the First Amendment Should Not Protect Hate Speech and White Supremacy* (New York: New York University Press, 2018).

53 Rich Noyes, "Never More Biased: TV Blasted Trump with 92% Negative Coverage; 66% Positive for Biden," *MRC News Busters*, October 27, 2020. At: <https://www.newsbusters.org/blogs/nb/rich-noyes/2020/10/27/never-more-biased-tv-blasts-trump–92-negative-coverage–66-positive>. Accessed May 13, 2025.

54 Ryan Minnaugh, "Media Research Center Finds 92% Negative Coverage of Trump in First 100 Days," *National News Desk,* April 29, 2025. At: <https://thenationaldesk.com/news/americas-news-now/major-networks-92-negative-coverage-of-president-trump>. Accessed June 15, 2025.

by pollsters show significant distrust of the American media, which correlates with the adoption of progressive ideology and DEI advocacy and policies over what had been traditional American expectations of factual and honest journalism.

II.B. Education

Education, from K–12 and in colleges and universities, and as Bolsheviks and neo-Bolsheviks from Gramsci and the Frankfurt School have recognized, is the major instrument for influencing children and young adults by shaping their knowledge and their political, economic, and cultural beliefs and opinions.[55] The framework for introducing critical theory into education is now commonly termed critical pedagogy.[56]

Critical pedagogy places emphasis on promoting changes in the political identity of students, not only through the curriculum but also by involvement in protests. Involvement in protests is necessary to develop the critical consciousness of students; "participation in contention creates new, politicized, identities" for students.[57] Changes occur in "political identities and commitment—a change in consciousness—from joining demonstrations, marching, singing, joining in the activities of social justice organizations in one's neighborhood."[58] Such participation "leads to groups developing their own collective activity as social change agents."[59] Critical pedagogy advocates progressive change by providing "students direct experience with social justice work, we can educate them to appreciate

---

55 See Jean Anyon, *Marx and Education* (New York: Routledge, 2011), pp. 13–14; and Henry Giroux, *Theory and Resistance in Education* (Santa Barbara, Calif.: Praeger, 1983). Also see William Hayes, *The Progressive Education Movement: Is It Still a Factor in Today's Schools?* (Lanham: Rowman and Littlefield, 2007).

56 Jean Anyon, *Radical Possibilities: Public Policy, Urban Education, and a New Social Movement*, 2nd ed. (New York: Routledge, 2014).

57 Anyon, *Marx and Education*, p. 99.

58 Anyon, *Marx and Education*, p. 100.

59 Anyon, *Marx and Education*, p. 100.

and value those forms of democratic process that are aimed specifically at creating a more equitable society—public contention toward progressive social change."[60]

Additionally, progressivism's rise changed the American campus significantly by permitting the rise of New Left neo-Bolshevik academics, who came to dominate the American academy, and of the Black Power movement, which helped to redefine the identity of African Americans in the 1960s. This movement became a major political force and spawned the academic discipline of Black Studies, which, in turn, inspired and legitimized the creation of similar study disciplines for women and additional ethnic, racial, and sexual minorities.[61]

These steps helped to ensure that universities in the U.S.—at first in humanities and social sciences, and later, the natural sciences—were recast as agents of social change to advance CRT and DEI, with their faculties its producer and their students its consumer.

II.C. Civil Society

All civil society, from churches to the Elks Lodge and Knights of Columbus to the Boy Scouts and Girl Scouts, must conform, as must all business and commerce to public spaces where "holiday" trees have replaced Christmas trees. What the exact "holiday" is, no one should say because Christmas must not be privileged but, rather, diminished as one of the steps to its destruction. The arts are not spared; film, literature, and streaming services, and even children's books must conform, as the canceling of Dr.

---

60 Anyon, *Marx and Education*, p. 100.

61 Fabio Rojas, *From Black Power to Black Studies: How a Radical Social Movement became an Academic Discipline* (Baltimore: Johns Hopkins University Press, 2007), pp. 22–44. Rojas argues that Black Studies arose due to a disappointment with the civil rights movement, the rise of groups such as the Black Panthers, and the increased numbers of black students on campuses.

Seuss' work in 2021 captured in stark relief.[62] Progressives aim to destroy political opposition by preventing the expression of alternative political parties or ideologies and thought. The private behavior of governmental employees must be as well, as progressivism labors to eliminate the private. Increasingly, it dictates that families must be politically correct, with expressions of politically incorrect speech cause for reporting to authorities and denunciation. Any independent source of thought, expression, or practice must conform to the dictates of progressive thought or be eliminated. These are the ideological origins of "cancel culture" in American political, economic, and social life. Thus, in contemporary American politics, we have an ideological struggle between the traditional ideology of liberalism and the neo-Bolshevism of progressivism.

II.D. Critical Race Theory

A direct ideological descendent of progressivism is CRT, whose immediate genesis dates from the 1970s, and whose rhetoric is used to justify DEI policies. As defined by its progenitors, CRT is "a collection of activists and scholars engaged in studying and transforming the relationship among race, racism, and power."[63] It is different from the traditional civil rights movement and civil rights discourse. They stress "incrementalism and step-by-step progress," whereas "critical race theory questions the very foundation of the liberal order, including equality theory, legal reasoning, Enlightenment rationalism, and neutral principles of constitutional law."[64]

---

62 Mark Pratt, "6 Dr. Seuss Books Won't Be Published for Racist Images," *Associated Press*, March 4, 2021. At: <https://apnews.com/article/dr-seuss-books-racist-images-d8ed18335c03319d72f443594c174513>. Accessed May 15, 2025.

63 Richard Delgado and Jean Stefancic, *Critical Race Theory: An Introduction*, 3rd ed. (New York: New York University Press, 2017), p. 3.

64 Delgado and Stefancic, *Critical Race Theory*, p. 3.

The core propositions of CRT begin with the centrality of race and racism for historical, political, social, and economic analysis and legitimacy.[65] For CRT, "race remains the dominant and consistent, yet sometimes elusive, factor that influences laws, policies, relationships, and practices."[66] As seminal thinkers of CRT, Richard Delgado and Jean Stefancic, wrote: "Racism is ordinary, not aberrational," and thus it is "the usual way society does business, the common, everyday experience of most people of color in this country."[67]

According to CRT advocates, racial aggression could not occur without the ideological beliefs in white supremacy that justify them.[68] Ta-Nehisi Coates argued that "white supremacy is a crime and a lie, but it's also a machine that generates meaning."[69] For Coates, white supremacy has created the meaning of race throughout U.S. history to justify racism, and is a violation of humanity that is based on socially constructed conceptions of race. The political ideology, institutions, and culture of the United States is based on the powerful myth of the superiority of white Americans over all others, and which still affects the lives of people of color through

---

65 Kimberlé Crenshaw, Neil Gotanda, Gary Peller, and Kendall Thomas, "Introduction," in Kimberle Crenshaw, Neil Gotanda, Gary Peller, and Kendall Thomas, eds., *Critical Race Theory: The Key Writings that Formed the Movement* (New York: The New Press, 1995), pp. xiii–xxxii.

66 Jessica T. DeCuir-Gunby, Thandeka K. Chapman, and Paul A. Schutz, "Critical Race Theory, Racial Justice, and Education," in Jessica T. DeCuir-Gunby, Thandeka K. Chapman, and Paul A. Schutz, eds., *Understanding Critical Race Research Methods and Methodologies: Lessons from the Field* (New York: Routledge, 2019), pp. 3–10, 5.

67 Delgado and Stefancic, *Critical Race Theory*, p. 8.

68 Daniel G. Solórzano and Lindsay Pérez Huber, *Racial Microaggressions: Using Critical Race Theory to Respond to Everyday Racism* (New York: Teachers College Press, 2020), p. 51.

69 Ta-Nehisi Coates, *We Were Eight Years in Power: An American Tragedy* (New York: One World, 2017), p. 215.

institutional racism but also via racial microaggressions, both of which seek to maintain racial subordination.[70]

The concept of "white fragility" advanced by Robin DiAngelo arises when whites question or reject suppositions concerning white supremacy and racial microaggressions. White fragility is an attempt to "maintain our [white] dominance within the racial hierarchy. . . . Although white fragility is triggered by discomfort and anxiety, it is born of superiority and entitlement" and remains "a powerful means of white racial control and the protection of white advantage."[71]

American society is based upon property rights, which "postulates that it is essential to examine social inequities, particularly educational inequities, from the understanding that racism is systemic and Whiteness has value."[72] The privilege of whiteness means that racism "is difficult to address or cure because it is not acknowledged."[73] As critical race theorist Cheryl Harris argues, "whiteness as a theoretical construct evolved for the very purpose of racial exclusion. . . . Recognizing oneself as 'white' necessarily assumes premises based on white supremacy. It assumes that

---

70 Solórzano and Pérez Huber, *Racial Microaggressions,* p. 51. For CRT proponents, people of color frequently endure countless racial microaggressions. A racial microaggression may be overt or covert and take one of three forms. It may be, first, "verbal and nonverbal assaults against People of Color, often carried out in subtle, automatic, or unconscious forms;" second, "layered assaults, based on race and its intersections with gender, class, sexuality, language, immigration status, phenotype, accent, or surname;" or third, "cumulative assaults that take a psychological and physiological toll" on people of color. Solórzano and Pérez Huber, *Racial Microaggressions,* p. 55.

71 Robin DiAngelo, *White Fragility: Why It's So Hard for White People to Talk about Racism* (Boston: Beacon Press, 2018), p. 2. Also see Layla F. Saad, *Me and White Supremacy: Combat Racism, Change the World, and Become a Good Ancestor* (Naperville, Ill.: Sourcebooks, 2020), pp. 33–39.

72 DeCuir-Gunby, Chapman, and Schutz, "Critical Race Theory, Racial Justice, and Education," p. 5.

73 Delgado and Stefancic, *Critical Race Theory,* p. 8.

black ancestry in any degree . . . automatically disqualifies claims to white identity, thereby privileging 'white' as unadulterated, exclusive, and rare."[74]

There is the intersectionality of race and racism with other forms of subordination. "Racism is intricately woven within all aspects of society and actively interacts with all forms of subordination," such as immigration status or LGBTQI (Lesbian, Gay, Bisexual, Transgender, Queer or Questioning, and Intersex) identity.[75] Harris submits that "inherent in the concept of 'being white' was the right to own or hold whiteness to the exclusion and subordination of blacks."[76] Indeed, whiteness was premised on white supremacy, which encompassed all forms of superiority, maleness, heterosexuality, and national identity and citizenship.[77] The last category is salient as Barbara Fields argues that "immigrants from Europe and the Middle East are able to become white" and change their economic status, but African immigrants, "even wealthy ones, are never able to change their 'blackness.'"[78]

Critical race theory is a challenge to the purported dominant ideology in the United States, which CRT assumes to be liberalism. "A major goal of CRT is to question and challenge the status quo or majoritarian perspective. CRT promotes skepticism toward how the law operates in terms of neutrality, objectivity, and color-blindness."[79] This is a clear link to the thought of Gramsci, the Frankfurt School, and Marcuse and demonstrates CRT's intellectual debt to these Marxists and critical theorists.

---

74 Cheryl I. Harris, "Whiteness as Property," in Sherrow O. Pinder, ed., *Black Political Thought: From David Walker to the Present* (Cambridge: Cambridge University Press, 2020), pp. 272–280, 272.

75 DeCuir-Gunby, Chapman, and Schutz, "Critical Race Theory, Racial Justice, and Education," p. 5.

76 Harris, "Whiteness as Property," p. 272.

77 Harris, "Whiteness as Property," p. 272.

78 Barbara J. Fields, "Whiteness, Racism, and Identity, in Pinder, ed., *Black Political Thought*, pp. 281–290, 285–287.

79 DeCuir-Gunby, Chapman, and Schutz, "Critical Race Theory, Racial Justice, and Education," p. 5.

CRT postulates that meritocracy is a myth. "This principle questions the existence of meritocracy or the idea that advancement in society only occurs because of hard work and ability."[80] Meritocracy is not possible because the institutions and rules have been implemented to the benefit of white males and to the exclusion of people of color. Meritocracy is an expression of white privilege who are socialized to perceive their dominance as normal and earned by their individual efforts.[81]

CRT proclaims a commitment to social justice. "CRT is a liberatory, transformative and emancipatory theory that focuses on racial justice," with its ultimate goal to "end racial oppression and other forms of oppression through social change."[82] This principle is also called critical social justice, which asserts that society is stratified in all significant ways along divisions of race, class, gender, sexuality, and ability.[83] Critical social justice recognizes that United States society is structurally racist.[84] Its intent is to change this.

CRT centers on experiential knowledge of people of color. Its analyses highlight the importance of the voice and "experiences of People of Color."[85] As a result of their different "histories and experiences with oppression, black, American Indian, Asian, and Latino writers and thinkers may be able to communicate to their white counterparts matters that whites are unlikely to know."[86]

---

80 DeCuir-Gunby, Chapman, and Schutz, "Critical Race Theory, Racial Justice, and Education," p. 5.

81 Özlem Sensoy and Robin DiAngelo, *Is Everyone Really Equal? An Introduction to Key Concepts in Social Justice Education*, 2nd ed. (New York: Teachers College Press, 2017), pp. 91–82.

82 DeCuir-Gunby, Chapman, and Schutz, "Critical Race Theory, Racial Justice, and Education," p. 6.

83 Sensoy and DiAngelo, *Is Everyone Really Equal?* p. xx.

84 Sensoy and DiAngelo, *Is Everyone Really Equal?* p. xx.

85 DeCuir-Gunby, Chapman, and Schutz, "Critical Race Theory, Racial Justice, and Education," p. 6.

86 Delgado and Stefancic, *Critical Race Theory*, p. 11.

CRT's theoretical contribution is manifest in the Black Lives Matter (BLM) movement. BLM started in 2013 after the acquittal of a Florida neighborhood watch captain, George Zimmerman, in the shooting of a young black man, Trayvon Martin.[87] The movement accelerated with the shooting of Michael Brown, a black man, by a white police officer in Ferguson, Missouri in 2014, and, more recently, after the 2020 death of George Floyd in Minneapolis.

Black Lives Matter was a significant force in United States politics with support in the Obama and Biden White Houses. The movement used the concept of staying "woke," which was drawn from Erykah Badu's 2008 song "Master Teacher," to describe their ideological beliefs, including an awareness of "white privilege."

Immigration is another front. CRT advances the notion that borders and sovereignty are artificial constructions by racist states in the West. They have no moral force and should not be respected by progressives.[88] This is particularly true of the United States, whose borders expanded by conquest of territory from Mexico and thus, for CRT, colonized indigenous people.[89] CRT seeks to erase the concept of citizenship dependent on laws of the United States in favor of documented or undocumented immigrants who possess the same right to live in the United States as United States citizens. CRT welcomes their presence because it will reduce the traditional political and cultural dominance of the historically dominant Americans and their political principles, influence, and values.

Additionally, CRT advocates changing how American history is conceived and taught through the work of Professor Nikole Hannah-Jones and *The New York Times*' "1619 Project." The Project was launched

87 Black Lives Matter, "About Black Lives Matter." At: <https://blacklivesmatter.com/about/>. Accessed May 10, 2025.

88 Ricardo Castro-Salazar and Carl Bagley, *Navigating Borders: Critical Race Theory Research and Counter History of Undocumented Americans* (New York: Peter Lang, 2012).

89 Castro-Salazar and Bagley, *Navigating Borders*, pp. 39–44.

in August 2019, the 400th anniversary of English pirates transporting twenty to thirty African slaves to Point Comfort in the English colony of Virginia. It seeks to "reframe American history by considering what it would mean to regard 1619 as our nation's birth year," that is, the country's origin, according to Jake Silverstein, the *New York Times Magazine* editor in chief.[90] This is part of the fundamental goal to "decenter whiteness," according to Nikole Hannah-Jones, the Project's principal creator, as the foundation of American history.[91] For the 1619 Project, slavery is the source of economic wealth and prosperity of the United States, and even the American Revolution of 1776, which purportedly was caused by the revolutionaries' desire to preserve chattel slavery in the face of British opposition.

The changes sought by CRT have implications for the U.S. position in the world. But an example of CCP behavior that may be increasingly anticipated occurred at the March 18, 2021, meeting in Anchorage, Alaska, between the Biden administration's Secretary of State Antony Blinken and National Security Advisor Jake Sullivan and their Chinese counterparts, Director of the Office of the Central Commission for Foreign Affairs Yang Jiechi and Foreign Minister Wang Yi made clear, the difficulties in the Sino-American relationship are many and profound.

Director Yang argued in his opening statement: "On human rights, we hope that the United States will do better on human rights. China has made steady progress in human rights, and the fact is that there are many problems within the United States regarding human rights, which

---

90 See Jake Silverstein, "Editor's Note by Jake Silverstein," in Nikole Hannah-Jones, et al., "The 1619 Project" *The New York Times Magazine*, August 18, 2019. At: <http://pulitzercenter.org/sites/default/files/full_issue_of_the_1619_project.pdf>. Accessed April 27, 2025.

91 Nikole Hannah-Jones, "Introduction" in Hannah-Jones, et al., "The 1619 Project" *The New York Times Magazine*, August 18, 2019. At: <http://pulitzercenter.org/sites/default/files/full_issue_of_the_1619_project.pdf>. Accessed April 27, 2025.

is admitted by the U.S. itself as well."[92] He continued: "The United States has also said that countries can't rely on force in today's world to resolve the challenges we face. And it is a failure to use various means to topple the so-called authoritarian states."[93] However, the "challenges facing the United States in human rights are deep-seated. They did not just emerge over the past four years, such as Black Lives Matter. It did not come up only recently. So we do hope that for our two countries, it's important that we manage our respective affairs well instead of deflecting the blame on somebody else in this world."[94]

Director Yang's statement is remarkable: A PRC official employed the discourse of progressivism against U.S. senior officials. PRC officials recognize that making accusations of racism, and systemic racism in U.S. society, would stymie Democrats. These accusations, however unseemly, could not be refuted by the Biden administration, which embraced the concept of systemic racism as a characteristic of the contemporary and historical United States.[95] This belief appears to be a significant component and belief of the contemporary Democratic Party and its senior leadership.

The discourse of progressivism is pernicious, as Director Yang's remarks reveal. He weaponized it to attack U.S. officials and to distract from the PRC's atrocious record on human rights, and deep and

---

92 "How It Happened: Transcript of the U.S.-China Opening Remarks in Alaska," *Nikkei*, March 19, 2021. At: <https://asia.nikkei.com/Politics/International-relations/US-China-tensions/How-it-happened-Transcript-of-the-US-China-opening-remarks-in-Alaska>. Accessed April 21, 2025.

93 "How It Happened," *Nikkei*, March 19, 2021. Accessed March 21, 2025.

94 "How It Happened," *Nikkei*, March 19, 2021. Accessed March 21, 2025.

95 See President Joseph Biden, "Remarks by President Biden on the Verdict in the Derek Chauvin Trial for the Death of George Floyd," The White House, April 20, 2021. At: https://www.whitehouse.gov/briefing-room/speeches-remarks/2021/04/20/remarks-by-president-biden-on-the-verdict-in-the-derek-chauvin-trial-for-the-death-of-george-floyd/>. Accessed April 21, 2025.

widespread racism at the elite and popular levels throughout the PRC.[96] PRC officials will continue to use the canard of systemic racism in their media to domestic and global audiences, as well as in political warfare attacks against the U.S.[97]

The systemic racism arguments have provided the PRC with a bludgeon to employ against the United States, to weaken the appeal of liberal ideology within the PRC, in the United States, and internationally; and second, to discredit the U.S. position as a human rights leader. Systemic racism is one element of the PRC's political warfare campaign to advance its fundamental goal of undermining the U.S. relationship with other states, including in the West. It is important that the rest of the world understands that the PRC, a Communist state with one of the worst human rights records in history, will employ any measure to undermine the U.S. Lies and deception are some of its favored political warfare tactics. Nonetheless, the neo-Bolshevism of the progressives within the U.S. and of the CCP abroad have been effective. At home, CRT and DEI policies have captured the federal and most state and local governments, as well as business, media, Hollywood, and popular culture. The CCP's efforts have borne fruit in many locations worldwide. While the Trump administration labors to correct the damage, Americans must have a realistic assessment of how much destruction has been wrought.

---

96 On the prevalence and consequences of racism in China, see John M. Friend and Bradley A. Thayer, *How China Sees the World: The Rise of Han-Centrism and the Balance of Power in International Politics* (Lincoln: Potomac Books, 2018).

97 Huang Huikang, "Racism Deeply Rooted in U.S.," *China Daily*, April 22, 2021. At: <http://global.chinadaily.com.cn/a/202104/22/WS6080c815a31024ad0bab9795.html>. Accessed April 22, 2025. Chinese media are particularly sensitive to discrimination against the ethnic Chinese in the United States.

III. The Assault on the American Trinity by Progressivism

The central political struggle in the United States for American identity is between the American trinity and progressivism. As is often the case in a period of ideological upheaval, it is not transparent whether progressivism will successfully fully supplant the American trinity. However, American politics at the elite level is moving to the political left. Whether progressivism replaces the American trinity will depend on the strength of liberalism versus that of progressivism.

In contemporary American politics it is unclear whether the American trinity will be able to reassert itself, since American history and identity for decades have been taught differently to the young, in contrast to the previous generations, the baby boomers (born 1946–1964) and Generation X (1965–1980), who were educated in a United States when liberalism was the dominant ideology. As a result, conceptions of American identity and ideology have changed.

To reinvigorate the American trinity requires a transition as great as that which has occurred from liberalism to neo-Bolshevik progressivism. It would require capturing the "ideas industry" that the critical theorists identified and successfully seized. The most important of the ideas industry are K–12 and university education, but also journalism and social media, film, music and other elements of popular culture, philanthropic foundations, and the major book presses. There is little evidence that this is occurring. To make progress in education would require the federal government, as well as state and local authorities, parents, and parent-teacher associations to intervene to halt progressivism's control of the American educational system from K–12 through universities.[98]

This would have to be a consistent and lengthy effort, and inevitably would be imperfect because private educational institutions, and particularly elite private institutions, would remain challenging but not impossible

98 The Trump administration and major states like Florida and Texas are acting to address CRT.

to reform. Of course, there also would be countermeasures. The example at the University of Oxford of Oriel College's refusal to remove the statue of British imperialist and philanthropist Cecil Rhodes at the face of the college, despite the demands of the "Rhodes Must Fall" Movement, was met with protest from academic staff and over 150 academics refusing to teach Oriel's students, hurting the educational opportunities and reputation of the Oriel College.[99] Thus, any steps taken will have to be sustained despite the inevitable legal and other challenges. Additionally, these efforts must be able to endure accusations of racism, sexism, homophobia, and white privilege, which so far have halted any successful effort of liberalism's proponents to defend their ideology or reverse its decline.

While there was some success at Oriel College, there has been defeat thus far with the greatest writer in the English language, William Shakespeare, who has to go through a humiliation ritual four centuries after his death. The neo-Bolshevik efforts to remake British and Western identity now target Shakespeare and his home in Stratford-upon-Avon. Since 2022, the Shakespeare Birthplace Trust, established in 1847, has been urged by academics at the University of Birmingham to purge its vast collection of "Anglocentric and colonist thought" because it could promote white supremacy. According to the criticism, which is led by Dr. Helen Hopkins of the University of Birmingham, the Trust's collections risked

---

99 Gareth Harris, "Oxford Professors Refuse to Teach Undergraduate Students If Cecil Rhodes Statue Stays in Place," *The Art Newspaper*, June 11, 2021. At: <https://www.theartnewspaper.com/news/uk-culture-wars-escalate-as-oxford-dons-refuse-to-teach-oriel-college-students-if-rhodes-statue-stays-in-place>. Accessed June 12, 2025. Also in June 2021, the University of Oxford's Magdalen College did not object when graduate students in the Middle Common Room removed the Queen's portrait due to concerns over the Queen's "colonial links." See "Cecil Rhodes: Oriel College Faces Teaching Boycott over Refusal to Move Statue," *The Guardian*, June 10, 2021. At: <https://www.theguardian.com/education/2021/jun/10/oriel-college-faces-teaching-boycott-over-refusal-to-remove-rhodes-statue>. Accessed June 12, 2025.

showcasing European culture as the world standard of culture and of using Shakespeare as a symbol of "British cultural superiority."[100] Moreover, "the narrative of Shakespeare's greatness has caused harm—through the [*sic*] epistemic violence" toward other communities.[101] Reverence for Shakespeare as a universal genius formed part of "white, Anglocentric, Eurocentric, and increasingly 'West-centric' worldviews that continue to do harm in the world today."[102] Furthermore, the critique, to which the Trust has acquiesced, claimed that the play *King Lear* was about "whiteness" and that the character Hamlet in the eponymous play held racist views of black people.[103] The Shakespeare Birthplace Trust secured funding from the Esmée Fairbairn Foundation, which finances projects that promote "diversity and inclusion," to make the changes.

The assault on Western civilization is endless and occurs on all fronts. It is not just Shakespeare or Rhodes; there is the advancement of a targeted decapitation campaign of the leaders, culture, and history of Great Britain which includes the elimination of Winston Churchill, Jane Austen, J. M. W. Turner, and Alan Turing, from Bank of England banknotes. They are being replaced by images of wildlife: a hedgehog, hare, red squirrel, and otter. Replacing august historical figures with wildlife is part of elimination of British history and Western identity. That will be a next step in the United States, too. President Andrew Jackson will be replaced on the twenty-dollar

---

100 Charlie Parker, "Shakespeare's Birthplace to Be 'Decolonised' Over 'White Supremacy' Fears," *The Times*, March 16, 2025. At: <https://www.thetimes.com/uk/society/article/shakespeare-birthplace-stratford-upon-avon-empire-qvb2zdvz8>. Accessed January 10, 2026.

101 Parker, "Shakespeare's Birthplace to Be 'Decolonised' Over 'White Supremacy' Fears."

102 Parker, "Shakespeare's Birthplace to Be 'Decolonised' Over 'White Supremacy' Fears."

103 Craig Simpson, "Shakespeare's Birthplace to Be Decolonised After "White Supremacy Fears," *Daily Telegraph*, March 16, 2025. At: <https://www.telegraph.co.uk/news/2025/03/16/william-shakespeare-birthplace-trust-white-supremacy-empire/>. Accessed January 10, 2026.

bill with Harriet Tubman in 2030. Unless reversed, no doubt that will be the first of many changes to U.S. banknotes.

This attack on Western civilization developed over decades, with its genesis in the late 1980s in university education. As Schlesinger noted at the time, there was a great danger from multiculturalism. He identified the importance of education: "Schools and colleges of the republic train the citizens of the future. Our public schools, in particular, have been the great instrument of assimilation and the great means of forming an American identity."[104] Identifying what Gramsci and the Frankfurt School, and thus progressivism, had appreciated sixty years before, he continued: "What students are taught in schools affects the way they will thereafter see and treat other Americans, the way they thereafter will conceive the purposes of the republic."[105]

However, for Schlesinger, the American educational system of the late 1980s and early 1990s had radically changed: "The militants of ethnicity now contend that a main objective of public education should be the protection, strengthening, celebrations, and perpetuation of ethnic origins and identities;" however, "separatism nourishes prejudices, magnifies differences and stirs antagonisms."[106] For him, "the consequent increase in ethnic and racial conflict lies behind the hullabaloo over 'multiculturalism' and 'political correctness,' over the iniquities of 'Eurocentric' curriculum, and over the notion that history and literature should be taught not as intellectual disciplines but as therapies whose function is to raise minority self-esteem."[107]

For many liberals, including former New York Governor Mario Cuomo, it was possible to embrace assimilation and diversity simultaneously. Cuomo said: "Most Americans can understand both the need to

---

104 Schlesinger, *The Disuniting of America*, p. 17.
105 Schlesinger, *The Disuniting of America*, p. 17.
106 Schlesinger, *The Disuniting of America*, p. 17.
107 Schlesinger, *The Disuniting of America*, p. 17.

recognize and encourage an enriched diversity, as well as the need to ensure that such a broadened cultural perspective leads to unity and an enriched sense of what being an American is, and not to a destructive factionalism that would tear us apart."[108] As the decades passed, Cuomo's position became antiquated, particularly the call for assimilation to avoid factionalism with progressivism's rise.

Fundamentally, what Schlesinger did not perceive was that American political institutions have been captured by the Communists and so are in a state of transition from the principles and practices defined by the American Revolution and the United States Constitution to neo-Bolshevism.

In the mid-1960s, in the middle of great prosperity, the country's political leaders decided to reform the United States to make it a more just and humane society. As sociologist Charles Murray wrote: "You have to be quite old to remember how uncomplicated it seemed to many of us, White and Black alike, in 1963. African Americans had been wronged for centuries, during slavery and after. It was time to set things right" with the 1964 Civil Rights Act.[109]

Thus commenced a series of moral and political crusades, for which the Civil Rights Act provided the template for women who entered professions and roles that had been exclusively male. Later, this was employed by the LGBTQI community, as well as immigrants, and advanced the rapid erosion of American liberalism's conception of immigration. Immigrants previously unwanted in the United States were welcomed and even recruited

---

108 New York Governor Mario Cuomo, "Governor Cuomo Issues a Statement on Multicultural Education," July 15, 1991, in *Public Papers of Governor Mario M. Cuomo—1991 (Part 2)* (Albany: State of New York, 1995), p. 1416. At: <https://nysl.ptfs.com/knowvation/app/consolidatedSearch/#search/v=list,c=1,q=field11%3D%5B18379742%5D%2CqueryType%3D%5B16%5D,sm=s,l=library1_lib%2Clibrary4_lib%2Clibrary5_lib>. Accessed April 17, 2025.

109 Charles Murray, *Facing Reality: Two Truths about Race in America* (New York: Encounter Books, 2021), p. 3.

as a result of the Immigration Reform Act (Hart-Celler) of 1965 and its subsequent modifications.

Hart-Celler supplanted the "national origins" immigration system passed in 1924 and reaffirmed in 1952, which kept the country's ethnic composition roughly what it was.[110] The consequences of Hart-Celler have been profound. As Christopher Caldwell argues, in the "three-and-a-half centuries between its discovery and 1965, the United States had received 43 million newcomers," which includes an estimated quarter-million slaves.[111] In the half-century after Hart-Celler, the United States would receive 59 million.[112] A consequence of this dramatic change in the country's immigration policy, indeed, is its reversal from centering upon immigration from Europe to immigration from the rest of the world and the minimization of those from Europe.

Hart-Celler changed the culture of the United States and committed the government to terminate the three-centuries-old connection between America and Europe and undermined each aspect of the American trinity to the point today where American identity is under tremendous strain.

As Caldwell captures in his analysis of this change, at some point in the years since, "what had seemed in 1964 to be merely an ambitious reform revealed itself to have been something more. The changes of the 1960s, with civil rights at their core, were not just a major new element of the Constitution," but were, in fact, "a *rival* constitution, with which the original one was frequently incompatible—and the incompatibility would worsen as the civil rights regime was built out."[113] Thus, for Caldwell, in 1964, Americans had inadvertently voted themselves a second constitution,

---

110 Indeed, even in the mid-1960s, immigrants from Great Britain and Germany made up half of the "quota" on immigration, and those countries plus Ireland, Italy, and Poland, comprised three-quarters of all legal immigration. Christopher Caldwell, *The Age of Entitlement: America Since the Sixties* (New York: Simon & Schuster, 2020), p. 113.

111 Caldwell, *The Age of Entitlement*, p. 115.

112 Caldwell, *The Age of Entitlement*, p. 115.

113 Caldwell, *The Age of Entitlement*, p. 6. Emphasis original.

repealing the one they had. Each constitution contained guarantees of rights that could be invoked against the other.[114] However, in any clash, the new constitution tended to prevail.

Much of the clash between the American trinity and progressives is not actually a disagreement over which of the two constitutions should dominate. It is a clash between American identity and Communism, with what Caldwell insightfully notes is the *de facto* Constitution of 1964, as the stalking horse for the Communist agenda.[115]

In contrast to the American trinity, progressivism is ascendent, particularly for Americans age forty and under who mark the end of Generation X, and the beginning of the millennials (also called Generation Y, 1981–1996) and Generation Z (1997–2012) and Generation Alpha (2013–today) who have come of age in the milieu of progressivism. This ideology's narratives concerning American identity and history are taught, and have been for decades, and are seemingly accepted at elite and popular educational institutions, from elementary schools to universities, and reinforced in media, popular culture, and government policies.

As those who are young and young-middle-aged move into positions of management and authority this will only solidify. One major factor may offset this. The Trump administration's efforts to reverse this indoctrination may have considerable impact because it is revitalizing American identity. If decades of indoctrination are to be reversed, appeals to American identity will be one of the most effective means.

III.A. Communist Muscle: The Role of Antifa

Dominating ideas can win much of the fight or keep the fight from happening in the first place. But Communist movements have always found that muscle is still needed. That is the role of Antifa—Communist muscle. Historically and today, it serves as the coercive force to dominate the streets

114 Murray, *Facing Reality*, pp. 3–7.
115 Caldwell, *The Age of Entitlement*, p. 6.

and other physical spaces for the Communists. Antifa performs major and interconnected roles that provide Communists with the ability to coerce Americans and deny them their political and civil rights.

Antifa serves the traditional role of the Communist Party going back to the Red Guards of the Bolsheviks in Russia and also in Weimar Germany—that is, as a shock troop force to be employed to serve Communist aims.[116] Today, Antifa shock troops can dominate any major city's public space for the Communists to do what they want in that sphere, which might be hindering or thwarting Immigration and Customs Enforcement (ICE) actions, effective policing of the city, or a demonstration or gathering of Trump supporters. Antifa recruits and trains the shock troops of the Communists so that there are always sufficient numbers of recruits but also leaders and organizers. Antifa deters the presence of others to conduct peaceful protests and to exist in the public sphere through demonstrations. It effectively denies the physical public sphere to its enemies, thus violating their political and civil rights. Antifa acts to intimidate, to keep those who would resist from appearing in the public sphere. It demonstrates to the local and state police that it can generate physical presence and force, and because its presence is strongest in Democratic-controlled cities like Chicago, Minneapolis, New York City, Portland, Oregon, and Seattle, city and state officials will support and provide top cover for its actions. As a result, local authorities often will tolerate its abuses, thuggery, and lawbreaking.

Antifa also plays an important political warfare role. By purportedly serving as an "anti-fascist" force, the name and activities mask an attempt to justify anti-American, criminal, and terroristic activity. The name permits supporters in the media, universities, the Democratic Party, and their donors to back Antifa's actions without having to confront publicly the reality that it is an anti-American terrorist organization. The designation

---

116 Mark Bray, *Antifa: The Anti-Fascist Handbook* (Brooklyn: Melville House, 2017). Bray provides the history of Antifa and lessons for its members in his handbook.

of Antifa as a domestic terrorist organization and other actions of the Trump administration are making this camouflage far more difficult and it is certain that investigations will reveal ties to the modern Comintern run by Soros and his son Alexander, and their ideological allies like Singham and The People's Forum. Their influence with groups like the Democratic Socialists of America (DSA) is important, but the DSA is just a front. Their true power comes from their influence in the Democratic Party.

The cases of Antifa attacks on MAGA contributor, commentator and broadcaster Jack Posobiec and, in a separate incident, journalist Andy Ngo, illustrate the two-tiered standard of policing.[117] That is another indication of Antifa's power. Its members can effectively intimidate local authorities to allow their coercive and terroristic actions.

The Trump administration has endeavored to reveal the scope and activity of the modern Comintern, both its domestic wing run by the Soros family and their allies in the U.S., Canada, and Europe. That investigation will reveal ties to the international arm of the Comintern run by the CCP, that is, formally the United Front Work Department, but also its associated and front organizations.[118] That revelation illuminates that the fight against Communism is one fight against its presence within the U.S. and West, but also the fight against the CCP. It has been so since 1917.

---

117 On the attack on Jack Posobiec see Allum Bokhari, *Breitbart News*, October 7, 2020. At: <https://www.breitbart.com/politics/2020/10/07/dc-antifa-ringleader-jason-charter-charged-with-assaulting-oanns-jack-posobiec/>. Accessed September 13, 2025. Also see Andy Ngo, *Unmasked: Inside Antifa's Plan to Destroy Democracy* (New York: Center Street, 2021). Ngo's account of Antifa's training manual, its violence, which was directed against him, doxing and other actions, is particularly telling about the terroristic nature of Antifa.

118 See Anne-Marie Brady, "Exploit Every Rift: United Front Work Goes Global," in David Gitter, et al., *Party Watch Annual Report, 2018* (Washington, D.C.: Center for Advanced China Research, 2018); Clive Hamilton and Mareike Ohlberg, *Hidden Hand: Exposing How the Chinese Communist Party Is Reshaping the World* (London: Oneworld Publications, 2020); and Alex Joske, *The Party Speaks for You* (Canberra: Australian Strategic Policy Institute, 2020).

Chapter 6

Winning the Hundred Years' War Against Communism: Implications for Americans

This chapter explains what Americans can do to win the Hundred Years' War against Communism. Fundamentally, the key to victory for Americans is to restore the American trinity, and that requires Americans to educate themselves about the external and internal threats from Communism and once again embrace the American spirit, ideas, and civilization. Communists will win only if Americans forget who they are. Of course, the Communists have labored for decades precisely to cause a great forgetting among the American people. The struggle against the CCP or Communists at home will not be easy, but, thankfully, there is still time to save American identity and thereby finally win the Hundred Years' War.

There is an inverse relationship between the strength of American or Western identity and Communism. The stronger American identity, the weaker Communism; the stronger Communist ideology, the weaker American identity. That is true of the states of Western civilization as well. The stronger Western civilizational identity, the weaker Communist identity. Unfortunately, today Communist identity is on the march in America and in the West, and American identity and Western civilization are under assault as never before in history.

I. The Costs of Leninism to the United States and the West

The costs of Leninism to the United States and Western civilization have been monumental. When the history of U.S. wars and interventions is viewed through the prism of Leninism, those costs are starkly illuminated. Certainly, Leninism resulted in the rise of fascism, Benito Mussolini's 1922 "March on Rome" was inspired by the Bolsheviks and brought fascism to Italy. The far-right reaction in Weimar Germany that yielded Naziism was largely due to Communists seizure of power and attempted seizures in many parts of Germany in the wake of World War I. Stalin ordered the German Communist not ally with the Socialists, and so Hitler came to power in 1933. The 1939 Molotov-Ribbentrop Pact gave Hitler what he wanted and resulted in World War II in Europe. Leninism caused the Cold War that the U.S. fought with the Soviet Union, which incurred tremendous risks and costs for the American people. As Leninism birthed the CCP, it has also yielded the current cold war between the PRC and the U.S. He started a civil war in the West over Western civilization and the West's identity. His children and grandchildren are responsible for the neo-Bolshevik progressivism that seeks to overthrow American identity. From 1917 to today, Leninism has cast a long shadow over the twentieth and twenty-first century.

When the history is examined in detail, a more extensive accounting is revealed, which captures the deleterious consequences for the United States.[1] In World War I, due to Lenin's betrayal of the Allied cause

1 There were domestic consequences, of course. The Palmer Raids to destroy Bolshevik cells in the U.S. and prevent their propaganda and later Sen. Joseph McCarthy's efforts to identify Communists in the United States Government were examples of the domestic side of the struggle. In addition, Bolshevik/Soviet/Warsaw Pact intelligence collection against the U.S. resulted in great costs. For example, the Cambridge Five, the Walker Family spy ring, Aldrich Ames, and Robert Hanssen caused great damage to the U.S. and its allies as well as the agents they betrayed and great U.S. military advantages and technology they compromised. Moreover, the changes to U.S. politics, culture, and society incurred by the Cold War should be included in a full accounting of

and the abandonment of Russian military operations against Germany, Austria-Hungary, and the Ottoman Empire, more Americans were killed than would have been the case had the Russians stayed in the war and occupied the German eastern front.

One of Lenin's top priorities was to end Russian involvement in the war, and he did so quickly. Soon after the Bolshevik Revolution, Lenin conveyed to the Germans the Bolshevik desire to terminate the fighting. Naturally, the Germans were receptive. The negotiations held by the German military and the Bolsheviks began on December 22, 1917. The Germans quickly tired of the Bolsheviks' tactics, captured by Trotsky's identification of the "neither war, nor peace" Bolshevik strategy—the Bolsheviks would not continue military operations, but they would not surrender to German demands.

Weary of Bolshevik wordplay and deceit, the Germans signed a separate treaty with Ukrainian nationalists on February 9, 1918, and resumed military operations against the Bolsheviks a day later. Under such pressure, the Bolshevik regime could not survive and so they requested a return to negotiations, which the Germans granted on February 23, giving the Bolsheviks only five days to conclude the agreement. On March 3, 1918, the Bolsheviks signed the Treaty of Brest-Litovsk.

It was a Carthaginian Peace. Russia lost Ukraine, its Polish and Baltic territories, and Finland. Germany gained their resources at a critical time of civilian suffering to prevent another "turnip winter" on the German home front. However, both the Ukrainian and Bolshevik treaties were annulled by the November 11, 1918, armistice, thus saving the Bolsheviks.

The peace was also critical for the war effort, as the Germans already had begun transferring divisions to the West. The British estimated on

---

the costs of Leninism. That would include the changes that brought the start of the Cold War from the National Security Act of 1947, universal military training, and the opportunity costs of the mobilization against the Soviet Union. At the same time, prodigious positive achievements were caused as well, from the Apollo program to the internet.

December 7, 1917, that the Germans would be able to transfer eight to ten divisions per month from the eastern to western front.[2] In November 1917, the British estimated that the Germans had 150 divisions on the western front. The British estimate on February 3, 1918, was that the Germans had 174 divisions on the western front, having transferred twenty-six from Russia and five from the Italian front. Finally, on March 11, 1918, the British estimated that the Germans possessed 185 divisions on the western front.

In fact, the Germans would have 192 divisions when they launched the *Kaiserschlacht* (Kaiser's Battle, also known as the Ludendorff Offensives). Those divisions made possible Germany's last effort to win the war before the full weight of the American mobilization could be brought into the fight. The German attack on the British line on March 21, 1918, was the start of the first of the five great *Kaiserschlacht* offensives (which was termed Operation Michael) launched seriatim between March and July 1918 that Quartermaster General Erich Ludendorff, the *de facto* leader of the German Army, had determined would win the war for Germany. In the first of the offensives, the Germans had amassed 110 divisions against fifty-seven defending British divisions. The Britain would lose more than 300,000 men—28,182 killed, 181,339 wounded, and 93,403 missing and captured. In the end, the Allies would win, but in the words of the Duke of Wellington after Waterloo, it was "a damned serious business . . . the nearest-run thing you ever saw in your life." That alone would have been sufficient for Britain to condemn Lenin for treachery and respond accordingly.

Likewise, the French and American armies suffered the hammer blows of the German army in these offensives. The Bolshevik decision to leave the war cost the Allies hundreds of thousands of lives, and might have

2 These estimates are from John Hussey, "The Movement of German Division to the Western Front, Winter 1917–1918," *War in History*, Vol. 4, No. 2 (April 1997), pp. 213–220, pp. 214–215.

cost them the war, had the *Kaiserschlacht* offensives been successful. The irony of that outcome was that the German army would have then defeated Bolshevism in Russia. Instead, the Allies paid the blood price of continuing the war until Germany's mutiny and the collapse of the home front. The U.S. alone suffered the loss of about 117,000 men killed in action or other deaths in World War I, not including those wounded and lives destroyed by the conflict.[3] By defeating Germany, the Allies had the immediate effect of saving Bolshevism.

In the interwar period, the cost of Leninism remained high. Lenin's government gave the world Stalin with all of his horrors, including bringing the CCP to power. The Comintern penetrated American labor unions through front organizations, and its spies infiltrated the U.S. government and much of the American political left. This set the stage for the loss of atomic secrets due to espionage rings. As discussed, when the Molotov-Ribbentrop Pact was in effect, August 23, 1939 to June 22, 1941, strikes called by Communist labor fronts or Communist-influenced unions—such as the CIO, United Electrical, Radio, and Machine Workers, United Mine Workers, United Rubber Workers, and United Auto Workers—hindered U.S. rearmament, such as by attacking the imposition of conscription in 1940, and aid to Great Britain.

The U.S. also incurred the price of Leninism in the Second World War. The Molotov-Ribbentrop Pact directly contributed to the origins of World War II in Europe. By securing Adolf Hitler's eastern front and supplying Hitler with raw materials and other aid—this was, in essence, a Soviet lend-lease to Hitler—this enabled aggression in the West against Denmark and Norway in April, the Low Countries and France and Great Britain in May 1940, the *Afrika Korps* deployment to aid the Italian military in

---

3 Defense Casualties Analysis System, "U.S. Casualties World War I 1917–1918." At: <https://dcas.dmdc.osd.mil/dcas/app/summaryData/casualties/principalWars>. Accessed July 11, 2025.

February 1941, against Yugoslavia and Greece in April 1941, and the airborne invasion of Crete in May 1941.

Hitler's invasion of the Soviet Union immediately reversed Stalin's appeasement of Hitler. But it was Stalin's effort to turn Hitler westward with the Molotov-Ribbentrop Pact that provided the permissive condition for World War II in Europe. Thus, the Soviets directly contributed to the origins of World War II, in which about 250,000 American deaths were incurred in the European (including Mediterranean) theater of war, again excluding wounded and the prodigious cost of the war on men who survived combat.[4]

Moreover, the fact that Stalin maintained neutrality against Japan prevented the U.S. military from using Soviet bases to attack Japan. Had U.S. forces been able to do so, the Doolittle Raid in April 1942 was only a slight indication of what U.S. airpower might have accomplished in conjunction with U.S. naval forces using Soviet ports to interdict Japanese sea lines of communication, to attack targets in the Japanese home islands, and to mine Japanese ports. But the Soviets maintained strict neutrality and so the U.S. incurred the costs of that position, taking years of bitter conflict through the Southwest Pacific Area (up the New Guinean northern coast) and Central Pacific Area (from the Gilberts to the Marshalls to the Marianas) to base forces, the 20th Air Force's B-29s (the XXI Bomber Command of the 20th Air Force), to be in a position to attack Japan effectively and in a sustained manner.

This campaign, which commenced in November 1944, had a tepid and ineffective start. But under Major General Curtis LeMay from January 1945, the XXI Bomber Command became supremely successful, unlike the XX Bomber Command B-29s based first in India and then

4 Total deaths, of all causes from 1941 to 1945, were 405,399. Defense Casualties Analysis System, "U.S. Casualties World War II 1941–1945." At: <https://dcas.dmdc.osd.mil/dcas/app/summaryData/casualties/principalWars>. Accessed July 11, 2025.

in China. This was the XX Bomber Command of the 20th Air Force, established in November 1943. Their attacks, which commenced in June 1944, were not as effective due to the excessive range of targets in Japan, great logistical difficulties of running a B-29 strategic bombing campaign first from China, and the vulnerability of those bases to attacks by the Japanese.

The U.S. suffered the loss of about 112,000 soldiers, sailors, and Marines killed in action in the war against Japan and over 253,000 wounded in action. Clearly, those numbers might well have been lower if Japan had been weakened sooner by the air and naval campaign against the home islands. Had that campaign against the home islands started in earnest in 1942, rather than in mid-to-late 1944, fewer Americans would have died.[5]

In addition, Stalin did not allow lend-lease aid to travel to China through Soviet territory due to the Soviet-Japanese Neutrality Act of April 1941. Lend-lease aid to the Soviet Union did use Iran as a conduit; the Soviets occupied the northern half of Iran, and the British did the southern half in 1941 to ensure that aid could reach Soviet territory from ports on the Persian Gulf. This was one of three principal ways that aid reached the Soviets, the others being to the Soviet far east from Alaska (known as ALSIB—Alaska to Siberia), and to Arkhangelsk, Murmansk, and other ports on the Barents and White Seas.[6]

Aid could have traveled to China from this route as well, through Soviet territory, which would have been a far safer one and would have allowed much greater tonnage to reach Chiang's armies. Instead, U.S. aid had to travel over the 717-mile Burma Road until that route was interdicted by

---

5 The major problems with U.S. Navy's torpedoes might have been discovered and addressed earlier, yielding greater loss of Japanese merchantmen and warships, and thus shortening the war.

6 See Robert Huhn Jones, *The Roads to Russia: United States Lend-Lease to the Soviet Union* (Norman: University of Oklahoma Press, 1969).

the Japanese in 1942.[7] For most of the war, aid had to fly over the Hump on the U.S. Army Air Force 10th Air Force (later Air Transport Command) cargo aircraft, mostly C-46s, C-47/C-53s, C-87s, and later C-54s, from bases in India to China. Aircraft flying over the Hump delivered just over 738,000 tons of supplies to China at the cost of 594 aircraft. That was a significant amount that involved a Herculean effort, but it is only a fraction of what might have been delivered by road and rail. Moreover, from April 1944 to January 1945, the Hump route also had to support the XX Bomber Command's B-29 raids against Japan. The use of the road route to China was restored in January 1945 after the completion of the Ledo Road.

By denying lend-lease aid to China, Stalin hindered the Allied war effort against Japan, weakened the KMT, and contributed to American and Allied casualties directly due to those killed and wounded in action on the Hump, as well as by prolonging the war.

Soviet support for the CCP led directly to its victory over the KMT in 1949. The CCP's victory, in turn, then also caused the Korean War, 1950–1953, because Stalin would not approve the invasion unless Mao committed, which he did. Thus, the Korean War was started by Stalin reaching an agreement with Kim Il-sung and Mao to conquer South Korea, resulting in about 36,000 Americans killed in action.[8] The Vietnam War, 1964–1973, sparked by Communist North Vietnam's aggression against South Vietnam, resulted in about 57,000 Americans killed from all causes.[9]

Of course, Soviet nuclear capabilities would have led potentially to the deaths of many millions of Americans had nuclear deterrence failed

---

7 In July 1940, the British had yielded to Japanese pressure to close the Burma Road and did so for three months.

8 Total deaths, of all causes from 1950 to 1953, were 36,574. Defense Casualties Analysis System, "Korean War 1950–1953." At: <https://dcas.dmdc.osd.mil/dcas/app/summaryData/casualties/principalWars>. Accessed July 11, 2025.

9 Total deaths, of all causes from 1964 to 1973, were 58,220. Defense Casualties Analysis System, "Vietnam War 1964–1973." At: <https://dcas.dmdc.osd.mil/dcas/app/summaryData/casualties/principalWars>. Accessed July 11, 2025.

and a limited or total nuclear exchange occurred. In sum, Soviet actions, principally encouraging and sustaining the Korean and Vietnam wars during the Cold War, resulted in the deaths of about a hundred thousand Americans.

The CCP's aggression also resulted directly or indirectly in the deaths of many tens of thousands of Americans. The PRC, not the Soviet Union, paid the blood price in the Korea War. But it was only the People's Liberation Army that had the mass, willingness to incur high casualties, and sufficient combat effectiveness to stalemate U.S. conventional military might.

In addition to Korea, the CCP conquered Tibet in 1950, which would lead to great tension with India after the failed Tibetan Uprising of 1959. Its support for North Vietnam made it possible for the North to continue that war.[10] Its belligerence toward Taiwan led to the Taiwan Strait Crises of 1954–1955 and 1958 and thus introduced the risk of escalation.

---

10 The PRC did actively support North Vietnam by providing a great number of PLA soldiers and other experts as well as a massive amount of supplies in Mao's "assist Vietnam and resist America" campaign from 1965 to 1970. By 1973, all PRC troops had been withdrawn from Indochina. The PRC presence was substantial. By March 1966, the PRC had over 180,000 troops in North Vietnam, or more than half of the size of the U.S. deployment in South Vietnam that year. The PRC allowed Soviet aid to transit its territory by rail, maintained the Ho Chi Minh trail, manned many antiaircraft artillery (AAA) sites—and AAA was deadly, claiming about 85 percent of the about 3,000 U.S. aircraft lost in Vietnam. The PLA also constructed offshore defensive works, laid naval mines, built and maintained pipelines, and provided infrastructure support to repair damaged bridges, rail lines, and roads. From September 1968, the PLA entered Laos, where it conducted similar functions. By August 1973, an estimated 1,715 PLA soldiers had been killed in Vietnam and 6,400 wounded. In Laos, 269 were killed and 1,200 wounded. See Xiaobing Li, *The Dragon in the Jungle: The Chinese Army in the Vietnam War* (New York: Oxford University Press, 2020), p. 3. It is now publicly known that the Soviets were manning the SA-2 Guideline Surface to Air missiles sites with an estimated 1,500 to 2,500 Soviets in North Vietnam from 1965. That number likely increased as the war continued. Li, *The Dragon in the Jungle*, p. 100.

The PRC's support for the Khmer Rouge contributed to the massacre of the Khmer people. What the Khmer Rouge did to the Cambodian people is beyond horrific. The Cambodians suffered under Pol Pot's Khmer Rouge democide (1975–1979), which still does not receive the attention it should. The Khmer Rouge killed an estimated 3 million Cambodians of a population of 7.5 million before the Vietnamese invasion in December 1978 and occupation of Cambodia from 1978 to 1988 ended it. The CCP made the Khmer Rouge mass killing possible.

I.A. Lenin Starts a Civil War in Western Civilization

In addition to the colossal burdens to the American people discussed, the costs are even greater as Lenin and the Bolsheviks also started a civil war in Western civilization. That war is ongoing and is played out on almost every post on X and most articles written over the last forty years. The Bolsheviks and their allies in Western Europe and the U.S. hated the societies in which they formulated their ideas, which allowed them to thrive, plan their seditious acts, and served as the launching pad for them to execute their revolution.

Their intent was to remake everything. What precisely they were attempting to create was not exactly clear: The Bolsheviks were brutal, cruel, organized, and ruthless, but they also could be supremely foolish, inchoate, naïve, and idealistic. The closest indicator to what they actually believed was War Communism—the tectonic shift from tsarist Russia to Communism. The Bolsheviks were really a fly-by-the-seat-of-pants organization regarding precisely what they were going to create. Lenin argued in *State and Revolution* (1917) that the state would "wither away" after the revolution.

Of course, remaking everything required destroying everything. The Bolsheviks were clear that their objectives required destroying history, social relationships, religion, and intellectual foundations so that individuals, whether Russian peasants in 1917 or schoolkids in Ohio or Oregon today, could be remade. Stripped of their past, their identity, and any understanding of their birthright bequeathed by previous generations, they could be reconstructed and replaced. That destruction necessarily included Western civilization because any understanding of it would checkmate Bolshevik designs. The Hundred Years' War against Communism is a war fought against the Soviet Union and the PRC, but it is also a civil war within the West.

The response to Lenin's civil war by those who would cherish and sustain Western civilization has never been strong enough. Too few in the West recognize that it is in a fight for their inheritance, for Western civilization. Again, that is by design. Popular culture, media, social media, and even AI are arrayed against it. In politics, Western countries' major political parties are no better. From the Democrats in the U.S., Labour in the UK, La République en Marche in France, and the Liberals in Canada, to Fine Gael and Fianna Fail in Ireland and the Christian Democrats in Germany and Italy, these parties either explicitly attack Western civilization or fail to defend it effectively or with any alacrity or vigor. In fact, they are parties captured by the Communists because their policies, responses, and activities are only within parameters set by the Communists. Post-Trump, the Republican Party may revert to its pre-Trump default position that was a party of tax cuts and genteel concession speeches.

The issue of immigration captures the civil war dividing lines like no other. The Communists want immigration by legal and illegal means to accelerate the destruction of the West and Western identities. In the context of the civil war, immigration is Lenin calling for replacements and reinforcements. And he is getting them in the numbers and with a rapidity that will ensure that West is destroyed. The same objectives and tactics are employed against the American spirit and political liberalism to annihilate them as well.

The supporters of Western civilization have not acted with the alacrity needed to defeat this civil war. The West needs to take a page from Lenin's book and wage political warfare more effectively than the neo-Bolsheviks today. Lenin has a lot to teach, even if the tuition is high.

Although it should never have come to this point, it has. Hence, the forces in support of Western civilization have the greatest civilization upon which to call. They need to act now. All denizens of the West need to decide on which side they are and whether their actions and words support their declaration. The victory over Communism beings with the renaissance of American identity and Western civilization described below.

II. Communism Is Illegitimate

Communism is illegitimate. The ideology has no right to impose its tyranny on any people or country. Victory in the fight against Communism begins with the recognition that it is a base, corrupting, dehumanizing, and illegitimate ideology. Nevertheless, Communists are successful at seizing power and maintaining their oppressive control. With feet of clay, this ideology has killed hundreds of millions of people and keeps a billion and a half people imprisoned in its iron cage. And it is not done yet. It seeks to imprison the American people.

The great power struggle with the CCP abroad and with Communism at home will define the twenty-first century. The U.S. objective is the same as in any of its previous titanic struggles the U.S. has fought: total victory. Total victory over Communism will require many steps, including understanding Leninism to comprehend the enemy's ideology. That permits the most fundamental recognition of its vulnerability: Communists within the U.S. are illegitimate because they are actively opposed to the Constitutional Republic that is the United States, and abroad they are because the CCP is an illegitimate regime. Developing strategies to prepare for the consequences of this illegitimacy, the certainty of conflict, is essential for American people to grasp and should be the key mission for the U.S. and allied governments and people of goodwill around the world, most importantly in China.

Recognizing the illegitimacy of the regime is the bedrock of a U.S. victory. Chinese Communism is a Western derivative, and the CCP is trapped because it is a colonial government. The result is that the PRC's Communism is fundamentally incoherent and vulnerable to strategies that would capitalize upon its divisions.

Communists are aggressive, ruthless, and rule by terror in no small measure because they know they are illegitimate. While they should never be underestimated—indeed, the twentieth century was defined by this struggle—they are vulnerable because their ideology, in theory and in application, is inhuman and dehumanizing because it rejects individuals as individuals, requiring instead that they are treated as a member of the collective. There is no individual identity for Communists. Moreover, Communism has inflicted a horrific blood price on peoples and civilizations from China to Cambodia, Angola to East Germany, from Russia to Spain. In that light, Americans and the American government must understand its threat, and once again defeat Communist ideology in this century, as Americans did in the last one.

In essence, as argued in chapter 3, the central issue is not what is Chinese about the CCP, but what is Communist about it. The answer is that most of it is Communist. Not much is Chinese. Communist ideology is inherently aggressive and thus the CCP believes it must defeat the U.S. Moreover, this polity has lasted, carried on the backs of the Chinese people since 1949, despite the grave injuries inflicted on them by Mao, the Gang of Four, and Deng. The CCP could not have survived without the prodigious help it received first from the Soviet Union and then from the United States and the liberal international order that Washington created, which permitted the PRC's prodigious growth.

The CCP is illegitimate for three major reasons. First, they were formed and nurtured by the Communist International, and its seizure of power in 1949 was made possible by U.S. vacillation and lack of support for the KMT and by Stalin's active support before and after the defeat of Japan. The CCP is a product of Soviet imperialism.

Second, as with the other poisonous fruits of the Bolshevik Revolution, the CCP is illegitimate because it seeks to sustain the tyranny of the odious and dehumanizing ideology of Leninism on the Chinese people anchored on the lie detailed in chapter 2 that Leninism possesses a "scientific" understanding of society. The dependence upon this imported Western ideology means that the CCP's ideology of Leninism, and its Chinese idioms—Maoism, Deng's "Socialism with Chinese Characteristics," and most recently "Xi Jinping Thought on Socialism with Chinese Characteristics for a New Era"—are illegitimate for China.

Think of this ideology for what it is: the last surviving form of Western colonialism. Despite the CCP's efforts, it cannot hide the fact that it is the product of this. The "Century of Humiliation," which defined Western imperialism in China from the First Opium War (1839–1842) to the CCP's victory (1949), has not ended. More accurately, given the CCP's colonial origins, China soon will realize its second century of humiliation.

This causes a legitimation crisis in the PRC that provides justification for the Chinese people to work to overthrow the CCP. Its fall would permit China to evolve into a polity that is in accord with the historical political culture of China. As a product of Western intellectual thought—Marx, Engels, Lenin, Trotsky, and Bogdanov—the CCP lacks even the legitimacy of the Qing Dynasty (1644–1911/1912), who were foreign, Manchu rather than Han, but who ruled successfully in accord with China's dynastic political traditions.

Third, the CCP is illegitimate because of its abhorrent and contemptible leadership, which continues today under Xi's misrule. Evil men rise to the top in Leninist regimes. Its odious rulers from Mao to Xi have forced China to endure seventy years of tyranny and has led to many tens of millions killed by the CCP. The widespread contempt for the CCP by the Chinese people and their recognition that the regime rules for itself, not for the people, is a final verdict on the regime.

II.A. Political Warfare Strategy Needed to Exploit the CCP's Illegitimacy

The political incoherence of the CCP is a profound vulnerability that the U.S. should exploit by waging political warfare against the regime. While political warfare in the U.S. is in purview of the Intelligence Community and Department of State, other actors could assist, including academics, journalists, think tanks, and non-governmental organizations (NGOs) in the U.S. and around the world. Hence, while political warfare is not one of the principal missions of the Department of War, senior civilian leadership should consider how War Department policy might contribute and support political warfare advanced by other components of the U.S. government.

For example, the U.S. could employ political warfare campaigns that deny the legitimacy of the PRC and evaluate policy options regarding how the U.S. may pressure the CCP. The utility of a political warfare campaign that supported the right and necessity of the Chinese people to overthrow it, so that it may be replaced by a true form of Chinese polity, would be useful. It might ensure that the U.S. wins this cold war with the CCP without it escalating to kinetic conflict.

Of course, the cold war with the CCP is multifaceted and fought in all domains—economic, diplomatic, military, intelligence, cyber, technological, space—and thus far short of kinetic war. It is important to consider the similarities between this cold war and the one with the Soviet Union. The similarities are myriad but the most important is that Communism is the cause of both. The motivation for aggression remains the same: the Communist ideology of the Soviet Union in the past and of the CCP today.

In essence, in the current cold war with the CCP, the U.S. is confronting the last gasp of Soviet ideology. The CCP has failed to become Chinese after more than seventy years in power. As I have argued, the success of Soviet imperialism in creating and sustaining the CCP means that the CCP is illegitimate. The pull of Western ideology—Communism—remains too great for the Party to overcome because Communist thought is inherently Western. Only by removing the fetishization of Western ideological constructs can a Chinese identity once again come to the fore. Only then may the Chinese step forward with civilizational confidence to realize a Chinese polity and society free from a foundational Western influence that is alien to Chinese civilization.

Because the CCP is the product of Soviet imperialism through the Comintern, the powerful legacy of the Soviet Communist Party remains in the CCP. It is a profoundly incongruous fact that the CCP, the product of Soviet imperialism, rules the people of China. Given their august civilization, the Chinese naturally possess a profound sense of pride in their civilization and its accomplishments and perceive themselves to occupy a unique place in the world. They have excelled in every aspect, including literature, philosophy, art, religion, and technology. Notable as well is the sheer size of the population, which is almost an order of magnitude more than the population of the Soviet Union during the Cold War.

This introduces a tremendous vulnerability for the CCP because its ideology is anchored and remains dependent upon a Western ideology, Leninism, which means that their worldview attempts to impose a Western ideology upon Chinese civilization. A dangerous civilizational incoherence and keen tension between the CCP and the Chinese people is the result. In sum, the CCP brutally and tyrannically oppresses their people. They have done so since they came to power in 1949 and will continue to do so as long as they remain in power.

Every political party, and every state, defines the key question of "who are we." The CCP's answer to this fundamental question is embarrassing. The CCP's founding fathers are Marx and Engels, as interpreted, influenced, and forged by Lenin and Stalin, through the idiom of Maoism and now "Xi Jinping Thought on Socialism with Chinese Characteristics for a New Era." Thus, Germans, Russians, and Georgians are the founding fathers and guiding influences of the CCP.

In the PRC today, the CCP faces the paradox of laboring consistently to hijack Chinese civilization to provide its legitimacy and popular support. But as it does so, the CCP reveals its illegitimacy to rule China and shows that it fetters Chinese civilization with a Western ideology and worldview. That is one of the CCP's Achilles' heels and must be at the centerpiece of Chinese efforts to overthrow the CCP.

A second political warfare message is to explore and publicize why the CCP leadership is wealthy.[11] This is a paradox for Communists and Communist governments, and this should be employed against the CCP. The U.S., its allies, and other states must find their wealth. This includes Xi as the General Secretary of the CCP, and senior leadership officials of the Central Committee, the Politburo, the Politburo Standing Committee, and regional Party Secretaries.

The answers to these investigations are certain to be startling and will capture the corrupt nature of the CCP.[12] Comprehending the wealth of the CCP leadership underscores that the CCP rules China, but it is not the legitimate government of China. To call attention to the tyrannical and corrupt nature of CCP leaders, states can employ their resources to reveal

---

11 See Paul Berkowitz and Bradley A. Thayer, Paul Berkowitz and Bradley A. Thayer, "Intelligence Community's Report on Wealth and Corruption of China's Rulers Is Overdue," *Washington Times*, October 8, 2024. At: <https://www.washingtontimes.com/news/2024/oct/8/intelligence-communitys-report-on-wealth-and-corru/>; Berkowitz and Thayer, "Key Report Helps Reveal the Wealth and Corruption of the CCP," *Sunday Guardian*, June 9, 2024. At: <https://sundayguardianlive.com/investigation/key-report-helps-to-reveal-the-wealth-and-corruption-of-the-ccp>; and Berkowitz and Thayer, "Publicize the Wealth and Corruption of the CCP Leadership," *Warroom*, March 25, 2024. At: <https://warroom.org/publicize-the-wealth-and-corruption-of-the-ccp-leadership/>. All accessed July 15, 2025.

12 The reports thus far generated in 2025 by the Congressional Research Service and by the Intelligence Community are insufficient. The fiscal year 2026 National Defense Authorization Act has tasked the Intelligence Community with again generating a report on the wealth of the leadership of the CCP, including personal wealth, financial holdings, and business interests of Xi and all member of the seven-man Politburo Standing Committee. See Bill Gertz, "Inside the Ring," *Washington Times*, December 10, 2025. At: <https://www.washingtontimes.com/news/2025/dec/10/inside-ring-trump-ends-controls-nvidia-chips-doj-says-boost-chinas/>. Accessed December 11, 2025.

the details of the corruption to the Chinese people and the world. This may be accomplished by employing their intelligence communities on this topic. Journalists also may find the topic worthy of investigation. Media, perhaps most importantly social media, may highlight the CCP's wealth and corruption to publicize and inform global populations.

Worldwide investigation into the wealth and corruption of the CCP leadership will reveal the outlines of that base regime. No doubt, it will find that the CCP's leaders are billionaires with untold wealth parked in banks and investments in Dubai, Switzerland, New York, Los Angeles, San Francisco, London, Singapore, and countless other locations. These secret wealth and investments in the U.S. might well exceed even those of Saudi Arabia, Kuwait, or the United Arab Emirates (UAE). While that has been long suspected, the revelation of the facts will be important for the Chinese people and the world to know. Knowing how many billions that Xi, his family, associates, and Party comrades have in overseas banks, properties, and other assets is significant to reveal the true corrupt nature of the CCP leadership, with specific amounts and locations documented. That will allow the victims of the CCP to move to seize those assets. Equally, it will allow the Chinese people and the world to see proof of the CCP's gross misrule and abuse of the country and the Chinese people. These actions may spark the events that lead to their overthrow.

Third, academics, journalists, and think tanks might consider research analyzing the creation of a Chinese government in exile to oppose the misrule of the CCP—a "Committee on Chinese Civilization and Governance." This committee might have several aims but one clearly would be to govern and address the needs of Chinese citizens while furthering the delegitimation of the CCP.[13] The CCP as an illegitimate political entity but with the

13 This might be accomplished by several international or domestic actors. It is useful to consider which actor, or coalition, would be the most effective in advancing this objective.

power of a peer competitor is unpredictable and unstable and the United States must prepare for this.

In the three-quarters of a century of its tyranny over the people of China, the CCP has never been held to account. It has never been forced to pay for its myriad crimes against humanity and human rights abuses against the Chinese people and those inflicted upon the global population through its support for illegitimate regimes, the mass murder of the Khmer Rouge or genocide against the Muslim peoples of Xinjiang, or by facilitating the spread of pandemics like Covid-19, or by promoting the horrors of drug addiction and millions of American deaths through fentanyl and other narcotics.

To hold the CCP to account, there might be the creation of a human rights tribunal, termed the Chinese People's Human Rights Tribunal (CPHRT), to document the CCP's abuses against the Chinese people and global community.[14] Documenting human rights violations would be accomplished through witness and other testimonies to provide evidence against the CCP's abuses while these abuses remain in living memory. The tribunal would be independent of any government or existing human rights organization. As a nongovernmental tribunal, it would be able to commence the documentation for an accounting of the CCP's human rights abuses.

This is important to accomplish even if the tribunal does not employ the force of international law. Its labors would be valuable because they would start the accounting and publicizing of the CCP's crimes. In turn, these steps are the foundation for changing how states, intergovernmental organizations like the United Nations, and Non-Governmental Organizations like Human Rights Watch, consider the legitimacy of the

14 Jianli Yang and I first advanced the idea of the CPHRT in Jianli Yang and Bradley A. Thayer, "The Chinese Communist Party Should Be Held Accountable for its Crimes," *National Review*, June 4, 2023. At: <https://www.nationalreview.com/2023/06/the-chinese-communist-party-should-be-held-accountable-for-its-crimes/>. Accessed December 10, 2025.

CCP. The tribunal could serve as the foundation to alter the global perception of the CCP so that it is revealed to be what it is—an illegitimate regime that has grossly abused human rights. The tribunal would be important for the Chinese people. It would convey global support in their struggles against the Party.

Equally, for the international community, it would signal to the CCP that countries and people around the world do not accept its legitimacy because of the human rights violations it has inflicted upon the Chinese people. The tribunal's objective would be to serve as a single source for the panoply of the CCP's crimes directed against the Chinese people, the Chinese diaspora, Party members, and the global community.[15] That would be a fulsome start to holding the CCP accountable for its crimes against humanity.

---

15 These crimes would fall into three broad tranches. The first tranche is that the tribunal would examine the historical record of the CCP's human rights abuses to identify what occurred with historical accuracy and to publicize the CCP's decision-making regarding these acts and the individuals responsible for these abuses, many of whom are still alive. This would include investigations into the human rights disasters caused by the Chinese Civil War and after the CCP came to power in 1949. The tribunal would conduct a year-by-year examination of the CCP's human rights record.

The second tranche is that the tribunal would document and hold the CCP to account for its crimes against other states. This would include support for the tyranny of North Korea, its intervention in the Korea War on behalf of Pyongyang, the conquest of Tibet and the suppression of the Tibetan population, violations of India's borders in 1962, against Vietnam in the seizure from South Vietnam of all of the Paracel Islands, the genocide of the Khmer Rouge in Cambodia, the violation of the 1984 PRC-UK agreement on Hong Kong, and repeated bellicose measures directed at Taiwan.

The third tranche is that the contemporary human rights record must be investigated, documented, and publicized. The present ubiquitous human rights violations against the Chinese people, including ethnic and religious minorities, Tibetans, and Muslims in Xinjiang, must be recorded and charges brought against the CCP.

II.B. The Ubiquity of Aggression: Always on the Offensive

Understanding Communism requires that the American people and U.S. national security planners prepare for war. The aggression of Communists, whether within the U.S. or the CCP, is ubiquitous and maximal, as required by Leninism. It is inexorable that the CCP has struggled against the U.S., is fighting against the U.S., and will do so until either it or the U.S. is defeated. In essence, Americans must recognize that they are truly, for the first time since the Cold War, in an existential fight for their national survival. The U.S. faces the certainty of aggression waged by political warfare. This form of warfare is occurring today. In addition, the risk of kinetic war is always present.

As explained in chapter 2 in the discussion of the core ideas of Leninism, the ideology possesses an urgency and immediacy for action *à outrance*. Always favoring the offense, Lenin forged the hyper-aggressive Communist Party that the world came to know. Like Lenin's party, the CCP has waged metaphorical and actual warfare on the Chinese people, the American people, and those of the world.

Leninists are belligerent. They want to push History—in the Hegelian sense—along to cause the revolution in spite of Marx and Engels' identification of the necessary stages of class conflict. Leninists, including Xi, cannot accept other ideologies and are required to confront and defeat them. Fundamentally, they must be aggressive because they are illegitimate forms of government. They must always have internal and external enemies to motivate their believers and sustain and justify their totalitarian grip on power. For Communists, there has been a perpetual, restless aggression against the West since 1917.

The U.S. needs to take a forceful, multifaceted response to target the CCP directly.[16] This will include the rollback of the PRC's gains in the South China Sea, and the defeat of the PRC in its attempts to seize other territory, such as of the Philippines at Sabina Shoal, Second Thomas Shoal,

16 Han and Thayer, *Understanding the China Threat*, pp. 163–186.

and elsewhere. The U.S. and its allies should be prepared to evict the PLA from facilities they have created in other countries like Djibouti, or Ream, Cambodia. Those are important and necessary measures to place Beijing on the strategic back foot.

But the center of gravity that the U.S. must attack is the CCP itself to ensure that the Party, the Chinese people, and all global audiences know that it is illegitimate and that the U.S.—collaborating with the Chinese people and allies and partners—is working to expel it from power. This requires employing all the arrows in the U.S. quiver, including a focus on political warfare that the U.S. did well during much of the Cold War, like the Active Measures Working Group, but has allowed to atrophy in the post-Cold War years.

This book has stressed that there are two fronts in this war—the domestic and international—but it is one fight. They are mutually reinforcing and must be fought through a coordinated response. Communism is present at home in the Democratic Party, its donors, base, law firms, media, think tanks, and Political Action Committees (PACs), who have penetrated almost every aspect of American life from education to popular culture to media, and labor to destroy it. Abroad, Communism is the CCP's ideology and thus explains the PRC's prodigious efforts to overthrow the U.S. position in the world and American way of life. Ruefully, U.S. trade, investment, and technology transfer aid the growth of the PRC, and make a successful NEP more likely. In turn, that makes the PRC a greater military threat to the U.S. and its allies but also permits it to support the Democrats' front organizations like Antifa.

The struggle against Antifa is a fight against Communism. Within the U.S., the government must target Antifa as the Trump administration is through its Executive Orders in September 2025, designating Antifa as a domestic terrorist organization, and the State Department's designation in October 2025 that Antifa-Ost, and three other Antifa organizations, were foreign terrorist organizations. Investigation of Antifa's direction, organization, funding, and leadership likely will reveal that Antifa is sponsored by major Democratic donors, politicians, media, businesses, and PACs, but it also is sponsored by the PRC through Beijing's intelligence community, front organizations, and indirect support for Democratic PACs and donors.

This fight allows the Trump administration to target in a unified manner both of these Communist threats and so remove the greatest danger to the security of the American people. Now is the time for the American people to demand the end of the Communist threat through a whole of government and whole of society response.

The continuation of bold action against Antifa must be joined by equally necessary steps against the PRC. The tranches of action against the PRC are to demonstrate connection between PRC front organizations and Antifa and related groups; reduce trade with the PRC; end of direct and indirect investment in the PRC; prohibit technology transfer; declare the PRC to be a state sponsor of terrorism within the United States; and hold the CCP accountable for the Covid-19 pandemic and the chemical warfare attacks against Americans through narcotics including fentanyl and other synthetic opioids.

Trump's December 2025 declaration of fentanyl as a Weapon of Mass Destruction (WMD) was an important step forward. As the PRC produces the precursor chemicals and aids in their transport to the Western Hemisphere where they are made into fentanyl, the PRC is contributing to a WMD attack against the American people and homeland.

III. Americans Fought Communism Better in the Past: Why There Is Great Variation in the Ability of the U.S. to Meet the Soviet versus PRC Threat

The ability of the U.S. to defeat Communism has undergone significant variation from the Cold War until the present. In the Cold War, the U.S. comprehended the threat of Communism at home and abroad and its success in that conflict provides important lessons for Americans and the U.S. government today. Two historical lessons are salient in this context.

First, the Cold War was fought by a generation that had direct experience in World War II and grasped the ideological dimensions of conflict. The ideological element of the Cold War was well understood, as was the threat that Communism posed to the free world. The danger of Communism was taught in schools, universities, in Joint Professional Military Education (JPME), and in popular culture from television, to magazines, to film. The contrast between freedom and tyranny was well understood, taught, and reinforced by America's two major political parties, educational system, major media, and popular culture.

Second, the overt nature of the Soviet Union's belligerence to the U.S. was clear. Soviet leaders' statements and hostility to the U.S. and its allies were commonplace. The Soviets aggressively recruited Americans to spy for them and, during the Cold War, there were Soviet spies caught in the U.S. or in allied countries. Two significant wars, in Korea and Vietnam, were fought with Soviet proxies; there were major nuclear crises in 1962 and 1973; and flashpoints in Berlin, Cuba, the Middle East, and in the Third World were almost constant reminders of the Soviet threat for the national security community and the American public.

In sum, the U.S. national security decision-makers and the American people knew the nature of the Leninist threat from the Soviet Union because they faced it every day, without end, in a bitter and dangerous Cold War.

The cold war against the PRC is very different. Since the end of the Cold War against the Soviet Union, the American people and U.S. national security decision-makers and analysts have largely lost the understanding of the danger of Communism to U.S. national security. While that has been positively addressed during the Trump administrations, the legacy of underestimating the PRC threat retains an impact.

This cold war is significantly unlike the previous one for four major reasons. The first is structural—the geography is very different. The geography of the confrontation is radically altered. While this cold war, as with the last, is fought globally, the U.S. does not face the PLA on a border, as NATO and the Warsaw Pact did along the Central Front. There is no divided Berlin that was always simmering when it was not the center of superpower crises. The closest to this today is the tension and security competition on the Indo-Chinese border and Taiwan. Taiwan and the PRC's expansion in the East and South China Seas are primarily the purview of the sea services and Air Force, and relatively isolated in contrast to Cold War Berlin or the Korean De-Militarized Zone (DMZ), and the PRC's expansion was relatively gradual in contrast to Soviet expansion and so did not attract the same attention from global media.

The second reason is also structural. The distribution of power is different. The Soviet Union and the U.S. were clearly the dominant military powers in 1946. While the U.S. was stronger and the Soviets needed to recover from the devastation of the war, they were roughly equivalent military powers on land, and by the late 1960s or early 1970s were so in the nuclear balance.

However, the distribution of power was radically different with the PRC. The U.S. was a military superpower without question and without peer once the Soviet Union fell in 1991. At that time, the PRC represented less than 2 percent of world GDP, with a military focused upon guerrilla warfare. Thirty years later, the PRC was about 19 percent of world GDP and a formidable military power. That rapid change in the distribution of power was almost without precedent in international politics.[17] In sum, the PRC had the ideological intent to fight the U.S. but not the capabilities.

Now the PRC has the intent and the capabilities. The U.S., and the West more broadly, made the PRC's rapid rise possible through the policy of engagement. Engagement permitted Western investment and manufacturing to occur in the PRC, while permitting widespread education of PRC

17 Arguably it was without precedent as the closest comparisons, the rise of the U.S., Japan, and Prussia/Germany in the nineteenth century all occurred within a multipolar distribution of power.

students in the West, as well as technology transfer and scientific transfer to the PRC. Fundamentally, the U.S. funded and supported the rise of the PRC from a poor, agrarian state to peer competitor.[18]

Third, such a rapid change should have generated balancing against the PRC but did not because of the PRC's political warfare strategy. Under Deng's leadership, the PRC employed a brilliant political warfare strategy to minimize its perception of a threat. Its strategy since Deng has been supremely successful, in part because of the PRC's expertise at threat deflation.[19] For decades, and even today, the U.S. threat deflated—that is, it did not perceive the reality of the PRC's danger to U.S. national security but rather consistently, year after year, discounted it in the face of ample evidence to the contrary. Threat deflation undermines any urgency to address the PRC's ambition and growth because of its inherent bias that the PRC does not pose a significant threat to the U.S. The effectiveness of the PRC's political warfare strategy, which deliberately minimizes the nature and imminency of the PRC's intent to overthrow the U.S.'s position in world politics and its ability to defend its national interests, which includes extending deterrence to its allies, means the U.S. has a major task to confront.

Deng witnessed the Soviet Union's disastrous efforts at political and economic reforms under General Secretary Andropov and then Gorbachev that led to abandonment of its empire shortly before its complete collapse. Deng was determined that this would never happen to the CCP. At the same time, the U.S. was emboldened by its victory, and furthering democratic regime change beyond Europe. The PRC remained a Communist state that appeared vulnerable to regime change, as the Tiananmen Square massacre had revealed. To save the CCP, Deng employed threat deflation while instituting a Leninist NEP to permit economic investment and manufacturing

18 See Fanell and Thayer, *Embracing Communist China*, pp. 15–56.

19 Fanell and Thayer, *Embracing Communist China*, pp. 16–18.

and thus, fundamentally, to make the U.S. a partner of the CCP. This was the foundation of the catastrophic policy of engagement with the PRC.

The PRC could host manufacturing at very low labor costs, with no labor unrest and no regulation—in essence, only corruption was an additional cost to manufacturing. Japanese, South Korean, and U.S. manufacturers poured into the PRC. In turn, Deng employed that investment to further technology transfer to assist the PRC's manufacturing, and invested in Western elites—universities, media, think tanks, politicians and political parties—to ensure they had a stake in the PRC's prosperity and would ensure threat deflation as the PRC grew, year by year, and its military power became significant, and then formidable. In a tremendous political warfare victory for the CCP, the pernicious twins of engagement and threat deflation yielded the inability of the U.S. to meet the threat. Hence, the effectiveness of the PRC's political warfare strategy is a major and stark difference between the cold wars.

Fourth, informed by engagement and threat deflation, the understanding of the ideology of Communism has greatly diminished.[20] The comprehension of that ideology is essential to understand the PRC, the principal national security threat the U.S. faces. As noted, the study of the ideology was ubiquitous during the Cold War with the Soviet Union. Today, it is largely absent from undergraduate and graduate international relations curricula and JPME. Consequently, decision-makers and analysts may miss or discount the important role of Communist ideology. At root, the U.S. national security community dropped its guard, to the great benefit of its enemy, when it stopped studying Communist ideology. By so doing, it lost great insight into the enemy's strategy and objectives.

There is a strong inclination in U.S. strategic thought to perceive international politics through an optimistic lens. U.S. history of the twentieth century introduced a pattern: First, the great power or peer competitive

20 See Fanell and Thayer, *Embracing Communist China*, pp. 84–87.

threat is defeated, proving U.S. superiority, which, in turn, permits a relaxation and even an end to great power security concerns—another "End of History" jubilation as the world is on the path to perpetual peace. Until that expectation of peace is corrected, the U.S. remains acutely vulnerable to manipulation through threat deflation. The costs of ignoring the rise of a peer are monumental. Yet, once again the U.S. confronts the challenge of having to defeat a nuclear peer competitor in a new cold war with all of the risks this entails for the American people.

The PRC was far more effective at penetrating Western societies than was the Soviet Union. Correcting the U.S. response is clearly multifaceted. It requires that once again the U.S. emphasize in JPME the importance of Communism, from Lenin to Xi, so that Americans understand one of the fundamental causes of the threat from the PRC.

The history of the twentieth and twenty-first centuries has been a Hundred Years' War against Communism and that must be inculcated and taught to Americans in their schools and universities. It must be taught to the Intelligence Community and Departments of State and War civilian and military workforces so that they understand the enemy and develop countermeasures, and exploit vulnerabilities to defeat the PRC.

To understand the CCP, its origins, behavior, and objectives, it is necessary to comprehend the core ideas of Leninism and its history. This ideology and its intellectual history must be familiar to the American people and to the Departments of State and War civilian and military workforces so that they may comprehend the nature and scale of the CCP threat. The Sino-American struggle is the major international conflict of this century, and one that the U.S. might lose if it does not comprehend Leninism. As with the Cold War with the Soviet Union, the conflict is to be found in every realm of international politics: diplomacy, economics, ideology, intelligence and covert action, lunar and planetary exploration, military, science and technology, popular culture, and athletic competition. But Communist ideology is the foundation of the competition.

The U.S. has been slow to recognize the danger it confronts. This was in large part because the Communists had penetrated the U.S. educational system, media, civil society, and Democratic Party. It is cold comfort to acknowledge that planning current U.S. strategy incurs the costs of decades of national security decision-makers' and analysts' insouciance to the threat. The threat deflation that the U.S. incurred narrowed the aperture of possible strategic options while increasing the necessity and urgency of the response. The Hundred Years' War against Communism was never seen to be either long or a war because the U.S. national security community does not respond well to ideological threats until they become potent military threats, as in the case of the Germans, Italians, and Japanese in World War II, the PRC today, or in the case of Islamic fundamentalist ideology, as with the 9/11 attacks.

Only in one case did the U.S. act with dispatch. It did respond to the Soviet Union early in the Cold War, certainly by Stalin's February 1946 address, because the Soviet Union had declared political war on the U.S. and was a potential hegemon on the European continent with formidable conventional power in place in Europe, in China, and in Iran with the Soviet occupation of Iranian Azerbaijan. The U.S. responded with dispatch because the hegemonic threat was clear and because U.S. national security leadership saw the threat and balanced it effectively.

The ideological cause of the threat is usually absent from the threat calculus and so the U.S. is vulnerable to the enemy's political warfare strategy of threat deflation. Given that the U.S. has struggled mightily against two Communist foes, understanding the ideology of Communism is necessary. Given the Hundred Years' War fought against Communism, it reveals a great flaw in U.S. strategic thought that the ideology still is not well understood by most U.S. national security decision-makers and the American people.

Understanding the ideology of the foe matters and is consequential in all wars, hot or cold. The ideology of the PRC explains its intention to defeat U.S. national security interests globally and why Beijing targets the

U.S. population. In the decades after the Cold War, U.S. officials dismissed the PRC's Communist ideology as trite and platitudinous, a legacy of the past that remained of diminishing utility while the PRC became a capitalist state, on its path toward becoming a democracy. They believed the CCP would disappear as an impactful force in time, leaving only a rump Party to provide a bridge from the PRC's Communist past to a democratic future.

That was a Western conceit, and a calamitous strategic mistake. It helped the PRC's strategy of threat deflation. Far from abandoning its Communist ideology, the PRC has always sustained it and at present is strengthening adherence to it under the current guise of Xi Jinping Thought. The PRC's Communist ideology has been and remains essential for comprehending its behavior.

Because few in the U.S. national security community took Communism seriously, there was considerable elite thought that the PRC would be positively transformed through the coterie of engagement policies. This assumption was based on the belief that the CCP's ideology was not credible by the metric of the "End of History" and was not really believed by the CCP leadership, who it was asserted were more interested in capitalism and, despite a lagging effect, it would result in greater freedom for the Chinese people.

Accordingly, Americans should have the same familiarity with the CCP's ideology and the PLA's doctrine as with Soviet Communism during the Cold War. The U.S. national security community, especially within the Department of War and the Intelligence Community, must understand the CCP's priorities for investment, research, and force structure development, and the missions and options that force structure would support. During the Cold War, the U.S. national security community intensively studied Soviet doctrine to discern where the Soviets were investing, what they were developing, and the force structure they were creating and the missions that force structure could support. Information about this should be brought into the public sphere to inform the debate regarding the PRC's bellicosity and capabilities for aggression.

Hence, senior civilian and military national security decision-makers—and all Americans—may profit from understanding Leninist thought, how Stalin contributed to that canon, and how Mao derived his ideology from the Bolsheviks and their agents and enforcers in the Comintern. Briefings regarding why Communism is illegitimate, the core ideas of its major thinkers, its history, how the ideology drives conflict with Western states, and why the CCP believes that History is on its side, should be provided regularly so that leadership and all Americans understand the ideological origins of the current cold war with the CCP.

When the sources of conflict due to the CCP's Communist ideology are understood, and that the CCP is at war with the U.S., then the American people and senior national security decision-makers may understand that the CCP is inherently aggressive. Senior officials and analysts must realize the value of political warfare for the CCP—that is, from the CCP's perspective, war is far more than kinetic. Anterior to kinetic war is political warfare, including the united front which is so well employed by the CCP.

Therefore, the CCP's ideology drives the new cold war and neo-Bolshevik progressivism within the U.S. to attack American identity. It could not be otherwise—that is, for ideological reasons, the CCP must confront and defeat the U.S. as Communists labor within America to accomplish the same end. Not taking Leninism seriously was and remains a profound and possibly fatal mistake. The belief that the PRC's increased wealth or engagement with the West would cure the CCP of Communism was a major misunderstanding of Communist ideology. When Americans view the last century through the Leninist lens, they will understand why Communist ideology will always trump economic growth and why control over the Chinese people will always be valued, as in Hong Kong, over economic prosperity, or tolerance of "two systems." Within U.S. borders, Communists will always work to defeat the U.S. There can be no compromise with them.

Americans, including senior national security civilian and military leadership, must recognize that there can be no accommodation with the

Communists. The U.S. must fight to win the cold war but must comprehend that domestic Communists or the CCP will not end their struggle until they are either defeated or victorious. That is the stark and necessary truth.

However, the great virtue of comprehending the foe's ideology is that Americans can understand its motivation for conflict and grasp how U.S. strategy must plan for the difficult task of defeating the CCP. The CCP will not evolve into a more moderate party or even into a democracy. That is not how Leninism works. This is unlikely in any case because of the illegitimacy of the regime and its need to cling to Leninism for its hold on power. It certainly will not do so as long as Xi is in power because of the emphasis he places upon ideology to advance his power as the "great leader" who will proclaim how Communism explains what the Party must do. Ideology also legitimizes the PRC's power. It is a sharp instrument that he employs to police his Party. Finally, to the CCP's satisfaction at least, Communist ideology legitimizes their rule of the Chinese people and their employment of coercion to control the populace.

IV. The CCP Is a Western Import, Not Part of Han Civilization

I have argued that the CCP, as a Leninist party, is the product of Soviet imperialism and so is the one of the last remaining colonial governments in existence. It is a Western import that has no legitimacy and is divorced from the greatest of the Chinese people and of Han civilization. Xi prominently provides examples of his lack of civilizational confidence. When Xi speaks of the influences on his life, he writes of Johann Wolfgang von Goethe's poetry and prose, not Han civilization literary masters. Xi was the son of Communist luminary Xi Zhongxun, who was once head of the CCP's propaganda department, but who was disgraced twice, first when he fell from power in 1962 and then later, with greater consequence for this family, during the Cultural Revolution. In 1968, the younger Xi was sent to work in Liangjiahe, a miserably poor mountain village in northern Shaanxi. Allegedly, he was lent a copy of Goethe's *Faust*, which he told German Chancellor Angela Merkel that he read again and again, knowing it by heart. Xi's endorsement is certainly informed by flattery but equally telling is that his inspiration and enchantment stemmed from the Western canon.

This is in direct opposition to Xi's and the Party's public proclamations about the greatness of Han civilization. At the same time and at a personal level, his daughter, Xi Mingze, reportedly using the alias Qu Chuchen, has lived in the United States for the last ten years. Purportedly, she has studied in the United States—Harvard University is often mentioned. To the great embarrassment of the General Secretary of the CCP and the Party itself, his daughter chooses to live in the United States, China's great adversary, enjoying Western civilization while evidently rejecting Communist rule in her homeland. His Party rivals and loyal cadres must have doubts about Xi's legitimacy since he cannot control his family and prevent it from humiliating the Party and underscoring the attractiveness of Western civilization. Other reports have Xi's daughter marrying Lu Hongfeng, who also studied and lived in the U.S. and returned to the PRC in 2021.

Despite the attractiveness of Western civilization to his family, as well as to himself, Xi frequently refers to the greatness of Han civilization. One of his best summations he provided at a CCP Politburo group study session in 2020:

> Our country has a million years of human history, 10,000 years of cultural history and more than 5,000 years of civilization [*sic*] history. The latest archaeological results show that China is the hometown of oriental mankind, and is tied with Africa as the first place where mankind originated; the Beijing apes invented the use of artificial fire 500,000 years ago, one of the first in the world; as early as 10,000 years ago, our ancestors planted millet and rice, and yet the origin of agriculture is tied with West Africa and North Africa as the first; China's inventions and discoveries in musical

> instruments, canoes, irrigation facilities, astronomy, etc., are also the first or among the earliest in the world.
>
> Our country was a world leader in the development of ancient civilizations during the neolithic, Bronze, and Iron Ages.
>
> Chinese civilization is the only civilization in the world that has continued uninterrupted since ancient times.
>
> The ancient Chinese agricultural technology, the "Four Great Inventions" [these refer to paper, painting, gunpowder, and the compass], as well as lacquer ware, silk, porcelain, iron and steel-making technology, the county system, and the imperial examination system are distinctive and original in the history of world civilization.[21]

This text is the perfect example of Xi's employment of the greatness of Han civilization while simultaneously identifying why this employment will fail so long as China is ruled by an imported Western ideology. Additionally, Xi's ignorance of human evolution is notable for its gross misunderstanding—rejecting the "out of Africa" origin of humanity for a dual genesis of humanity. It permits Xi to reject the almost universally recognized "out of Africa" thesis for human origins and dissemination and so serves to underscore the solipsism and absurdity of Xi's and the CCP's worldview.

In this version of history, the "century of humiliation" from the First Opium War to the CCP's victory in 1949 was a horrible aberration. Now, under the CCP and Xi in particular, the PRC is poised to regain the position it had enjoyed. This conveys the historical inevitability about the PRC's emergence as a superpower and its inevitable victory over the U.S. The

21 Annabelle Timsit, "Read Xi Jinping's Full Speech from the 100th Anniversary of the Communist Party," *Quartz*, July 1, 2021. At: <https://qz.com/2028306/xi-jinping-speech-transcript-for-the-ccps-100th-anniversary/>. Accessed September 13, 2025.

narrative that the CCP and Xi advance is significant because it informs the world how they perceive themselves and expect to be perceived—as an eternal hegemonic power and acknowledged as such by all other states—what they seek to create, and that they will hide their power and aggression in the mantle of legitimacy, but this actually reveals their insecurities and self-doubts.

When considering Xi's position in historical perspective, there is a relevant insight from Sir Nevile Henderson's memoir of his time as British ambassador to Nazi Germany from 1937 until the outbreak of the war in 1939.[22] Henderson demonstrated acuity in his assessment of Hitler's deep insecurity, which he argued had a major effect upon his foreign policy decision-making. In Hitler's characterization of himself, like Xi's, it was always that Germany was maltreated and abused and yet, at the same time, a supremely powerful, unstoppable country, whom Destiny had chosen to define the future.

In Henderson's reflection of his time as the British ambassador to Nazi Germany, he wrote that Prime Minister Neville Chamberlain "so aptly and feelingly described the 'sickening technique' of Hitlerism. It was always poor little Germany, which was being ill-treated."[23] At the same time, "Hitler was always preaching to Germans that they should forget their inferiority complex, which is so often attributed to them [Germans]. I used to ask my Nazi friends how they combined Hitler's doctrine of the superiority of Germans over all other races with this habit of describing Germany as the 'poor little downtrodden victim' of unscrupulous neighbors."[24] Henderson remarked that "it would revolt me to hear my own country so alluded to." In reply, "One, possibly more perspicacious

22 NB: Henderson's first name was indeed spelled Nevile rather than Neville, which was the spelling of the first name of the Prime Minister he served at this pivotal time.

23 Sir Nevile Henderson, *Failure of a Mission: Berlin 1937–1939* (New York: G.P. Putnam's Sons, 1940), p. 184.

24 Henderson, *Failure of a Mission*, p. 184.

than the others, remarked to me that Hitler's excessive insistence on the point of the Germany inferiority complex only meant that he still had it himself."[25] Henderson reasonably concludes: "He was probably right."[26]

While the differences between Xi and Hitler are great and manifold, in this instance they share a common tie. Whatever Hitler's motivations, he did advance the nearly paradoxical point that the Germans are superior and yet everywhere downtrodden. Xi's message is the same. Xi has a sense of inferiority, as he constantly informs the Chinese people that they are great under the CCP and yet always have been taken advantage of by Europeans, Manchus, Mongols, Japanese, and Americans.

That reveals a great insecurity in Xi's, the Party's, and the Han's conception of China—certainly powerful, but not powerful enough, and indeed, not good enough to supplant the West, but determined to do so because of Communist ideology.

Thus, Xi, the CCP, and the Han face a logical contradiction. The intellectual tension it creates is clear in Xi's and the Party's utterances. The CCP is Communist and were it to supplant the West, what would occur is one Western ideology is supplanting another Western ideology. For China to triumph over the West, it would be necessary for a Han polity to best the West. That can never happen under the CCP because the Party would not permit another form of government to rule China. So, Xi's argument implicitly is that China under the CCP will always be inferior to the West. Only by abandoning the CCP's ideology could China—that is, the Han civilization—demonstrate superiority over the West.

Xi cannot square this circle. Thus, China under the CCP will not have sufficient civilizational confidence to overthrow the West, unless the West loses its civilizational confidence. To accept Communism—Marxist, Leninist, Maoist thought—requires the rejection of Han civilization as a foundation for China's polity. To accept Han civilization requires the

25 Henderson, *Failure of a Mission*, p. 184.
26 Henderson, *Failure of a Mission*, p. 184.

acceptance of the traditional Han polity, imperial rule, and the rejection of imported ideologies and polities based on them. The fact that Xi and the Party embrace both means they are simultaneously incoherent and profoundly insecure regarding their legitimacy.

However, Han civilization does not have this insecurity when it compares itself with other civilizations. It is only when it compares itself with the West that it considers itself inferior. This is seen most clearly when the Han compare themselves to Hindu civilization. For the CCP, Hindu civilization is innately inferior.

For the United States, this also raises the possibility of outreach to India. The West could approach India in a new manner: along civilizational lines. That is, the West—Washington, London, Paris, Berlin, Canberra, Wellington—may appeal to India as the British did a century ago, as the representative of Western civilization that can work with Hindus against the common adversary, as they did before—two great civilizations uniting to defeat the Han, which seeks to overturn the position and tenets of both civilizations.

That is a positive development for the U.S. in the Sino-American confrontation. Importantly, viewed from the perspective of civilizational confidence, India has as least as much if not greater confidence than China. While this may not be determinative in any clash between these civilizational titans, it is a powerful force multiplier for India and would contribute to its ability to sustain a long conventional war against China.

Given the rapid expansion of its military, the PRC is a threat to India because of the CCP's aggressive ideology and the distribution of power, where the PRC still has an edge on India. Their respective conventional and strategic military power and proximity ensure that each will perceive the other as a threat. This threat will be magnified because China and India have a civilizational identity and major territorial disputes, which ensures that the Sino-Indian relationship is ripe for conflict.

Finally, Xi's rule in the PRC has proven that the CCP does not have the solution to creating a modern and just polity. Grafting a Western import to define and govern China was certain to generate ideological and political incoherence for the Han people. Economic growth cannot solve this problem. A fatal flaw of the Leninist economy is its inability to mobilize individuals. This flaw cannot be eliminated by coercive pressures or by adding market mechanisms. Likewise, a Leninist political environment is unlikely to produce innovation on a sustainable basis. Of course, one hopes that Western countries are beginning to recognize the political and economic motivations of the CCP's efforts to seize the "commanding heights" of technology, by implementing some countermeasures, such as restricting Huawei and restricting technology transfers to the PRC, like from Nvidia.

As part of a political warfare campaign, the West could advance messages to illuminate the CCP's confusion as discussed above. From Xi down, the CCP's leadership is tied to the Western idea of Communism and is enamored of the greatness of Western civilization, as Xi's discussion of Goethe's impact upon him reveals. This is a contradiction with the historical polity of the Han civilization and the civilizational confidence of Chinese emperors.

The consequence is that Xi, the CCP, and the Han face a logical contradiction. The CCP is Communist by definition and were it to supplant the West, what would occur is one Western ideology supplanting another Western ideology. For China to triumph over the West, it would be necessary for a Han polity—derived from the greatest of Han civilization—to provide more effective governance than any provided by the West. That can never happen under the CCP because the Party would not permit another form of government to rule China.

Hence, Xi's argument implicitly is that China under the CCP will always be inferior to the West. Only by abandoning the CCP's ideology could China—that is, Han civilization—demonstrate superiority over the West. As argued, Xi cannot square this circle. The nearest equivalent would be if the U.S. president suddenly, as the result of political and social turmoil or revolution, began advancing Confucianism as the proper and only political ideology and ordering principle for the society and culture of the United States. Many Americans might mouth the sayings to go along but the disconnect with traditional American polity would be enormous. Such a change would generate tremendous resentment, incredulity, and alienation that a great country would be ruled by a strange and foreign ideology.

To accept Communism requires the rejection of Han civilization as a foundation for China's polity. To accept Han civilization requires the acceptance of the traditional Han polity, imperial rule, and the rejection of imported ideologies and polities based on them.

That is a profound vulnerability that the U.S. and its partners may exploit to weaken the CCP through political warfare. Political warfare campaigns may be centered on three avenues of attack. First, the Chinese people have the right, obligation, and motivation not to support the CCP but rather, to overthrow it so that it may be replaced by a government of their choosing, which might be a genuine form of Han polity. Second, because the CCP is Communist, it lacks political legitimacy. Its absence provides the United States, its allies and partners, and the international community with justification to support the removal of the CCP, and to undermine the actions of the PRC in international politics and international organizations. Moreover, this is a powerful reason to support Taiwan as a model of how a post-Communist Chinese polity might govern. The third element of the ideological warfare campaign messaging would be that the CCP has failed to become Han after more than seventy years in power. That is, not only is the Party founded in Western ideology, but the pull of Western ideology remains too great for the Party to overcome. Thus, the CCP is inherently Western. Only by removing the fetishization of Western ideological constructs, such as Communism, can a Han identity come to the fore. Only then can the Han step forward with civilizational confidence to realize a Han polity and society free from a Leninist influence that is inherently alien to Han civilization.

V. Restore Confidence in the American Trinity and Western Civilization

Americans must once again have confidence in the American trinity and in Western civilization. They never should have lost it. The fact that American identity was under attack has been known for decades and yet few did anything to stop it. That passivity, whether the result of timidity or because they were captured by Communist influence, must end. Year after year, American identity has been under assault. Now is the time for Americans to once again have confidence in American identity and the American trinity based on their accurate understanding of their history and greatness. That is linked to the restoration of Western civilization confidence.

Western civilizational confidence is essential and necessary to win the fight against the CCP and neo-Bolshevism within the U.S. Fortunately, appeals to it will resonate because of the recognition of what the American people and Western civilization have accomplished. Its strength remains and was touted unambiguously within living memory, and certainly for Americans and other Westerners born after the mid-1970s when educational systems identified, taught, and touted its greatness. Western governments must unify states under the aegis of Western civilization to face the threat from the CCP and Communists within Western countries.

In many respects, from the civilizational perspective, this will be easier than it was during the Cold War. The Soviet Union was Russia, a close cousin of Western civilization who shared much of the same history and religion as the West. Russian philosophers, statesmen, and poets debated perpetually whether they were of the West and should be so regarded or possessed a unique identity and therefore should not be part of the Western community of nations. In the same vein, Western statesmen saw Russia as part of the Western order since Peter the Great's opening to it. Russia was a peer at international conferences of the nineteenth and twentieth centuries before the Bolshevik Revolution disrupted its position as an equal and welcome member of the European order.

With the PRC, it is the opposite; there is no ambiguity. The West may clearly define itself as apart from Han civilizational identity. There is no history of interaction because Western influence on Han civilization was minimal before the end of the eighteenth century, and so was Han influence on the West.

The West has the opportunity to draw a sharp division between the path the CCP envisions and that of the freedom of the West. This requires an accurate image of CCP rule in China, unalloyed by CCP propaganda or partial or misinformation from their allies in the West. It also requires that the media, foundations, think tanks, and universities also provide accurate assessments of CCP rule. Moreover, the matter ultimately rests with the citizens of the West to educate themselves on how the CCP rules and seeks to expand its influence into other countries. Thus, threat awareness is necessary after decades of threat deflation regarding the intent and objectives of the CCP.

The second requirement is for Western populations and governments to embrace confidence in their civilization. While both populations and governments have dramatically changed over the last several decades, ascriptive (age, ancestry, kin, and ethnicity), cultural (clan, tribe, language, religion), political (faction, clique, movement, cause, party, ideology), economic (job, occupation, profession, work group, employer, industry, union, class), and social (friends, clubs, teams, colleagues, status) sources of identity have weakened and altered due to the end of the Cold War and political and population changes within the West. There is the opportunity for civilizational identity to serve as a cohesive force.

The recognition of the greatness of Western civilization should provide populations and governments with tremendous strength in what their ancestors accomplished and bequeathed to the world. It was Western civilization that provided its denizens with the recognition that humans are individuals and developed the relationship between the individual and his society. The West understood the importance of liberty and freedom for fulfillment and for political rights and other human rights. It was this civilization that developed the philosophy of science, as well as modern science and even the critique of science. In turn, that provided the understanding of physics, chemistry, biology, evolution and ecology, medicine, the human psyche, and the wonders of the natural world and the universe beyond. In the military realm, it was the West that developed the military art and science and provided the foundation and development of military thought. It taught the world how to employ high-intensity warfare, the rules and norms regarding the use of force, and created most of the weapons on the modern battlefield and the doctrines governing their use.

Thus, Western civilization is far from over, but it does face a crisis of confidence introduced by its Communist enemies. The West needs its populations and governments to generate its renaissance. There must be within the West itself the rebirth of appreciation of what the West accomplished to restore civilizational confidence—that requires the U.S. to lead, as Trump is the *de facto* leader of Western civilization. All of the concerns of the modern day, from rights to freedoms, have their foundation in Western thought. Were the West to be diminished, these rights and freedoms would suffer as well. Additionally, were Western civilization to be shattered or lost, it is probable that the new principles, norms, and values would be totalitarian—or Islamist in some locales—which would not tolerate such behavior.

Western civilization may be employed in the fight against Communism that will motivate its members to confront the CCP and Communists at home. It will also sustain that motivation in the struggle. Western civilization is more than languages and religious beliefs. It is also assumptions about social and political values, what is right and wrong, seemly and unseemly, appropriate and inappropriate, beautiful and hideous, and the objective institutions and behavioral patterns that reflect these elements. This provides the answer to the three fundamental questions confronting Western civilization today: First, it provides the reason why Communism is an implacable enemy of Western civilization; second, why the U.S. and its Western civilizational allies should defeat the CCP; and third, why the West should be confident that it can defeat Communism at home and abroad.

Western civilizational confidence is a national security issue. If the West possesses it, it can take advantage of Communism's incoherence as an asymmetry. If the West loses its civilizational confidence, then it has lost the world's best civilization and a powerful motivator in the peer competitive fight it now faces against the PRC and its enemies within the U.S. If the West squanders it, then the CCP's complete absence of civilizational confidence will not be the Achilles' heel it is now but will be a massive weakness of no consequence in the fight against the West.

To be sure, thus far, the CCP has been supremely fortunate in the fight against the West. The West did not seek to execute regime change after the Tiananmen massacre, but rather, welcomed the PRC into the liberal economic order. The West did not stop the PRC's economic or military growth, its penetration of Western markets, or check its aggression in the South China Sea, India, or elsewhere during the Clinton, George W. Bush, and Obama administrations.

The measures to limit trade enacted by the first Trump administration were largely reversed by President Biden, and in turn, are being reinstated by the second Trump administration. The PRC's genocide against the Muslim peoples of Xinjiang has been reported and generated a modest response, but not one equal to its barbarism. The PRC was able to negate its obligations to the UK over Hong Kong to crush the democracy movement and bring it fully under the CCP's control. It was able to unleash a pandemic upon the world and escape condemnation or reparations for the lives lost and irreparable damage done to the world.

None of this will be easy. President Trump must sustain the fight against the European elite to make this happen. The Trump administration's difficulties with the European and UK elite are only starting. Differences over the amount of military spending by members of NATO, the future of Greenland, the lack of support for Epic Fury, and their work to sustain the war in Ukraine versus Trump's labors to end it have received the most attention. Most European states are reluctantly increasing defense spending, and Trump's great efforts may bring an end to the war. Once the war ends, there will be the issue of rebuilding Ukraine. The costs will be gargantuan, and inevitable debates regarding how reconstruction will occur—who will do it, how the great costs will be paid, as well as the right security measures for post-war Ukraine—will stress the relationship between the UK and Europe on the one hand and the Trump administration on the other.

However, contentious as reconstructing Ukraine will be, by far, the greatest trouble between Trump and the UK and European elites centers on immigration. The European and UK elites want the status quo, which is endless immigration of millions of mostly young men from Africa, the Middle East, South Asia, and Southwest Asia to Europe. This affects almost every European state from Ireland to Greece; only a small number of states, including Hungary and Poland, have avoided this fate. In every sense that matters, Europe and the UK have an open borders policy that is rapidly changing the economic, political, and social life of Europe. This is a bit like Mark Twain's remark about the weather: Everyone notices it, but no one does anything about it. That suits the European elites just fine. Every hour, every day, every year brings in more immigrants.

The Trump administration's 2025 *National Security Strategy of the United States* (NSS) boldly identifies this problem and is directly critical of the European elites. However significant economic stagnation is in Europe, that difficulty "is eclipsed by the real and more stark prospect of civilizational erasure" through mass immigration and low birth rates among Europeans.[27] The NSS suggests that Europe is enfeebled by its immigration policies, declining birthrates, "censorship of free speech and

27 The White House, *The National Security Strategy of the United States*, November 2025, p. 25. The report was released to the public in early December 2025. At: <https://www.whitehouse.gov/wp-content/uploads/2025/12/2025-National-Security-Strategy.pdf>. Accessed December 6, 2025.

suppression of political opposition" and a "loss of national identities and self-confidence."[28]

The report foresees a dark future for Europe if it does not change course: "Should present trends continue, the continent will be unrecognizable in 20 years or less. As such, it is far from obvious whether certain European countries will have economies and militaries strong enough to remain reliable allies."[29] That is a national security threat to the U.S. but one that the Europeans are not only not solving but accelerating through their open borders immigration policy. "Many of these nations are currently doubling down on their present path. We want Europe to remain European, to regain its civilizational self-confidence."[30]

The UK once thought it was protected from invasion by the English Channel. While it protected the UK from Napoleon, today it does not save the UK from human traffickers using small boats to ferry people across. For the UK alone, 162,677 illegal migrants crossed in the 2018–2025 period. Over 11,000 have crossed the Channel from France to the UK in 2025, up 50 percent from 2024. Net migration into the UK is estimated to be about 525,000 people a year, or the equivalent of adding a city the size of Edinburgh each year. The victory of the Reform Party in the local elections on May 7, 2026, was an indicator of public opinion and outrage at the fecklessness of the Labour government and the Tory governments before it. Shared political elite opinion, that is, the uniparty, in the UK, Europe, and the U.S. want ceaseless immigration. They are getting it in the UK and Europe. They are not in the U.S. under Trump.

British citizens and Europeans know that the UK and Europe will be forever changed if those policies are not reversed, just as Americans knew that their country would be lost had Trump not won in 2024. Of course, there is no indication that the UK and European elites want to do so. To

---

28 *The National Security Strategy of the United States*, p. 25.

29 *The National Security Strategy of the United States*, p. 25.

30 *The National Security Strategy of the United States*, p. 25.

the contrary, every indication is that they seek more immigration. There may be a policy or two that fiddles around the edges, or Keir Starmer will once again tout Labour's empty promise to "smash the gangs" that traffic people into the UK. But everyone knows they will do nothing to stop or even curtail immigration. Wallis Simpson, the Duchess of Windsor, said that you could never be too rich or too thin. If she were a Labour politician today, she would have added "or have too much immigration."

The U.S. faced a similar problem because of the Biden administration's open borders policy when 15 million to 20 million illegal immigrants entered the U.S.—in fact, no one really knows how many millions arrived. The Trump administration has closed the border and started the task of deportations. Trump shows what the UK and Europe also could accomplish with the will to do so.

But there is no will, and that reveals much. The central question is: *Why* is there endless mass immigration? The answer is that the neo-Bolsheviks want it. Mass migration is a weapon of mass destruction to employ against American identity and Western civilization. It has been incredibly effective at destroying both, in a relatively short time. The neo-Bolsheviks are deploying new armies to win the West's civil war.

The immigration issue is a stalking horse for two competing conceptions of the value of the West and its civilization. In essence, mass immigration is the weapon the UK, European, and U.S. elites have chosen to destroy Western civilization. For these elites, including those behind the Biden administration's open borders strategy, that is precisely the point. Mass immigration is the most effective weapon the elites employ to alter their countries fundamentally and forever, with little fear of reversal due to their hold on power.

That was before Trump. He has broken their headlock on political control and so provides the chance for the U.S. to save Western civilization. Some early skirmishing has occurred. Vice President J.D. Vance's February 14, 2025, speech to the sixty-first meeting of the Munich Security Conference was the start. Vance noted that immigration is Europe's greatest security problem, and that the elites are ignoring this problem, thereby weakening democratic institutions and free speech. This was a critically important address, and the NSS, published about nine months later, amplified those concerns. But the European establishment did not heed the lessons. In fact, they rejected them.

The battle lines are drawn.

The European elites want to destroy Western civilization. They are on Lenin's side in the West's civil war. So they will reject any measure to stop immigration because it is the supremely effective tool to end traditional European nation states and unhinge Western civilization. The UK and European elites will not accept populism or populist parties, despite what the people want through their voting and demonstrations.

In fact, the European elites have caused their own legitimacy crisis. This is the source of tension between the Western European elites and their own people. It is also a source of tension between the Trump administration and the Western European elites. In this unequal fight, the British and European peoples need help from the American people and people of goodwill around the world.

It falls to the Trump administration to work with allies in Europe to save Europeans from increasingly tyrannical governments. The U.S. finds itself arrayed against a tyrannical CCP, an authoritarian Russia, and increasingly draconian governments in Western Europe. While trouble with the PRC is to be expected due to the actions of the CCP, there is possibility of improving relations with Russia once the Ukraine war ends. The European elites also pose unique challenges and compel a response.

If there is no change in behavior, mass immigration will begin to evince greater political impact in Western countries. The political elites will steer a course that involves greater political suppression of native Europeans and political parties that seek to advance their interests. At the same time, they will reward rising sectarian groups that are flexing their political muscles. That is a recipe for sectarian violence in the UK and Western Europe and for profound trouble in the North Atlantic relationship.

In the UK, the Labour government all but tells the British people to drop dead. It seeks to avoid any serious investigation and accountability into the ongoing rape gang scandal, in which many hundreds of thousands of white, working-class girls and women have been victimized over forty years by adult men of overwhelmingly Pakistani Muslim background. Many leftist politicians, including at the time of writing serving and former Cabinet members, former Deputy Prime Minister Angela Rayner, Health Secretary Wes Streeting, Parliamentary Under Secretary of State for Safeguarding and Violence Against Women and Girls Jess Phillips, and former Home Secretary Yvette Cooper are increasingly dependent upon Muslim votes. Because of this dependence, the Labour government in 2025 rejected and then approved a national inquiry into the rape gangs. It is likely that an additional study will simply be thrown onto the pile of previous studies. Criminal punishment and deportations are needed. A human rights court should be created to investigate and charge the leaders and members of these rape gangs with crimes against humanity. Civil lawsuits should be brought as well.

In France on March 31, 2025, Marine Le Pen, the former leader of the National Rally Party, was found guilty by a Paris court and sentenced to four years in prison, two years of which were suspended. As a result, she was *de facto* prevented from running in the 2027 presidential election. In May, the German establishment employed its *Bundesamt für Verfassungsschutz*, Federal Office for the Protection of the Constitution (BfV), its FBI or MI5, to surveil with the ultimate objective of banning what is—by some polls—the largest political party in Germany, the Alternative for Germany (AfD), which seeks to end mass immigration.

These examples illustrate that the European elites have all but declared war on their people and populist parties and continue to ignore them while employing the levers of state power against them. If they continue on their path, the UK and European states will devolve into countries with increasingly open sectarian conflict, jeopardizing what it is not theirs to endanger—the continuation of the West and its civilization. They will not change their path of their own volition and are certain that they can outlast the Trump administration. They will do their utmost to ensure a Democrat wins America's presidential election in 2028.

In 1593, when the Huguenot King of France Henry IV converted to Catholicism to unite his kingdom, he purportedly told a friend that "Paris is worth a Mass." And saving Western civilization is worth a fight. The Trump administration needs to develop strategies to prevent UK and Western European elites from destroying it through mass immigration.

To pressure these governments for change, President Trump, Vice President Vance, and senior U.S. officials must raise the big issue of the negative consequences of immigration at every meeting and in most speeches. The bully pulpit can go a long way to call attention consistently to the UK and Western European elites' actions and to keep these issues front and center when Trump meets with these leaders. Trump might ask the Labour government directly about the rape gangs and what is being done to stop them or ask German Chancellor Friedrich Merz about the suppression of the AfD. Other steps include travel advisories and cautions to let Americans know that their right to free speech on social media platforms will be violated by the UK, France, and Germany when Americans are in these countries. Trump administration officials can also raise the profile of groups like "Blue Labour" in the UK—that is, a group in the Labour Party that advances working class, culturally conservative policies and values, and of political parties like Reform, National Assembly, and Alternative for Germany. Trump's support for these will ensure immigration remains a center of attention precisely as their populations want.

In addition to steps that the Trump administration is taking in education, another useful measure would be for the Trump administration to create a Commission on Western civilization, with UK and Western, Central, and Eastern European members, to identify actions that should be adopted.

Tough love is needed. Senator Tom Cotton has proposed to the Director of National Intelligence that the U.S. Intelligence Community refrain from sharing intelligence with Germany's BfV and deny requests for surveilling AfD until the German government treats the AfD as a legitimate opposition party. Curtailing cooperation in intelligence sharing and a U.S. refusal to surveil political parties like Reform, National Rally, or AfD, is important but the Trump administration should evaluate the next step of warning these political parties if they are surveilled by domestic intelligence services. In 2016 and 2017, Trump, his campaign, and members of his campaign, and then his administration knew what it is like to be under government surveillance. Aiding these parties with lessons learned and other means will help them avoid and thwart their governments' race to totalitarianism.

Trump's greatest contribution is to state simply that he will support UK and Western European political parties and political movements that support Western civilization and oppose those that do not. In truth, there is a civil war in the West, and supporters of the West need to win it.

Social media might be useful in some instances. Unfortunately, the use of social media in the EU and UK is dangerous. The EU and the UK are panopticons and closely monitor their populations, who may receive a police visit or be incarcerated for free expression. The number of Europeans who have been persecuted is legion and includes journalist and *Daily Telegraph* columnist Allison Pearson. In November 2024, she received a visit from Essex police for a tweet she posted, which the police classified as "a non-crime hate incident." Totalitarians do love their neologisms. In the history of totalitarian thought, one has to return to Dzerzhinsky, Beria, or Pol Pot, to find another equally chilling synonym. As frightening as Pearson's experience was, there are many other, far worse examples of British citizens, once known as the freest people in the world, now persecuted by their government. The need for Western Europeans to be able to communicate with a low possibility of government interception, not needed since World War II, has now returned.

The illegal and legal immigration crises should be seen for what they are: armies by the tens of millions from non-Western countries to destroy the West forever. They are Lenin's foot soldiers, and if not stopped today, they will win.

Thus, decades in the making, Western civilization faces a profound crisis in its political leadership. The problem the West confronts is clear: For too long, Western leaders in Australia, Canada, Europe, and the U.S. willfully abandoned the core principles of Western civilization. Intentionally, they adopted policies that were both foreign and antithetical to the historical civilization of their countries, of the societies that their fathers and mothers knew, and which, in fact, nurtured the very leaders who then labored to destroy it.

These policies, including multiculturalism and progressivism, were anchored in Leninist thought. Their impact has been catastrophic. Their consequence is that the future of Western civilization is now in the balance. This was done deliberately.

The policies had the effect of weakening the Christian and Enlightenment core principles of the West. These included intentional and sustained efforts to evict these principles from the public space while opening their borders to mass immigration from non-Western peoples. This has been done so massively and so quickly that most Western European states, including Ireland, France, Germany, Great Britain, the Netherlands, and Sweden, are at great risk of destabilization. Importantly, those states that rejected mass immigration—Hungary and Poland—are not.

The populations of these great nations demand an end to mass immigration while their leaders refuse to accept their demand as legitimate. This cruel fact is the source of the legitimacy crisis that so many Western European governments face. It fuels the public's deep cynicism and suspicion that elites have betrayed them. Indeed, they have.

In reality, the elites will not change their policy and end mass immigration. The public, having learned the lessons from previous betrayals, expect that their elites will merely announce policy gossamer to deceive them while not actually meeting the demands of their populations.

The West is thus in the perverse position of permitting its icons to be vandalized, its statues to be toppled, its churches defiled and burned in arson attacks, its women and girls raped, and its civilization destroyed by those who have the freedom to hold the West in contempt, a freedom that was made possible by that civilization. Of course, the West's enemies do not care about that irony. The point is to destroy the West, and Western freedoms will be weaponized against Western peoples. In the end, it was Western Europe's leaders who have intentionally and consistently made this situation possible.

Now is the time to ask *quo vadis* of the West: Where is it going? Two paths are evident.

The first is the continuation of the destructive Leninist path which Western European, Australian, and Canadian leaders, as well as most of the American elites, have chosen, but that their people reject, clearly and consistently. This is the civil war Lenin started. It is the path that will dissolve the West—and do so very quickly. It will also deepen tensions with the Trump administration, because the Trump administration has declared it is on the side of the populations.

The second path is to save Western civilization and win the West's civil war. Like the story of Peter encountering Christ on the Appian Way, now is the time to gain courage, to reverse course, and confront the problems our civilization faces. Now is the time for Western leaders to have the confidence in Western civilization that their predecessors possessed. Now is the time for current Western leaders to value what they did and what their populations do now: Governments must have the consent of the governed. Consent of the governed is a foundation of the political life of the West. But the elites simply will not tolerate it on the issue of mass immigration.

This issue illustrates, like no other matter, the fork in the civilizational road. On this issue, most egregiously, the elites do not have the consent of the governed. From Ireland to Sweden to Germany, they reject their elites, who have chosen the path of profound social disruption through mass immigration that now threatens the stability of their countries and the existence of their civilizations.

The crisis of legitimacy for the Western elites will be resolved either by crushing their publics, by weaponizing the state against them, or by heeding their people. The former is happening now. It must end immediately to save the political contract between people and their government, to save their societies and Western civilization. Western governments need to heed their people and to stop abusing them by violating their human rights.

To accomplish this, the West needs leaders it does not appear to possess outside of Presidents Donald Trump and Viktor Orban of Hungary before his April 2026 defeat. They possess a strong civilizational confidence based upon an understanding of the greatness of Western civilization. New leaders and new political parties are needed in the UK, Ireland, and on the Continent. A new generation of Western leaders of their own parties must rebuild what has been destroyed in the West.

What should unite these leaders with their populations is civilizational confidence. The civilizational confidence of the elite and the people of the West is warranted precisely because of what the West is. Western civilization differs from others not in the way it has developed but in the distinctive character of its principles, values, and institutions, and the way they are able to adapt to new environments yet sustain core attributes. Christianity, the value and worth of the individual and of his natural rights, the rule of law, the West's august history, its arts, and its sciences, made it possible for the West to invent the modern world, to expand through the world, and to become the envy of other civilizations. Civilizational confidence entails the strength to say no to the architects of the destruction of the West, to say no to the policy of mass migration, to say no to the decline of the West, and to say yes to its renaissance.

Within living memory, the elites of the West understood and embraced this. The source of the ideas of dignity and worth of the individual, of freedom, liberty, political democracy, and the rule of law, are Western ideas; they are not Asian, nor African, nor Middle Eastern ideas, except by adoption. These ideas and principles make Western civilization unique, and Western civilization is valuable to its members and the world not because it is universal but because it is unique, and its leaders and public must understand it to be so. It is unique, it is capable of being destroyed forever, it is under threat, and so it urgently deserves protection by its leaders.

The West must be saved—and indeed it can be. The Trump administration is helping mightily by calling attention to the issue, for example, as Vance has done by declaring some Antifa groups in Europe as terrorist organizations. Leaders must join with their people in embracing their unique civilization without apology and with their confidence fully justified.

Demonstrating this will end the legitimacy crisis that plagues the elites. Western civilization keeps representative democracy viable and credible for its citizens. It connects the past with the present. It unifies them and identifies for them what Western civilization has accomplished: the creation of the best societies known to mankind. The West does indeed face a decision-point. Most of its elites are toying with its destruction.

In truth, the answer for its future is anchored in its 2,500-year past. The elites' embrace of their past will ensure that the West remains what it should be: prosperous and stable, a home to pious religious belief and scientific rationality, to sacred and profane art and literature, and to individual identity, rights, and freedoms. The West has been failed by its political parties and their leaders. It is time for the people of the West to restore their confidence in the greatness of Western civilization.

Despite the obstacles and the urgency of the hour, there is reason for optimism and courage, both of which have returned to Western civilization in no small measure due to Trump's election and the energy of his administration. Political change is possible. Populist movements are on the rise because Western populations see the damage to Western civilization and want to repair it. This spirit was evinced by the renovation of Notre-Dame de Paris Cathedral. It revealed the startlingly beautiful architecture and sublime features of an archetype of Western civilization.

At its reopening in December 2024, French President Emmanuel Macron called it a "shock of hope." It was, but in more than just the narrow sense Macron meant. It was a "shock of hope" for Western civilization. It shows that the skills needed for the restoration were not lost but remain, and were linked by their historic trades and abilities to the men who built it over eight hundred years ago. The restoration also united people, demonstrating that the nation—indeed, the civilization and its supporters around the world—were behind it.

The restoration is also a metaphor for the return of the West. Like Notre-Dame, the West may be restored too. Trump's visit there was fitting because he is a leader who champions the West and so should be at one of its iconic and most beautiful locations as its restoration was revealed.

Both the church and the civilization went through fire. Both now have a renaissance. However horrific, damage done can be repaired.

The repair of that damage requires accurately identifying how bad it is so that the laborious repair work can commence. Immigration is the barometer. The UK and European elites need an intervention to recognize the damage and discuss how to repair the destruction to their societies, as the populist parties demand.

The legitimacy crisis of the UK and European elites must be resolved in favor of the European people. The Western European elites must once again truly heed their populations. Of course, the elites will not do so, and so the legitimacy crisis will continue to worsen and the problem for the Atlantic relationship will become acute.

There is trouble ahead in the relationship between the U.S. and the elites in the UK and Europe. It has little to do with differences over defense spending and Ukraine. It has everything to do with valuing the West and saving it from those who are destroying it. Trump and the populist movement in the U.S., UK, and Europe and their many allies elsewhere in Europe and around the world, value Western civilization. The Western elites do not. It is a stark choice. The West never should have been brought to this point, but here it is, and the damage must be repaired. Confidence in Western civilization must return. Everything depends upon Trump and the populist movements' success to save the West from its elites. Bismarck once said that "A statesman must wait until he hears the footsteps of God sounding through events; then leap up and grasp the hem of His garment."[31] Now is the time to act to save Western civilization.

31 Otto von Bismarck, *The Oxford Dictionary of Quotations*, 5th ed. (Oxford: Oxford University Press, 1999), p. 116.

Chapter 7

Conclusions: The Greatest Generation—Those Who Finally Defeat Communism and Win the Hundred Years' War

The U.S. is engaged in a modern Hundred Years' War against the ideology of Communism. The ideology burst forth with the 1917 Bolshevik Revolution. It was spread in world politics by Soviet power and the Comintern. Soviet imperialism captured China and turned that great country into a colony, where the colonial masters still rule in the name of Marx and Lenin.

In the domestic realm, Lenin started a civil war in the West between those who wanted to sustain Western civilization and those who wanted to destroy it. In this arena, too, Communists have been remarkably successful, to the point where America and other Western states are on the verge—one election away, in a truly "1776 Moment"—from a complete Communist victory.

Americans may speak of a "cold civil war" in the U.S. Actually, as this book has argued, it is a civil war in Western civilization, and the Bolsheviks started it over a century ago. They have been supremely successful at capturing almost every political party, institution, aspect of civil society, and the ideas industry in every Western country. In sum, Communism may conquer the West.

Lenin's political warfare strategy to penetrate the West was far more successful than the U.S.'s efforts to penetrate the Soviet Union in the past or the PRC now. Until the MAGA movement, the Communists had effectively prevented the rise of any populist movement in the U.S. before Trump by targeting and eliminating potential leader. They captured the Democrats, and many of the Republicans, neutering most of the rest, and working through the EU and NGOs, they still prevent the rise of populism throughout much of Europe.

The aim has been the same—that is, to bring about the destruction of individual freedom and liberties, democratic government, strong civil societies, and Western civilization and societies, replacing these with totalitarian rule that professes to have a "scientific" understanding of society that crushes American identity and Western civilization. The costs to Americans and to citizens of Western states have been colossal. Communists may rob Americans of their birthright. They may destroy Western civilization. That remains to be seen. America is at a "1776 Moment" and could go either way.

However, if Communists win, it will not be for lack of empirical evidence regarding what happens when they come to power. Their historical record is plain to all. In almost every case, Communists have entered power through coercion and violence.[1] Over 100 million people have died

1 The exception was Chile in 1970 when the Communist Salvador Allende won a plurality of the vote, and possibly the 1998 election of Hugo Chávez in Venezuela. New to power, the Bolsheviks permitted one free, nationwide election for the Constituent Assembly, which was held on November 25, 26, and 27, 1917. The fact that balloting occurred at all and that it resulted in Bolshevik defeat was proof of a liberality in Russia then that the Soviet system soon extinguished. This made the vote all the more important as a form of poll-taking at the very moment when Russia crossed the divide between democracy and dictatorship. The Social Revolutionaries won 410 of 707 seats—a clear majority. The Bolsheviks won 175; Mensheviks sixteen; the Kadets (Constitutional Democrats) seventeen; national groups eighty-six; and miscellaneous parties won the small remnant. Thus, 24.7 percent of

because of Communism. That horrific total does not count the millions of forced abortions in the PRC and instances of female infanticide, which may cause the total to rise to at least 200 million. From Stalin to Mao to Pol Pot, Communist totalitarian governments have caused gross human rights abuses, famine, deportations, executions, and hyper-aggression, including two cold wars and, potentially, a hot World War III.

Consigning Communism to the ash heap of history begins by recognizing it is illegitimate and it must be fought, or it will destroy everything you value and even kill you. Americans must not underestimate Leninism. They need to understand it to defeat it.

Communism's incoherence and absence of a civilizational grounding are opportunities upon which the American people must capitalize to defeat that odious ideology. Abroad, its defeat begins with the recognition that the CCP is a colonial government, the product of the Western intellectual tradition, and was put in power by Soviet imperialism. It is no more legitimate to rule the Chinese people than was a Western imperial government during the nineteenth or twentieth centuries. To defeat the CCP, the U.S. must totally cut off its access to American capital, American high technology, including microchips, and access to American intellectual capital, including universities where hundreds of thousands of Communist Chinese students have trained. As discussed in chapter 3, the CCP must be denied the prospect of a modern NEP to save it. That will drive the stake through the heart of the Party.

At home, in American politics, destroying Communism requires the recognition of what is at stake and its evil. Leninists are extremely good at political warfare and Americans must employ American identity to defeat them. This requires understanding the threat, being able to "think

---

the electorate cast their ballots for the Bolsheviks when they had just come to power. The Assembly met on January 18, 1918, at the Tauride Palace in Petrograd. It adjourned at 4:40 a.m. on the 19th, after deciding to reconvene the same day at 5 p.m. Armed Bolsheviks prevented further sessions and thus ended revolutionary Russia's brief parliamentary experience until the 1990s.

like a Communist," and boldly asserting and defending the American trinity while identifying and checking Communist sources of funding, organization, propaganda, and agitation through Antifa and other groups. Americans checked Communist influence in the past. Now is the time to defeat it at home and abroad through a renaissance of American identity.

In essence, understanding Leninism allows the American people to grasp why the CCP and the Democratic Party are the two major threats to American identity. To some degree, they employ different tactics, but both have been successful at targeting traditional American identity by undermining the American trinity with a focused and unrelenting effort. This is because the American identity was and remains today the greatest barrier to their victory. This is why Communists relentlessly attack the American spirit, the freedoms of liberalism, and Western civilization. Americans should always view the actions of the CCP and the Democratic Party through the lens of Leninism, and always be cognizant that whatever they say or the policies they advance, they seek to make Americans' lives worse—"the worse, the better."

A huge part of the problem in winning the Hundred Years' War against Communism is that the American people do not understand the nature of the enemy because *the enemy* has been educating them for decades and *the enemy* dominates the media, and so has been framing the issues that impact their lives and how Americans see their society and the world, and *the enemy* has been waging supremely successful political warfare against Americans and Western states by supporting, that is, capturing Wall Street, businesses, universities, politicians, political parties, legacy media, and social media. The American people are not yet thinking about victory over Communism because they are not seeing the big picture, so many do not yet understand they are in a war, and do not yet understand Leninist strategy and tactics.

Americans must have the political nous to be able to perceive contemporary American politics through Americanism and Leninism. Those are the two lenses that allows Americans to understand today's politics and what is at stake. The American lens is how most Americans see America and American politics: It is and should remain as it has been defined throughout the country's history. They want their country to thrive. The second is the Leninist lens, which hostile to everything American, and seeks to destroy America and the West. When President Trump asks "why don't Democrats stand" to acknowledge American heroes at the State of Union, Americans have to be able to see this not only through the American lens but also the Leninist one. The Democrats do not want to celebrate America; they want to destroy it. That is why they do not stand, that is why they do not celebrate America, this is why they advance policies to erode and eliminate American identity and each element of the American trinity. Driven by an incandescent hate for America, they are here to destroy it.

Americans need to be able to grasp both perspectives to save American identity. They need to comprehend their own identity but also the enemy's. It falls upon Americans to accomplish this, rather than the government. Indeed, the U.S. government, including the Department of War, and the American people do not think of themselves as fighting ideologies, to say nothing of Communism. The American people and their government are not organized to fight a Hundred Years' War. Americans do not conceive of wars in that time frame. Neither are most Americans aware of the nature and parameters of this war, this single fight against Communism.

That is to the tremendous benefit of the foe. Americans need to get smart about Communism, and quickly. Not perceiving Communism as a hyper-aggressive ideology has been a massive mistake that has allowed them to weaken American identity at home and permit the growth of the PRC's power to the point where now the U.S. is in a second cold war. Importantly, it was not an error made by Americans in the Cold War with the Soviet Union. Americans were cognizant of Communism's dangers at home and abroad. They were educated in the thought of Marx, Engels, and Lenin, and the history of the Bolshevik Revolution and its consequences. Today Americans must understand that Communism is the greatest threat

America has faced. It was the principal national security policy impact for most of the twentieth century and is for this one as well.

Communism has killed over 100,000 Americans in hot wars in Asia and incurred the risk of causing many millions of Americans to be killed in a potential nuclear conflict with the Soviet Union in the past or with the PRC now. This ideology profoundly shaped U.S. strategy, planning, and force structure during the Cold War and today. The American people, and the Departments of State and War, and the Intelligence Community all made Herculean efforts to defeat the Soviet Union. Since Moscow's defeat, no such efforts were made to vanquish the CCP—just the reverse, the U.S. aided the CCP. Only in the first Trump administration did the U.S. try to end some of these policies.

In America, Communism targets the morale and economic and social well-being of Americans. It kills Americans daily through CCP-backed fentanyl and other drugs, truly WMDs as Trump has declared them, to which many Americans turn because their morale is low. They are lost because American identity has been hollowed out—there is a lack of understanding among young Americans about the American spirit, liberalism, and the greatness of Western civilization. American identity must be regained by calling attention to what it is, its importance, and why it is the birthright of Americans.

The Chinese people are suffering too. The CCP's ideology imprisons them and compels its hyper-aggression in international politics, including against U.S. partners like India and Taiwan, and U.S. Treaty allies like Japan and the Philippines. Just as the United States must rapidly build the platforms and weapons necessary to deter and defeat the PRC, and in the numbers needed to deter and defeat the CCP, the U.S. government must also fight the PRC's political warfare operations that have so badly subverted America's defenses and the American homeland. This is a war of ideas just as much as it is one of the number of nuclear warheads, tanks, aircraft, and ships possessed by the U.S. military. Ideas can kill the CCP more efficiently than conventional or nuclear munitions, if only the U.S. would fight to win the war of ideas.

Understanding the CCP's Leninist ideology permits the American people to recognize that there can be no accommodation with the CCP. Whatever its future, a successful NEP, stagnation, or efficient Stalinism, it is determined to fight the U.S. Hence, the U.S. must fight to win the cold war and must comprehend that the CCP will not end its struggle until it is defeated. During the Cold War with the Soviet Union, to combat Soviet materiel power, the United States strengthened its economy, military and alliance relationships. To combat Soviet ideational power, the appeal of Communism, the Truman administration turned to America's ideology. Americans must employ ideology again. Drafting ideas is more efficient than drafting men. The blood price of fighting with ideas is far less than with bullets.

As in America's previous wars, the role of political warfare in this struggle critically reinforced the material aspect. A U.S. victory in the ideological realm begins by recognizing that the CCP's Leninist ideology is illegitimate and the source of its profound belligerency. As this book has emphasized, the CCP is a Soviet colonial product imposed upon the Chinese people and the world by the Soviet Union and its tools. This point must be repeated until it penetrates the American media, government, and population: The CCP is the world's last colonial government. It is illegitimate. Understanding the history of Communism permits Americans to comprehend why this is. In turn, they may understand the CCP for what it is and then formulate a political warfare strategy that avoids a kinetic conflict but that defeats the CCP in the political realm.

The Hundred Years' War against Communism is the great struggle of the twenty-first century and promises to resolve the century's dispositive question—whether the world will be free or fall into a totalitarian abyss as sought by the PRC and their allies, the Communists in the West. The twentieth century encountered the same question and freedom defeated Communism. Indeed, Americans thought they had finally defeated Communism in 1989 when the Berlin Wall fell. That elation returned when the Soviet Union dissolved in 1991.

That great victory was winning a battle, not the war.

Had the U.S. denied the CCP access to its economy, technology, and investment, and had American education addressed the domestic Communist threat and reinforced American identity when it was in robust health, the world might have witnessed the final defeat of Communism.

Time is short to correct past mistakes. History has shown that American identity is superior and more durable than the incoherent, tyrannical, and failed political ideology of Communism and its accompanying hyper-aggression in world politics. But history is not determinative—the good guys do not always win. America's "1776 Moment" will be resolved, one way or another. Moreover, Americans will not win if they do not fight. At present, America and the West are at risk of losing its identity and segueing into Communism with the concomitant gross human rights abuses that are the hallmarks of the CCP's one-Party state. Already the dark prospect of an efficient Stalinism is possible, not just in the PRC but even in Western Europe and the U.S. if they do not change course. The U.S. would be well along that road had Vice President Kamala Harris won the White House in 2024, and the U.S. may well be there again in 2028 or subsequent elections if Americans do not heed the dangers of Communism.

The fact that AI is being developed by the intellectual grandchildren and great-grandchildren of Lenin means that neo-Bolshevist ideas may dominate the big LLMs. If ever there were a case of "garbage in, garbage out," this is it—although more accurately it is "evil in, evil out." The consequences of AI anchored in and biased toward neo-Bolshevik progressive thought may well ensure that Lenin wins as AI increasingly dominates intellectual life, culture, education, employment, and people's worldviews.

The question—Will freedom or tyranny define the twenty-first century?—will be answered ultimately by the American people. The Trump administration, Congress, U.S. allies and partners will play roles, but the American people are the most important today, as they were 250 years ago at the country's founding. They must ensure that the answer will be the same in this century as it was in the last: Freedom will triumph over Communism's tyranny in its CCP guise or in its American ones.

As an envoi, it falls to the American people to defeat Communism. This generation can be the greatest generation of Americans since the nation's founding if they defeat Communism and win the Hundred Years' War. To be the "Greatest Generation," the American people must see that the threat of Communism is existential. They must appreciate the great costs the U.S. has incurred in the past to defeat the ideology—in its CCP guise or within the U.S.—as their grandparents and great-grandparents vanquished the Soviet Union. Understanding American history and the American trinity provides the necessary insights to defeat Communism at home and abroad.

The U.S. is at a turning point in the confrontation with Communism. It may choose to employ its arsenal in support of victory, or it may choose to fight with incomplete mobilization. The American people must lead the government and rest of society to embrace and encourage the American trinity, not only to maximize its power of resources and the motivation of its citizenry to fight Communism but also to provide its citizens with the understanding of what it is they must defend—a citizenry, a country, a past, their forebearers, and a civilization.

While the struggle with the CCP and with Communism at home will define this century and will compel the U.S. to employ every tool at its disposal, a U.S. victory will require many steps. The most important is the most fundamental: to motivate the American people and their allies to understand, enjoin, and sustain the fight.

Americans can win this war and finally defeat Communism at home and abroad. This requires the recognition that American identity is a fundamental concern. It is a national security concern, to be sure, but it actually is more important because American identity is synonymous with the American people. American identity is America. It has been attacked year after year to undermine it with the intent to destroy it. This must end. American identity must be restored. The societies that the Founding Fathers forged in the U.S. and that Western civilization created in Europe, if fully and completely embraced and encouraged without apology, will serve the aims of explaining and motivating people for the fight. The West's unique civilization, and America's place in it as its leader, have demonstrated its effectiveness at sustaining the greatest political system and civilization in history, even as now they confront their greatest test. In contrast, its enemy is anti-American, anti-Western civilization, illegitimate, and a complete fraud, even as it is as deadly as a viper.

Yet, Americans have the power to defeat Communism once and for all by winning the Hundred Years' War against Communism. Doing so will make this the greatest generation since America's founding. The stronger American identity is, the weaker is Communism. The more powerful Western civilization is, the more exposed, ineffectual, and insubstantial is Communism. In sum, a renaissance of American identity is needed, as only strong American identity will defeat Communism and save Western civilization.

The CCP and the Communist movement in the U.S. are fundamentally incoherent and vulnerable to the strategies advanced in this book that capitalize upon their lies, incoherence, and illegitimacy, while advancing the American trinity to cause both the final defeat of Communism and a renaissance of American identity and of Western civilization. The American people will vanquish Communism. Understanding the greatness of American identity and the sublime achievements of Western civilization, while boldly and proudly asserting and acting upon both, are the keys to winning the Hundred Years' War against Communism.

Bibliography

Note:

In addition to books cited in the text, starting with Vladimir Lenin's *What Is to Be Done?* and *Left Wing Communism—An Infantile Disorder*, the following books are helpful for any readers who want to understand the Communist threat in more specific detail. Many hundreds of books published over the last century could be discussed, but here are ten exceptional fiction and non-fiction authors who will help you understand the evils of Communism.

Whittaker Chambers, in *Witness*, documents his personal account of what attracted him to Communism, why he spied for the Soviet Union, and why he rejected that odious ideology and exposed Communists' penetration of the United States government.

Stéphane Courtois, Andrzej Paczkowski, Nicolas Werth, et al., *The Black Book of Communism: Crimes, Terror, Repression* is a comprehensive account of the victims of Communism. From 1917 to the date of publication, 1997, this book details the crimes of all Communist governments. This is a masterpiece.

Isaac Deutscher's incredible account of the Bolshevik revolution and Leon Trotsky's role in it, Trotsky's battles with Joseph Stalin, and Trotsky's life in exile are captured in this great trilogy, *The Prophet Armed: Trotsky, 1879-1921; The Prophet Unarmed: Trotsky, 1921-1929; and The Prophet Outcast: Trotsky, 1929-1940.*

J. Edgar Hoover, in *A Study of Communism*, provides a clear and concise explanation of the foundations and history of Communism. This book explains how Communists seize power, their brutality once in power, how they have penetrated American society, and why Communism is an existential threat to Americans. It is as relevant today, in the age of Antifa, as it was sixty years ago.

The God that Failed is an account by former Communists, Arthur Koestler, Ignazio Silone, Richard Wright, André Gide, Louis Fischer, and Stephen Spender, of what attracted them to Communism in their youths, and how each wrestled with his conscience as Stalin's crimes and aggression became undeniable. This remarkably revealing book about the lives of these major thinkers of the political left in the twentieth century that captures why, despite its bloody history, Communism has an appeal generation after generation. As relevant today for understanding "democratic socialists" like Zohran Mamdani or Alexandria Ocasio-Cortez, and the modern Democratic Party as the book was when it was written.

Arthur Koestler's *Darkness at Noon* is a fictional account of a senior Communist Party leader, an old Bolshevik, who was a creator and enforcer of the Party's ideology before being arrested for treason on Stalin's orders (called Number One in the book), tried, imprisoned, and then executed. A stark and brutal account of an individual who was an enforcer of a Communist revolution but was consumed by the system that he helped to create.

Leszek Kolakowski's three-volume *Main Currents of Marxism* is an exceptional account of Marxism from the utopia socialists of the eighteenth century to the scientific socialism of Karl Marx and Friedrich Engels, through Eduard Bernstein to Karl Kautsky and Georges Sorel. All of the major Marxist-Leninists are included in this comprehensive accounting of Communist thought.

The Private Life of Chairman Mao, written by Dr. Li Zhisui, Mao Zedong's personal physician, is rivaled only by Milovan Djilas' *Conversations with Stalin* as a personal account of what it is like to be in the presence of a monster. Whereas Djilas only had to dine with Stalin from time to time, Li was Mao's doctor for decades. Li recounts the paranoia and viciousness of Mao, his indifference to the tens of millions he killed, and Li's constant fear of execution. This is an account that allows us to understand the type of men who rise to the top in Communist systems.

George Orwell's (Eric Blair) *1984* is an unparalleled fictional account of life under Soviet totalitarianism. It demonstrates how language "Newspeak" is remade constantly to keep the Party's power, to prevent critical thinking, and one slip of the tongue or use of outdated language will be fatal. History is also remade constantly to fit the Party's demands. Orwell demonstrated that he who controls the present controls the past, and he who controls the past controls the future. Orwell understood how education is essential for Communists. Historical truth and clarity of thought and language are antidotes to Communism.

Alexandr Solzhenitsyn's classic, *The GULAG Archipelago*, is a three-volume account of the horrors of the Soviet concentration camp system. Solzhenitsyn, a survivor of the camps, wrote it between 1958 and 1968, and it was first published in the West in 1973. Solzhenitsyn lays the responsibility of the camps at Lenin's feet, not Stalin's because Stalin inherited what Lenin had created. It is an account that cannot be surpassed. The work is a monument to the tens of million tortured and murdered in the Soviet Union, and a timeless indictment of Communism.

Adorno, Theodor, and Max Horkheimer, *Dialectic of Enlightenment* (New York: Seabury Press, 1972).

Alinsky, Saul D., *Rules for Radicals: A Practical Primer for Realistic Radicals* (New York: Vintage, 1989).

Anderson, Benedict, *Imagined Communities: Reflections on the Origins and Spread of Nationalism* (New York: Verso, 1991).

Anyon, Jean, *Marx and Education* (New York: Routledge, 2011).

Anyon, Jean, *Radical Possibilities: Public Policy, Urban Education, and a New Social Movement*, 2nd ed. (New York: Routledge, 2014).

Arato, Andrew, and Eike Gebhardt, eds., *The Essential Frankfurt School Reader* (New York: Continuum, 1982).

Arquilla, John, *The Reagan Imprint: Ideas in American Foreign Policy from the Collapse of Communism to the War on Terror* (Chicago: Ivan R. Dee, 2006).

Ashley, W. J., *Surveys Historic and Economic* (London: Longmans, Green, and Co., 1900).

Berkowitz, Paul, and Bradley A. Thayer, "Intelligence Community's Report on Wealth and Corruption of China's Rulers Is Overdue," *Washington Times*, October 8, 2024. At: <https://www.washingtontimes.com/news/2024/oct/8/intelligence-communitys-report-on-wealth-and-corru/>.

Berkowitz, Paul, and Bradley A. Thayer, "Key Report Helps Reveal the Wealth and Corruption of the CCP," *Sunday Guardian*, June 9, 2024. At: <https://sundayguardianlive.com/investigation/key-report-helps-to-reveal-the-wealth-and-corruption-of-the-ccp>.

Berkowitz, Paul, and Bradley A. Thayer, "Publicize the Wealth and Corruption of the CCP Leadership," *Warroom*, March 25, 2024. At: <https://warroom.org/publicize-the-wealth-and-corruption-of-the-ccp-leadership/>.

Biden, President Joseph, "Remarks by President Biden on the Verdict in the Derek Chauvin Trial for the Death of George Floyd," The White House, April 20, 2021. At: https://www.whitehouse.gov/briefing-room/speeches-remarks/2021/04/20/remarks-by-president-biden-on-the- verdict-in-the-derek-chauvin-trial-for-the-death-of-george-floyd/>.

Bigler, David L., and Will Bagley, *The Mormon Rebellion: America's First Civil War 1857–1858* (Norman: University of Oklahoma Press, 2011).

Biondi, Martha, *The Black Revolution on Campus* (Berkley: University of California Press, 2012).

Black Lives Matter, "About Black Lives Matter." At: <https://blacklivesmatter.com/about/>.

Bokhari, Allum, *Breitbart News*, October 7, 2020. At: <https://www.breitbart.com/politics/2020/10/07/dc-antifa-ringleader-jason-charter-charged-with-assaulting-oanns-jack-posobiec/.

Borkenau, F., *World Communism: A History of the Communist International* (Ann Arbor: University of Michigan Press, 1962).

Brady, Anne-Marie, "Exploit Every Rift: United Front Work Goes Global," in David Gitter, et al., *Party Watch Annual Report, 2018* (Washington, D.C.: Center for Advanced China Research, 2018).

Bray, Mark, *Antifa: The Anti-Fascist Handbook* (Brooklyn: Melville House, 2017).

Brown, Anthony Cave, and Charles B. MacDonald, *On a Field of Red: The Communist International and the Coming of World War II* (New York: Putnam's Sons, 1981).

Caldwell, Christopher, *The Age of Entitlement: America Since the Sixties* (New York: Simon & Schuster, 2020).

Cardenal, Juan Pablo, and Heriberto Araujo, *China's Silent Army: The Pioneers, Traders, Fixers and Workers Who Are Remaking the World in Beijing's Image*, trans. by Catherine Mansfield (New York: Crown, 2013).

Castro-Salazar, Ricardo, and Carl Bagley, *Navigating Borders: Critical Race Theory Research and Counter History of Undocumented Americans* (New York: Peter Lang, 2012).

"Cecil Rhodes: Oriel College Faces Teaching Boycott over Refusal to Move Statue," *The Guardian*, June 10, 2021. At: <https://www.theguardian.com/education/2021/jun/10/oriel-college-faces-teaching-boycott-over-refusal-to-remove-rhodes-statue>.

Coates, Ta-Nehisi, *We Were Eight Years in Power: An American Tragedy* (New York: One World, 2017).

Collins, Patricia Hill, *Intersectionality as Critical Social Theory* (Durham: Duke University Press, 2019).

Crenshaw, Kimberlé, Neil Gotanda, Gary Peller, and Kendall Thomas, "Introduction," in Kimberle Crenshaw, Neil Gotanda, Gary Peller, and Kendall Thomas, eds., *Critical Race Theory: The Key Writings that Formed the Movement* (New York: The New Press, 1995), pp. xiii–xxxii.

Cuomo, Mario, "Governor Cuomo Issues a Statement on Multicultural Education," July 15, 1991, in *Public Papers of Governor Mario M. Cuomo—1991 (Part 2)* (Albany: State of New York, 1995), p. 1416. At: <https://nysl.ptfs.com/knowvation/app/consolidatedSearch/#search/v=list,c=1,q=field11%3D%5B18379742%5D%2CqueryType%3D%5B16%5D,sm=s,l=library1_lib%2Clibrary4_lib%2Clibrary5_lib>.

Daniels, Roger, *Guarding the Golden Door: American Immigration Policy and Immigrants Since 1882* (New York: Hill and Wang, 2004).

DeCuir-Gunby, Jessica T., Thandeka K. Chapman, and Paul A. Schutz, "Critical Race Theory, Racial Justice, and Education," in Jessica T. DeCuir-Gunby, Thandeka K. Chapman, and Paul A. Schutz, eds., *Understanding Critical Race Research Methods and Methodologies: Lessons from the Field* (New York: Routledge, 2019), pp. 3–10.

Defense Casualties Analysis System, "U.S. Casualties World War I 1917–1918." At: <https://dcas.dmdc.osd.mil/dcas/app/summaryData/casualties/principalWars>.

Defense Casualties Analysis System, "U.S. Casualties World War II 1941–1945." At: <https://dcas.dmdc.osd.mil/dcas/app/summaryData/casualties/principalWars>.

Defense Casualties Analysis System, "Korean War 1950–1953." At: <https://dcas.dmdc.osd.mil/dcas/app/summaryData/casualties/principalWars>.

Defense Casualties Analysis System, "Vietnam War 1964–1973." At: <https://dcas.dmdc.osd.mil/dcas/app/summaryData/casualties/principalWars>.

Degras, Jane, ed., *The Communist International 1919–1943 Documents, Vol. I, 1919–1922* (London: Oxford University Press, 1956).

Degras, Jane, ed., *The Communist International 1919–1943 Documents, Vol. II, 1923–1928* (London: Oxford University Press, 1960).

Degras, Jane, ed., *The Communist International 1919–1943: Documents, Volume III* (London: Oxford University Press, 1965).

Delgado, Richard, and Jean Stefancic, *Critical Race Theory: An Introduction*, 3rd ed. (New York: New York University Press, 2017).

Delgado, Richard, and Jean Stefancic, *Must We Defend Nazis? Why the First Amendment Should Not Protect Hate Speech and White Supremacy* (New York: New York University Press, 2018).

DiAngelo, Robin, *White Fragility: Why It's So Hard for White People to Talk about Racism* (Boston: Beacon Press, 2018).

Dikötter, Frank, *Mao's Great Famine: The History of China's Most Devastating Catastrophe, 1958–52* (New York: Bloomsbury, 2010).

Djilas, Milovan, *Conversations with Stalin* (New York: Harcourt, Brace, and World, 1962).

Dower, John W., *War Without Mercy: Race and Power in the Pacific War* (New York: Pantheon, 1986).

Draper, Theodore, *The Roots of American Communism* (New York: Viking, 1957).

Draper, Theodore, *American Communism and Soviet Russia: The Formative Period* (New York: Viking, 1960).

Eicher, David J., *The Longest Night: A Military History of the Civil War* (New York: Simon & Schuster, 2001).

Eisenhower, Gen. Dwight D., "D-Day Statement to Soldiers, Sailors, and Airmen of the Allied Expeditionary Force," Dwight D. Eisenhower Presidential Library, National Archives and Records Administration. At: <https://www.archives.gov/historical-docs/todays-doc/?dod-date=606 >.

Engels, Friedrich, *Anti-Dühring (Herr Eugen Dühring's Revolution in Science)*, 8th printing (Moscow: Progress Publishers, 1978 [1877]).

Fanell, James E., and Bradley A. Thayer, *Embracing Communist China: America's Greatest Strategic Failure* (New York: Skyhorse Books, 2024).

Fields, Barbara J., "Whiteness, Racism, and Identity, in Sherrow O. Pinder, ed., *Black Political Thought: From David Walker to the Present* (Cambridge: Cambridge University Press, 2020), pp. 281–290.

Fiori, Giuseppe, *Antonio Gramsci: Life of a Revolutionary*, trans. by Tom Nairn (London: New Left Books, 1970).

Flood, Charles Bracelen, *Grant's Final Victory: Ulysses S. Grant's Heroic Last Year* (Boston: Da Capo Press, 2011).

Foote, Shelby, *The Civil War: A Narrative Fort Sumter to Perryville* (New York: Random House, 1958).

Forgacs, David, ed., *The Antonio Gramsci Reader: Selected Writings, 1916–1935* (New York: New York University Press, 2000).

Friend, John M., and Bradley A. Thayer, *How China Sees the World: The Rise of Han-Centrism and the Balance of Power in International Politics* (Lincoln: Potomac Books, 2018).

Fukuyama, Francis, "The End of History?" *The National Interest*, No. 16 (Summer 1989), pp. 3–18.

Fukuyama, Francis, *The End of History and the Last Man* (New York: Free Press, 1992).

Fussell, Paul, *Wartime: Understanding and Behavior in the Second World War* (New York: Oxford University Press, 1989).

Gertz, Bill, "Inside the Ring," *Washington Times*, December 10, 2025. At: <https://www.washingtontimes.com/news/2025/dec/10/inside-ring-trump-ends-controls-nvidia-chips-doj-says-boost-chinas/>.

Gilbert, Felix, ed., *The Historical Essays of Otto Hintze* (Oxford: Oxford University Press, 1975).

Gilbert, Martin, *Winston S. Churchill*, Vol. 4, *1916–1922* (London: Heineman, 1975).

Giroux, Henry, *Theory and Resistance in Education* (Santa Barbara, Calif.: Praeger, 1983).

Glasser, Theodore L., ed., *The Idea of Public Journalism* (New York: Guilford Press, 1999).

Gramsci, Antonio, *Selections from Cultural Writings*, ed. David Forgacs and Geoffrey Nowell-Smith, trans. William Boelhower (Cambridge, Mass.: Harvard University Press, 1985).

Gramsci, Antonio, *Selections from the Prison Notebooks*, ed. Quintin Hoare and Geoffrey Nowell-Smith (New York: International Publishers, 1971).

Gray, John, *Liberalism* (Milton Keynes: Open University Press, 1984).

Gray, John, *Enlightenment's Wake* (London: Routledge, 1995).

Guillermaz, Jacques, *A History of the Chinese Communist Party 1921–1949*, trans. by Anne Destenay (New York: Random House, 1972).

Habermas, Jürgen, *The Structural Transformation of the Public Sphere: An Inquiry into a Category of Bourgeois Society,* trans. by Thomas Burger (Cambridge, Mass.: MIT Press, 1989).

Hamilton, Alexander, James Madison, and John Jay, *The Federalist Papers*, ed. by Clinton Rossiter (New York: Penguin Putnam, 1961).

Hamilton, Clive, and Mareike Ohlberg, *Hidden Hand: Exposing How the Chinese Communist Party Is Reshaping the World* (London: Oneworld Publications, 2020).

Hamilton, John Maxwell, *Manipulating the Masses: Woodrow Wilson and the Birth of American Propaganda* (Baton Rouge: Louisiana State University Press, 2020).

Han, Lianchao, and Bradley A. Thayer, *Understanding the China Threat* (London: Routledge, 2023).

Han, Lianchao, Post on X, October 19, 2025. At: <https://x.com/lianchaohan/status/1979865610629546336?s=46&t=MWvVaFwWHHbqRtfknqZUlA>.

Hannah-Jones, Nikole, "Introduction" in Hannah-Jones, et al., "The 1619 Project" *The New York Times Magazine*, August 18, 2019. At: <http://pulitzercenter.org/sites/default/files/full_issue_of_the_1619_project.pdf>.

Harris, Cheryl I., "Whiteness as Property," in Sherrow O. Pinder, ed., *Black Political Thought: From David Walker to the Present* (Cambridge: Cambridge University Press, 2020), pp. 272–280.

Harris, Gareth, "Oxford Professors Refuse to Teach Undergraduate Students If Cecil Rhodes Statue Stays in Place," *The Art Newspaper*, June 11, 2021. At: <https://www.theartnewspaper.com/news/uk-culture-wars-escalate-as-oxford-dons-refuse-to-teach-oriel-college-students-if-rhodes-statue-stays-in-place>.

Hartz, Louis, *The Liberal Tradition in America* (New York: Harcourt, Brace and World, 1955).

Hastings, Max, *Nemesis: The Battle for Japan, 1944–1945* (London: William Collins, 2016).

Haynes, John Earl, and Harvey Klehr, *Venona: Decoding Soviet Espionage in America* (New Haven: Yale University Press, 1999).

Haynes, John Earl, and Harvey Klehr, *Early Cold War Spies: The Espionage Trials that Shaped American Politics* (Cambridge: Cambridge University Press, 2006).

Henderson, Sir Nevile, *Failure of a Mission: Berlin 1937–1939* (New York: G.P. Putnam's Sons, 1940).

Hopkirk, Peter, *Setting the East Ablaze: Lenin's Dream of an Empire in Asia* (New York: Norton, 1984).

Horkheimer, Max, *Critical Theory: Selected Essays* (New York: Seabury Press, 1972).

Horkheimer, Max, *Eclipse of Reason* (New York: Oxford University Press, 1947).

Horsman, Reginald, *The Causes of the War of 1812* (Philadelphia: Perpetua, 1962).

"How It Happened: Transcript of the U.S.-China Opening Remarks in Alaska," *Nikkei*, March 19, 2021. At: <https://asia.nikkei.com/Politics/International-relations/US-China-tensions/How-it-happened-Transcript-of-the-US-China-opening-remarks-in-Alaska>.

Howe, Irving, and Lewis Coser, *The American Communist Party: A Critical History, 1919–1957* (Boston: Beacon Press, 1957).

Huang, Huikang, "Racism Deeply Rooted in U.S.," *China Daily*, April 22, 2021. At: <http://global.chinadaily.com.cn/a/202104/22/WS6080c815a31024ad0bab9795.html>.

Hunt, Michael H., *Ideology and U.S. Foreign Policy* (New Haven: Yale University Press, 1987).

Huntington, Samuel P., *The Clash of Civilizations and the Remaking of World Order* (New York: Simon & Schuster, 1996).

Huntington, Samuel P., "Foreword: Cultures Count," in Lawrence E. Harrison and Samuel P. Huntington, eds., *Culture Matters: How Values Shape Human Progress* (New York: Basic Books, 2000), pp. xiii–xvi.

Huntington, Samuel P., *Who Are We? The Challenges to America's National Identity* (New York: Simon & Schuster, 2005).

Hussey, John, "The Movement of German Division to the Western Front, Winter 1917–1918," *War in History*, Vol. 4, No. 2 (April 1997).

Interagency Report, "East-West Policy Study," Washington, July 8, 1981, in *Foreign Relations of the United States 1981–1988 Vol. III, Soviet Union January 1981–January 1983* (Washington, D.C.: United States Government Publishing Office, 2016).

Jacobs, Dan N., *Borodin: Stalin's Man in China* (Cambridge, Mass.: Harvard University Press, 1981).

Jefferson, Thomas Jefferson, First Inaugural Address (1801). At: <https://constitutioncenter.org/the-constitution/historic-document-library/detail/thomas-jefferson-first-inaugural-address-1801>.

Johnson, Chalmers A., *Peasant Nationalism and Communist Power: The Emergence of Revolutionary China 1937–1945* (Stanford: Stanford University Press, 1962).

Jones, Robert Huhn, *The Roads to Russia: United States Lend-Lease to the Soviet Union* (Norman: University of Oklahoma Press, 1969).

Joske, Alex, *The Party Speaks for You* (Canberra: Australian Strategic Policy Institute, 2020).

Kallis, Giorgos, *In Defense of Degrowth: Opinions and Minifestos* (Brussels: Uneven Earth Press, 2017).

Kampelman, Max, *The Communist Party vs. the C.I.O.: A Study in Power Politics* (New York: Praeger, 1957).

Kennedy, David M., *Over Here: The First World War and American Society* (New York: Oxford University Press, 1980).

Klehr, Harvey, *The Heyday of American Communism: The Depression Decade* (New York: Basic Books, 1984).

Klehr, Harvey, John Earl Haynes, and Fridrikh Igorevich Firsov, *The Secret World of American Communism* (New Haven: Yale University Press, 1995).

Klehr, Harvey, John Earl Haynes, and Kyrill M. Anderson, *The Soviet World of American Communism* (New Haven: Yale University Press, 1998).

Koch, Adrienne, *Jefferson and Madison: The Great Collaboration* (New York: Alfred A. Knopf, 1950).

Latouche, Serge, *Farewell to Growth*, trans. by David Macey (Cambridge: Polity, 2009).

Leffler, Melvin P., *A Preponderance of Power: National Security, the Truman Administration, and the Cold War* (Stanford, Calif.: Stanford University Press, 1992).

Leffler, Melvyn P., *The Specter of Communism: The United States and the Origins of the Cold War, 1917–1953* (New York: Hill and Wang, 1994).

Lenin, Vladimir, *What Is to Be Done?* (Moscow: Progress Publishers, 1971 [1902]).

Lenin, V. I., "Revision of the Agrarian Programme of the Workers' Party," in V. I. Lenin, *Collected Works*, Vol. 10 (Moscow: Progress Publishers, 1962).

Lenin, V. I., "Speech at the Opening Session of the Congress," March 2, 1919, in V. I. Lenin, *Collected Works*, Vol. 28 (Moscow: Progress Publishers, 1965).

Lenin, V. I., "Letter to American Workers," August 18, 1918, *Collected Works*, Vol. 28 (Moscow: Progress Publishers, 1965).

Lenin, V. I., "Eighth Congress of the R.C.P. (B.): Report of the Central Committee," March 18, 1919, *Collected Works*, Vol. 29 (Moscow: Progress Publishers, 1965).

Lenin, V. I., "Left Wing Communism—An Infantile Disorder," in V. I. Lenin, *Collected Works*, Vol. 31 (Moscow: Progress Publishers, 1966).

Lenin, V. I., "Preliminary Draft Theses on the National and Colonial Questions," in V. I. Lenin, *Collected Works*, Vol. 31 (Moscow: Progress Publishers, 1966).

Li, Nan, "Party Congress Reshuffle Strengthens Xi's Hold on Central Military Commission," *The China Brief*, Vol. 18, No. 3, February 26, 2018. At: <https://jamestown.org/program/party-congress-reshuffle-strengthens-xis-hold-central-military-commission/?mc_cid=3132e01c7f&mc_eid=7bf8bdbc8d>.

Li, Xiaobing, *The Dragon in the Jungle: The Chinese Army in the Vietnam War* (New York: Oxford University Press, 2020).

Locke, John, *Two Treatises of Government* (Cambridge: Cambridge University Press, 1960 [1689]).

Locke, John, *The Second Treatise of Government*, ed. Thomas P. Peardon (Indianapolis: Bobbs-Merrill, 1952).

Lovell, Julia, *Maoism: A Global History* (New York: Knopf, 2019).

Lyons, Eugene, *The Red Decade: The Stalinist Penetration of America* (Indianapolis: Bobbs-Merrill, 1941).

Mao Tse-tung [Mao Zedong], *On Guerrilla Warfare*, trans. by Samuel B. Griffith (Washington, D.C.: Headquarters United States Marine Corps, Department of the Navy, 1989).

Mao, Tse-tung [Mao Zedong], "On Practice" July 1937, in *Four Essays on Philosophy* (Peking: Foreign Languages Press, 1966).

Mao Tse-tung [Mao Zedong], "Report on an Investigation of the Peasant Movement in Hunan," March 1927, *Selected Works of Mao Tse-Tung* (Peking: People's Publishing House, 1965), Vol. 1, pp. 23–59.

Mao Tse-tung [Mao Zedong], "On Contradiction," *Selected Works of Mao Tse-Tung* (Peking: People's Publishing House, 1965), Vol. 1, pp. 311–347.

Mao Tse-tung, [Mao Zedong], "Introducing *The Communist*," *Selected Works of Mao Tse-Tung*, Vol. 2 (Peking: People's Publishing House, 1965), pp. 285–296.

Mao Zedong, "On the Correct Handling of Contradictions Among the People" *Selected Works of Mao Tsetung*, Vol. 5 (Peking: Foreign Languages Press, 1977), pp. 384–421.

Mao Zedong, *Mao on Warfare* (New York: CN Times Books, 2013).

Marcuse, Herbert, *Eros and Civilization: A Philosophic Inquiry into Freud* (Boston: Beacon, 1966).

Marx, Karl, *Grundrisse: Foundations of the Critique of Political Economy* (New York: Harper & Row, 1972 [written in 1857–1858, first published in 1939]).

Marx, Karl, *Capital*, 3 Vols. (New York: International Publishers, 1980 [1867, 1885, 1894]).

Marx, Karl, and Friedrich Engels, *The Communist Manifesto* (New York: International Publishers, 2014 [1848]).

Marx, Karl, and Friedrich Engels, *The German Ideology* (New York: International Publishers, 2016 [written in 1846, first published 1932]).

Mill, John Stuart, *On Liberty*, ed. David Bromwich and George Kateb (New Haven: Yale University Press, 2003 [1859]).

Minnaugh, Ryan, "Media Research Center Finds 92% Negative Coverage of Trump in First 100 Days," *National News Desk,* April 29, 2025. At: <https://thenationaldesk.com/news/americas-news-now/major-networks-92-negative-coverage-of-president-trump>.

Montesquieu (Charles-Louis de Secondat, Baron de Montesquieu), *Reflections on the Causes of the Rise and Fall of the Roman Empire* (Glasgow: Robert Urie, 1758).

Montesquieu (Charles-Louis de Secondat, Baron de Montesquieu), *The Spirit of the Laws* (Cambridge: Cambridge University Press, 1989 [1748]).

Morgenthau, Hans J., *Scientific Man vs. Power Politics* (Chicago: University of Chicago Press, 1946).

Murray, Charles, *Facing Reality: Two Truths about Race in America* (New York: Encounter Books, 2021).

National Security Decision Directive 75 (NSDD-75), "U.S. Relations with the U.S.S.R." January 17, 1983, Box 91287, NSDD Files, Executive Secretariat Files, Ronald Reagan Presidential Library.

Nechayev, Sergey, *Catechism of a Revolutionary* (New York: Pattern Books, 2020 [1869]).

Ngo, Andy, *Unmasked: Inside Antifa's Plan to Destroy Democracy* (New York: Center Street, 2021).

North, Robert C., *Moscow and the Chinese Communists*, 2nd ed. (Stanford: Stanford University Press, 1963).

Noyes, Rich, "Never More Biased: TV Blasted Trump with 92% Negative Coverage; 66% Positive for Biden," *MRC News Busters*, October 27, 2020. At: <https://www.newsbusters.org/blogs/nb/rich-noyes/2020/10/27/never-more-biased-tv-blasts-trump-92-negative-coverage-66-positive>.

The Oxford Dictionary of Quotations, 5th ed. (Oxford: Oxford University Press, 1999).

Paine, Thomas, *Common Sense* (New York: Peter Eckler Publishing, 1918 [1776]).

Parker, Charlie, "Shakespeare's Birthplace to Be 'Decolonised' Over 'White Supremacy' Fears," *The Times*, March 16, 2025. At: <https://www.thetimes.com/uk/society/article/shakespeare-birthplace-stratford-upon-avon-empire-qvb2zdvz8>.

Patenaude, Bertrand M., *The Big Show in Bololand: The American Relief Expedition to Soviet Russia in the Famine of 1921* (Stanford: Stanford University Press, 2002).

Pocock, J. G. A., *The Machiavellian Moment: Florentine Political Thought and the Atlantic Republican Tradition* (Princeton, N.J.: Princeton University Press, 1975).

Pratt, Mark, "6 Dr. Seuss Books Won't Be Published for Racist Images," *Associated Press*, March 4, 2021. At: <https://apnews.com/article/dr-seuss-books-racist-images-d8ed18335c03319d72f443594c174513>.

Pyman, Avril, *The Life of Alexander Blok*, Vol. 2 (Oxford: Clarendon Press, 1980).

Richards, Leonard L., *Shays's Rebellion: The American Revolution's Final Battle* (Philadelphia: University of Pennsylvania Press, 2003).

Rojas, Fabio, *From Black Power to Black Studies: How a Radical Social Movement became an Academic Discipline* (Baltimore: Johns Hopkins University Press, 2007).

Rose, Tom, "The View from the Gulag: An Interview with Natan Sharansky," *The Weekly Standard*, Vol. 9, No. 21, June 21, 2004. At: <http://www.weeklystandard.com/Content/Public/Articles/000/000/004/224ncdel.asp>.

Rosen, Jay, *What Are Journalists For?* (New Haven: Yale University Press, 1999).

Ryan, Alan, *The Making of Modern Liberalism* (Princeton, N.J.: Princeton University Press, 2012).

Saad, Layla F., *Me and White Supremacy: Combat Racism, Change the World, and Become a Good Ancestor* (Naperville, Ill.: Sourcebooks, 2020).

Sagar, Rahul, ed., *To Raise a Fallen People: The Nineteenth-Century Origins of Indian Views on International Politics* (New York: Columbia University Press, 2022).

Saich, Tony, *Finding Allies and Making Revolution: The Early Years of the Chinese Communist Party* (Leiden: Brill, 2022).

Schlesinger, Jr., Arthur M., *The Disuniting of America: Reflections on a Multicultural Society* (New York: Norton, 1991).

Schwartz, Benjamin I., *Chinese Communism and the Rise of Mao* (Cambridge, Mass.: Harvard University Press, 1951).

Sensoy, Özlem, and Robin DiAngelo, *Is Everyone Really Equal? An Introduction to Key Concepts in Social Justice Education*, 2nd ed. (New York: Teachers College Press, 2017).

Silverstein, Jake, "Editor's Note by Jake Silverstein" in Nikole Hannah-Jones, et al., "The 1619 Project" *The New York Times Magazine*, August 18, 2019. At: <http://pulitzercenter.org/sites/default/files/full_issue_of_the_1619_project.pdf>.

Simpson, Craig, "Shakespeare's Birthplace to Be Decolonised After "White Supremacy Fears," *Daily Telegraph*, March 16, 2025. At: <https://www.telegraph.co.uk/news/2025/03/16/william-shakespeare-birthplace-trust-white-supremacy-empire/>.

Slaughter, Thomas P., *The Whiskey Rebellion: Frontier Epilogue to the American Revolution* (New York: Oxford University Press, 1988).

Smith, Anthony D., *Nations and Nationalism in a Global Era* (Malden, Mass.: Polity Press, 1995).

Smith, Rogers M., *Civic Ideals: Conflicting Visions of Citizenship in U.S. History* (New Haven: Yale University Press, 1999).

Solórzano, Daniel G., and Lindsay Pérez Huber, *Racial Microaggressions: Using Critical Race Theory to Respond to Everyday Racism* (New York: Teachers College Press, 2020).

Stephanson, Anders, *Manifest Destiny: American Expansion and the Empire of Right* (New York: Hill and Wang, 1995).

Stuart, Reginald C., *United States Expansionism and British North America, 1775–1871* (Chapel Hill: University of North Carolina Press, 1988).

Studer, Brigitte, *Travellers of the World Revolution: A Global History of the Communist International*, trans. by Dafydd Rees Roberts (London: Verso, 2023).

Thayer, Bradley A., "Our '1776 Moment:' Either a Liberal or Progressive America," *American Greatness*, January 21, 2022. At: <https://amgreatness.com/2022/01/21/our-1776-moment-either-a-liberal-or-progressive-america/>.

Thayer, Bradley A., "Just Say No to Xi's 'Four Red Lines,'" *Warroom*, November 23, 2024. At: <https://warroom.org/just-say-no-to-xis-four-red-lines/>.

Thayer, Bradley A., "*Quo Vadis* for Western Civilization: The Rebirth of the West's Confidence," *American Greatness*, November 18, 2025. At: <https://amgreatness.com/2025/11/18/quo-vadis-for-western-civilization-the-rebirth-of-the-wests-civilizational-confidence/>.

Timsit, Annabelle, "Read Xi Jinping's Full Speech from the 100th Anniversary of the Communist Party," *Quartz*, July 1, 2021. At: https://qz.com/2028306/xi-jinping-speech-transcript-for-the-ccps-100th-anniversary/.

Tocqueville, Alexis de, "To Ernest de Chabrol, 9 June 1831," in Roger Boesche, ed., *Selected Letters on Politics and Society* (Berkeley: University of California Press, 1985), pp. 37–40.

Tocqueville, Alexis de, *Democracy in America*, 2 Vols., ed. F. Bowen (Boston: J. Allyn, 1873 [1835]).

Tocqueville, Alexis de, *The Ancien Régime and the French Revolution*, trans. and ed. Gerald Bevan (New York: Penguin, 2008 [1856]).

Trotsky, Leon, *Problems of the Chinese Revolution* (New York: Pioneer Publishers, 1932).

Trotsky, Leon, *The Permanent Revolution and Results and Prospects* (New York: Merit, 1969).

Tucker, Robert W., and David C. Hendrickson, *Empire of Liberty: The Statecraft of Thomas Jefferson* (New York: Oxford University Press, 1990).

van de Ven, Hans J., *From Friend to Comrade: The Founding of the Chinese Communist Party, 1920–1927* (Berkeley: University of California Press, 1991).

Weinstein, Allen, and Alexander Vassiliev, *The Haunted Wood: Soviet Espionage in America—The Stalin Era* (New York: Random House, 1999).

The White House, *The National Security Strategy of the United States*, November 2025. At: <https://www.whitehouse.gov/wp-content/uploads/2025/12/2025-National-Security-Strategy.pdf>.

Wiggershaus, Rolf, *The Frankfurt School: Its History, Theories, and Political Significance* (Cambridge, Mass.: MIT Press, 1994).

Wittfogel, Karl A., "The Marxist View of China (Part I)," *The China Quarterly*, No. 11 (July–September 1962), pp. 1–20.

Wittfogel, Karl A., "The Marxist View of China (Part II)," *The China Quarterly*, No. 12 (October–December 1962), pp. 154–169.

Wolff, Robert Paul, Barrington Moore, Jr., and Herbert Marcuse, *A Critique of Pure Tolerance* (Boston: Beacon, 1965).

Wong, Chun Han, "Next Task for Xi Jinping: Rebuild the Military He Wiped Out," *Wall Street Journal*, March 7, 2026. At: <https://www.wsj.com/world/china/china-xi-jinping-military-command-4b0c6338?mod=hp_lead_pos6>.

Xi, Jinping, *The Governance of China*, 2nd ed., 2 Vols. (Beijing: Foreign Language Press, 2018).

Xinhua, "Senior CPC Official Stresses Deeper Study of Xi Jinping Thought among Officials," November 16, 2019. At: <http://www.xinhuanet.com/english/2019-11/16c_138560537.htm>.

Xu, Jian, "Rethinking China's Period of Strategic Opportunity," *China International Studies* (March/April 2014), pp. 51–70. At: <http://www.ciis.org.cn/english/2014-05/28/content_6942258.htm>.

Yang, Jianli, and Bradley A. Thayer, "The Chinese Communist Party Should Be Held Accountable for its Crimes," *National Review*, June 4, 2023. At: <https://www.nationalreview.com/2023/06/the-chinese-communist-party-should-be-held-accountable-for-its-crimes/>.

Index

M

N

O

P